A Place in the Sun

The Real Goods Solar Living Books

Wind Power for Home & Business: Renewable Energy for the 1990s and Beyond by Paul Gipe

The Independent Home: Living Well with Power from the Sun, Wind, and Water by Michael Potts

Real Goods Solar Living Sourcebook: The Complete Guide to Renewable Energy Technologies and Sustainable Living, Ninth Edition, edited by John Schaeffer

The Straw Bale House by Athena Swentzell Steen, Bill Steen, and David Bainbridge, with David Eisenberg

The Rammed Earth House by David Easton

The Real Goods Independent Builder: Designing & Building a House Your Own Way by Sam Clark

The Passive Solar House: Using Solar Design to Heat and Cool Your Home by James Kachadorian

A Place in the Sun: The Evolution of the Real Goods Solar Living Center by John Schaeffer and the Collaborative Design/Construction Team

Hemp Horizons: The Comeback of the World's Most Promising Plant by John W. Roulac

Real Goods Mission Statement

Through our products, publications, and educational demonstrations, Real Goods promotes and inspires an environmentally healthy and sustainable future.

Real Goods Trading Company in Ukiah, California, was founded in 1978 to make available new tools to help people live self-sufficiently and sustainably. Through seasonal catalogs, a periodical (Real Goods Renewables), a bi-annual Solar Living Sourcebook, as well as retail outlets, Real Goods provides a broad range of tools for independent living.

"Knowledge is our most important product" is the Real Goods motto. To further its mission, Real Goods has joined with Chelsea Green Publishing Company to co-create and co-publish the Real Goods Solar Living Book series. The titles in this series are written by pioneering individuals who have firsthand experience in using innovative technology to live lightly on the planet. Chelsea Green books are both practical and inspirational, and they enlarge our view of what is possible as we enter the next millennium.

John Schaeffer
President, Real Goods

Ian Baldwin, Jr.
President, Chelsea Green

A Place in the Sun

The Evolution of the Real Goods Solar Living Center

John Schaeffer
and the Collaborative Design/Construction Team

David Arkin, A.I.A.
Nancy Hensley
Adam Jackaway
Bruce King
Stephanie Kotin
Stephen Morris
Baile Oakes
Jeff Oldham
Christopher Tebbutt
Sim Van der Ryn
Mark Winkler

Chelsea Green Publishing Company
White River Junction, Vermont

About the manufacturing of this book

In keeping with the spirit of innovation and the principles of sustainable living demonstrated so convincingly at the Real Goods Solar Living Center, we have tried to print and produce this book making the most appropriate choices of available materials. In the process, we discovered that in printing, as with building, decision-making involves a balance between the ideal and the practical.

The text is printed on 70# Roland New Life Opaque, a recycled sheet containing 30 percent post-consumer material. Sheets with higher content sacrifice print and archival quality. Several contributors lobbied to print the book on 100 percent tree-free paper. We did significant research on papers made with kenaf, hemp, bamboo, and various combinations using agricultural waste, such as kenaf/wheat straw. Many look promising, but questions of cost, availability, lead-time, and reliability made them risky choices for a job of this magnitude. Choosing 100 percent hemp papers, for instance, would have more than doubled the price of the finished book, which would have been in conflict with our desire to have the story of the Solar Living Center as broadly read as possible.

The color section is printed on 80# Rubicon, a 100 percent tree-free, acid-free stock that is manufactured by the Fox River Company in Wisconsin. Although this is a beautiful paper, it, too, reflects a compromise in that the bamboo is grown in the Philippines on sustainably harvested plantations. Transporting fiber products such a distance so that a company in Vermont (in the midst of America's great remaining hardwood forest) can publish a book on a building project in the midst of California redwoods is hardly the model for sustainability that we are seeking. At best it is a small step in the right direction.

The cover of this book is printed on recycled stock, but is protected by a laminate for which there is no commercially available, benign substitute. Booksellers and book buyers demand books that resist scratching and that maintain a bright appearance for many years. They should not have to lower their expectations or standards. Instead, it is incumbent on those of us who trade in the written word to insist on products that better reflect our goals of sustainability. For a small company to make a difference requires diligence, patience, and a lot of persistence, but as Real Goods has shown with the Solar Living Center, this is how progress is made.

Printed in Canada

1 2 3 4 5 97 98 99 00

Chelsea Green Publishing Company
P.O. Box 428
White River Junction, VT 05001
(800) 639-4099

Library of Congress Cataloging-in-Publication Data

Schaeffer, John, 1949-
A place in the sun : the evolution of the Real Goods Solar Living Center / John Schaeffer and the collaborative design/construction team, David Arkin ... [et al.].
p. cm.
Includes index.
ISBN (invalid) 0-89013-201-2
1. Real Goods Solar Living Center (Hopland, Calif.) 2. Architectural museums--California--Hopland. 3. Showrooms--California--Hopland--Design and construction. 4. Tourist camps, hostels, etc.--California--Hopland. 5. Renewable energy sources--California--Hopland. 6. Solar energy--Museums--California--Hopland. 7. Environmental protection--Equipment and supplies--Museums--California--Hopland. 8. Green products--Museums--California--Hopland. I. Title
TH6.U62H627 1997
720' .472'09794--dc21 97-31121

to the devoted employees of Real Goods, whose untiring efforts on behalf of the company have made it possible for the dream of a Solar Living Center to become a reality; to the project team who accepted the challenge to collaborate and suppress their egos; to the shareowners without whose financial resources it wouldn't have been possible; and to my son Jesse who taught me how valuable and transitory life and relationships can be.

—J. S., 1997

Contents

Foreword *by Ralph Nader*

Edited transcript of the Keynote Address at SOLFEST 97 sponsored by Real Goods and Greenpeace at the Solar Living Center, June 20–21, 1997.

As I stand here at the Solar Living Center buffeted by the wind—who says there's no such thing as wind power?—I'm impressed by the very interesting experiment here, that John and others have underway. Apparently in the first year of operation, one hundred thousand people visited, a hundred thousand people with virtually no publicity, just word of mouth. What does that tell you? Well, it tells you first that there will probably be a million people coming here in another five or ten years. But it's more than just eco-tourism. It's very much an increasing recognition by people that there are two different kinds of technologies competing in this world. One is the technology of the global corporations, which has certain characteristics. And the other is the technology that serves people needs first, which we call democratic technology.

This distinction is drawn very clearly in the area of energy. Global energy corporations choose energy sources that maximize the company's control over the source, complicate the technology so few can compete, influence government policy for subsidies and tax escapes, persuade members of Congress to go along with more than a little campaign money, and develop a public attitude toward conventional sources as inevitable—coal, oil, gas, nuclear: inevitable. I was just talking with a nuclear physicist I met on a plane a few weeks ago, and I said, "It looks like you're going to be out of a job pretty soon other than to deal with radioactive wastes and closing down nuclear plants." And he said, "Yeah, it looks like that's all that's left." Except of course passing the costs on to you, the ratepayers and consumers, through a mechanism called stranded costs. Nuclear power—atomic energy as it used to be called—was sold to us right after World War II as a technology capable of producing electricity "too cheap to meter." This ended up being the most expensive electricity of all, immediately and in the long-term. It's not only that we had to subsidize nuclear energy in its construction, in its limited liability (in case of a disaster), in its free government research and development, with the taxpayer paying the bills, but now we have to buy these lemon nuclear plants that are not competitive with other forms of energy and have to be closed down by the utilities. So the taxpayer pays going in, the taxpayer pays going out; in between the consumer pays; and future generations have to deal with the deadly residues of radioactive nuclear waste.

And yet, even now, do you see anybody involved and responsible for this massive technological debacle? The way the laws are operating, no one's responsible for this, no one gets prosecuted, no one gets sent to jail, companies don't go bankrupt, instead they go to Washington for bailouts. Nuclear energy is a technology that has not been allowed to fail, year after year, until it collapsed of its own internal contradictions, defects, and costs. When you have a technology that is so bolstered by the taxpayer, so limited in terms of its liability to lawsuits, and protected by so much secrecy that it cannot be allowed to fail, it can blunder and plunder and heap risks on present and future generations for years before the public catches up.

Anyway, to continue with this conversation with the nuclear physicist: I said, "So what do you think of solar energy?" Now, this is a man who has gone through college physics, graduate school physics, nuclear physics, and he gives me the same answer I and others have heard from most of the nuclear physicists we've ever talked to. Here it comes:

"What do you think of solar energy?"

"Well, it's okay, but it's too diffuse."

"What do you mean, 'too diffuse'?"

"Well, you can't focus it, you can't concentrate it, you can't store it."

To which I say, no wonder you're a nuclear physicist. Do you know that over 95 percent of our energy since the world began has been solar? What do you think keeps the Earth at a temperature where need to add only a few degrees in winter or subtract a few degrees down in the summer to stay comfortable by conventional energy? It's called the Sun. If anyone tells you there's no such think as a free lunch, tell them *yeah*, there's one up above, a few tens of millions of miles away. Now our job is to bring the Sun's energy back to replace the conventional energy sources.

Let's assume that you are an individual and you are making a choice as to what kind of energy you want for your family. It's not Exxon, it's not Peabody Coal, it's not the Department of Energy, it's not the oil companies that's deciding, it's just you. Would you pick a kind of energy that shrouds cities in smog, contaminates groundwater, produces acidic runoffs in strip mine areas, loads up future generations with risks of deadly radioactive wastes, damages forests, warms up the Earth toward potentially catastrophic levels, damages the ozone layer, and produces national security risks? Well, our rulers did that. And will continue to do so, until we develop this distinction—and move behind it—between corporate dominated technologies, and democratically validated technologies.

Here's the essential immorality of our conventional fuels in a nutshell. If every person in the world consumed the same kind of fuels that we consume at the same per capita levels, with the same kinds of technologies, from the internal combustion energy to the coal-burning plants, the Earth would be uninhabitable. The only way we get away with the ways we use, and how much we use, of coal, oil, gas, and nuclear is that we in the United States are only about 4 1/2 percent of the world's population. We consume almost 30 percent of the energy, while most of the world's population uses merely a tiny fraction of that per capita consumption. How long is that going to last? Take a look at what's going on in China, and India, and Indonesia. Look at the rising consumption of fossil fuels. Look at all the highways and all the cars that they want to buy and build, just the way we did. And who are we to tell them otherwise, because we've already done it, and we've lost credibility. In another twenty to thirty years, if we add another five hundred to eight hundred million net motor vehicles with the same internal combustion engines, and probably even less in the way of smog controls, we're in deep trouble. In another fifty years, if we add another two billion motor vehicles and increase the consumption of fossils by about eight-fold, we're in serious global trouble.

The advantages of solar energy have been known for centuries. The ancient Greeks and Persians used passive solar architecture for their buildings and residences. In East Africa, air conditioning using wind power to cool through tunnels off the coast was developed many centuries ago. Wind mills were invented several hundred years ago. Likewise, biomass has been a form of energy for centuries. We have had decades to refine solar technology, to make wind turbines more efficient and longer lasting. Now we know how to develop solar water heaters far more economical than the ones that were on the roofs of Miami before natural gas came in and replaced them in the 1920s. Now we can see how to take biomass—the wastes from our harvests—turn it into gases and put it through existing pipelines. Now we can see how fast the price of photovoltaic-produced solar electricity is dropping: it has dropped over 90 percent since 1965 and it's continuing to drop. Now we know how to use the Sun in its various manifestations to give us a decentralized form of energy. Never again will we have to spend 50 billion dollars a year and human casualties in the Persian Gulf to protect the oil companies because we're so reliant on them. Fifty billion dollars per year of our military budget goes to the Persian Gulf—50 cents per gallon of gasoline or heating fuel that you buy—that's the hidden tax.

The Sun has a remarkable characteristic: Even Exxon cannot order an eclipse to create a shortage. We want a solar decentralized system of energy that can never be cartelized and monopolized, never subjected to intimidation. A form of decentralized energy where you, the homeowner, consumer, or small business person, can produce it, use it, or sell it within the local community economy. A form of decentralized energy that does not promote the destruction of the planet through ozone depletion and global warming. A form of decentralized energy that doesn't require plans for mass evacuations around nuclear power plants such as those now on file in libraries throughout the country by requirement of law. A form of decentralized community energy that is democratic by definition, that doesn't increase dependency on long lines of supply, that doesn't make people vulnerable to disruptions and bluster and intimidation, and that does not damage that slice of life around the planet, a mere three or four miles, where we find all the water, all the air, and all the soil essential to sustain the livelihoods of six billion people and every other living thing on Earth.

Now, what are the conventional arguments against solar energy?

We know for example, that each form of solar energy is operating competitively somewhere in the world. Solar water heaters are now competitive, yet the structure of the U.S. housing industry is such that when you buy a conventional house, you have to pay for the fuel every year. If on the other hand you could buy a solar house, you would pay for much of your energy expenses at the beginning. The initial cost would be somewhat higher, but throughout the life of the house, the operating costs would be significantly lower. We don't have a marketing system that prices the life cycle of the house, not to mention its environmental costs. If we did, solar energy would win hands down.

Over a million houses have been solarized in this country; thousands of buildings have been partially solarized. There's even an office complex not too far from here, the Lockheed-Martin building, where they're saving $500,000 a year, since the building was built in a way that not only improves worker moral because it is daylit, filled with sunshine and air instead of sealed and artificially "conditioned," but is also more efficient. And of course the Real Goods Solar Living Center offers solar solutions for you to examine on site.

The conventional arguments against solar are arguments dripping with ridicule, like the nuclear physicist saying solar cannot be focused or cannot be stored. But they basically come down to four myths.

First myth: solar energy and solar designs work well only in warm, sunny climates. This is false. Solar energy is successfully operating in every region of the United States, whether using wind power, thermal solar, passive design, or PV direct applications. The Navy is installing 20,000 solar photovoltaic modules in its installations around the country and the world, not out of any idealism, but purely because these are more economical than turbine generators. A dozen small lighthouses off the New England coast run on solar power. Passive solar design heats and illuminates a nonprofit health facility in Frederick, Maryland, hardly the solar capital of the world.

Second myth: solar power is too costly. Obviously, any new technology is behind the curve of economies of scale. The more units of a technology that are sold, the cheaper it becomes. Barry Commoner, a leading environmentalist, said during the 1970s that if the Pentagon had directed a couple of hundred million dollars a year to buy photovoltaics, as the Navy is now doing in a smaller way, it would have helped build a solar economy with increasing economies of scale, cutting costs so that solar would now be easily the most economical form of energy, even on a short time scale. But that wasn't done.

Third myth: solar energy is not as reliable as conventional energy technologies. The National Renewable Energy Laboratory has found photovoltaics to be "the most reliable source of electrical power ever invented." According to the

Solar Energy Industries Association, surveys taken over the last decade show that over 94 percent of solar water heater owners consider their solar heater to be a wise investment. The main reason for solar's superior reliability is that, as a decentralized power source, it is not subject to power blackouts or breaks in the system network. Because they are highly reliable, solar technologies are used to power highway warning signals, navigational buoys, aircraft warning lights, and railroad crossing signals. You don't do that with an intermittent source of energy.

Fourth myth: solar power is not practical in urban areas. New forms of solar technology that now make it very, very practical include solar walls, venetian blinds, glazing, and water heating systems that are an economical replacement for electric heaters in almost any urban setting. The issue is whether we can tailor solar technology to different economic purposes, and whether we can make them economical enough in shorter and shorter time spans—solar is indisputably very economical in a long time span. (Just think, radioactive waste has to be guarded and dealt with for hundreds of thousands of years; that's what we leave behind for others to pay for when we turn on an electric bulb to read our newspaper at night if it comes from a nuclear power plant.)

The only real obstacle to solar energy is the massive fossil fuel/nuclear corporate juggernaut that controls our government, misinforms or controls the media, and makes people actually believe that solar energy is too diffuse. But do you know what the polls show on solar energy? By a wide margin, solar is the most popular and desired form of energy of all the available choices. These polls have been registering that response since 1975.

There are times when societies have to overcome their superstitions and their confusions, and ask themselves, What do we want to do? Rip out the belly of the Earth extracting petrochemicals and hydrocarbons with their deadly effects on health, safety, and the global environment? Or take advantage of the unlimited, life-giving power beaming down everywhere on the Earth every day? These questions have been discussed for years. When is it going to change? There are entrepreneurs now who are innovating in solar energy, innovating in renewables—you see the results at the Solar Living Center! This is no Mickey Mouse Disneyland. The diffusion of what you see at a place like the Solar Living Center is potentially global-saving. Useful, simple, down-to-earth, consonant with nature, and respectful of future generations. Solar energy has arrived.

Acknowledgments

In its own way, this book has been as much of a construction project as the Solar Living Center. Building with words and images, we found, can be more challenging than working with straw bales and shovels. In the construction process, each participant was an expert in his or her specialty, while in writing this book, we were almost all novice authors. Thanks to all for patience, confidence, and forbearance.

Besides the names and faces in this book, some other key players' contributions deserve recognition. Thanks to Norm Bourassa and Leslie Lorimer, important members of the design team from the Ecological Design Institute. Phil Otto and Scott Stewart from the Otto Design Group are responsible for the beautiful fixturing in our showroom. Terry McGillivray, our civil engineer, was a model of professionalism and consistency. The builders from TDM Construction went from skeptics to true believers during the course of this project. Tom Myers, the principal, and crew foreman Manuel Paz, were open-minded to our crazy ideas, and helped to ground them in reality.

Steve Gresham of Mendocino Solar Works was our construction superintendent and all-around savior. Also in that category is Steve Heckeroth, who helped out on everything from design to pouring concrete. Another Real Goods associate of long standing is Ross Burkhardt, who has emerged as one of the nation's foremost authorities on straw bale construction. Ed Winelman, president of North Coast Construction, went to extraordinary lengths to accommodate our need to use only Certified Sustainably Harvested lumber. Joe Garnero donated wood for the dock, and I think of him every time I look out across the ponds. Greg Steliga should be thanked on behalf of all the contractors who rose to the occasion at the midnight hour in order to have us ready for the grand opening.

Mary Buckley, our Feng Shui consultant, is responsible for much of the harmonious feel of the showroom. Peter Erskine designed the Rainbow Sundial Calendar that brings a smile to so many store visitors. Victoria Oldham, Jeff's wife, receives special spousal recognition for her relentless care of a husband who was habitually late, tired, and in need of a massage.

Collectively, we thank the Energy Center of Pacific Gas & Electric for their design input, and the "green" design professionals around the country who were unfailingly supportive in taking our calls and generously sharing their wisdom. We're grateful to the Hopland community for putting out the welcome mat. Special thanks to the people at Fetzer Vineyards for collaboration on many projects.

The upfront team that helped to develop the initial vision included Dave Smith and Jim Robello. Thanks also to John Horne, our loan officer from National Bank of the Redwoods. We'll pay you back, honest!

On the publishing side, we thank Jack Howell for so rigorously holding us to deadlines, and Rachael Cohen and Jim Schley for making us seem more eloquent than we are in reality.

And finally, thanks to the real "owners" of Real Goods, our shareowners and staff. The Solar Living Center is a monument to your commitment.

A Place in the Sun

John Schaeffer is president and founder of Real Goods. An anthropology major from University of California at Berkeley, he migrated to Mendocino County in the early 1970s. Real Goods was originally a retail store in Willets, California. The company is now the largest consumer retailer of renewable energy products. John lives in Ukiah with his daughters, Sara and Ashley.

Chapter 1

The Big Idea

John Schaeffer

Dwell as near as possible to the channel in which your life flows. —*Henry David Thoreau*

I had waited all of my forty-six years to see an eagle fly in its natural habitat. February 6, 1996, felt like a propitious day when I awoke to cold and rain. I was excited at the lineup of creative visionaries whom we had assembled for our morning meeting to discuss the site features at the Solar Living Center (SLC), which after three years of planning was finally beginning to take shape. We assembled at the site bundled in our raincoats: Jeff Oldham, our project manager; David Arkin and Sim Van der Ryn, our architects; Chris Tebbutt and Stephanie Kotin, our landscape designers; Baile Oakes, our sculptor; Nancy Hensley, our store manager; Mark Winkler, our new SLC director; and me. After an hour of brainstorming some of our clearest and most creative ideas to date, I glanced up and saw a young bald eagle cruising over our property. It was at this defining moment, chills and goosebumps running up my spine from this powerful omen, that I realized that we were involved in something very, very important, and that we were doing it right.

I have been called a contrarian all my life. I've always enjoyed bucking the system and challenging authority. My education at UC-Berkeley in the late 1960s was comprised of 25 percent in-the-classroom learning, leading to a degree in anthropology, and 75 percent in-the-streets learning, leading to my immersion in radical politics and alternative lifestyles. Just after graduation in 1971, I followed the back-to-the-land movement to an archetypal hippie commune on 290 acres in Mendocino County to learn how to re-create society with new rules. The idea of Real Goods was born as it became readily apparent that our ideas about consumption and conservation needed to change radically if our species was to survive over the long term. The political society that we twenty-five idealists were creating somehow had to be replicated massively if we were to have any effect at all. There was no way to get hundreds of thousands of visitors to see our way of life up there in the middle of nowhere, so I had to figure out a way to take this "ecotopia" to the mainstream. The original Real Goods was a retail store in Willits, California, which eventually grew to a three-store mini-chain with additional outlets in Ukiah and Santa Rosa.

In 1986, Real Goods began its second incarnation as a mail-order business. Perched in my 8- by 10-foot office doing $18,000 per year in sales, I tried to educate via a small catalog mailed to five thousand people. As the business grew one-thousand-fold over the next ten years to $18 million in sales via seven million catalogs mailed annually, it became clear that we were not so much a company that marketed products as one that marketed ideas. Our slogan—"Knowledge is our most important product"—rang true because we couldn't possibly sell solar systems when a large portion of the public believed it when the government and utility companies claimed that these systems just didn't work. It was clear that demonstration and inspiration were the only effective ways to teach people about our products.

About the same time that we were learning about the benefits of educating our customers through demonstrations, the inherent hypocrisy of what we were doing began to surface. Here we were, preaching the gospel of solar systems and energy conservation, yet using utility company fossil-fueled power, driving gas-guzzling cars to work, wasting water, and in short failing to "walk our talk" at almost every turn. After April 1990, when the twentieth anniversary of Earth Day turned on the green light for many Americans, both the guilt of our energy hypocrisy and the opportunities for marketing through demonstration became much stronger. Buoyed by the success of our pioneering "direct public offering," by which we raised $1 million directly from our customers without the use of investment bankers or stockbrokers, we realized that we had the power to make our dreams come true and that it was high time to build a demonstration center where we could put into practice everything that we had been preaching in our catalogs for years. And it could become a test bed for new technologies that came down the pike.

In early 1993, we set out our strategy to do a second direct public offering to our customers to raise $3.6 million to build what we began to call the Solar Living Center. Shortly thereafter, the money began to roll in. In fact, not only did the $3.6 million roll in from over four thousand new shareowners, but in the last week of the offering, another $1 million came in that we had to return to disappointed potential investors. Soon after the

Growing from shopping trips for a back-to-the-land community, to a chain of retail outlets, to a mail-order business run out of John's garage, by 1996 Real Goods was mailing seven million catalogs annually to educate people about the wisdom of solar living.

John Schaeffer's vision for a "Solar Living Center," where Real Goods could "walk its talk" and demonstrate the practicality and beauty of renewable energy and conservation, became possible in 1993 with a public offering that brought in $3.6 million.

SEAN O'MALLEY

money had been raised, one of our employees who had been commuting to Ukiah from Berkeley found our site: a desolate, ravaged 12-acre piece of property in the Hopland flood plain that was being used as a dumping ground for highway rubble. The good news was that it was very cheap, and the bad news was that it would take a lot of energy and money to develop it. The challenge to turn a nearly treeless piece of waste property into an oasis of inspiration was awesome. That's when the fun began for me. I sat down in November 1993 and wrote a six-page vision statement setting my wildest fantasies onto paper (see sidebar).

The next step was to put together the team that could put life into these lofty ideas, on time and within budget. We started a design competition with five architects and selected Sim Van der Ryn, former State of California architect under Governor Jerry Brown, who had worked in ecological design and sustainable architecture for twenty years. Sim seemed to have the best understanding of our purpose and our vision. Next we found an incredible husband-and-wife team of landscape designers who are visionaries in their own right. Stephanie Kotin and Chris Tebbutt converted the vision statement into a brilliant planting plan complete with solar calendars, living structures, waterways, ponds, exotic and native

John Schaeffer's Vision Plan

The **Site Plan** and style of layout and construction should maximize elements of beauty, serenity, and spirituality—this should be a sanctuary and a testament to sustainable building practices, sustainable energy systems, sustainable living, agriculture, and community. It must evoke a feeling of wholeness that will touch each and every visitor and ultimately inspire employees, shareowners, lifetime members, the media, and customers. This can be done largely through landscaping, sculpture, design, and the quality and aesthetic of the buildings. When folks pull off Highway 101 and proceed through the entryway, they must be overwhelmed with a sense that they have crossed into another world. From the sterile highway, they are now in a green, cool, comfortable "parallel universe." Perhaps the showroom building could shield view and sound from the highway and face out to a Spanish-style courtyard in the center facing east.

The **Showroom** should be 3,000 to 4,000 square feet to accommodate everything we have now as well as a good-sized "bioregional" display (200 square feet), wood stoves and accessories (1,200 square feet), a gardening section (400 square feet), and plenty of room for expansion. All powered by photovoltaics (PVs). All built with state-of-the-art nontoxic building materials and maximizing the use of recycled and local building materials. There needs to be an area of reception where people can sit down and rest, a "Wall of Fame" where all the Real Goods accolades, letters, media stories, catalog covers, etc., are displayed, where the weary traveler can browse through catalogs, sign up for the mailing list, feel at home, feel part of the RG family, like they have finally come home.

species, wetlands, orchards, and vegetable gardens that would make any gardener drool. Best of all, they understood the vision and had worked in permaculture, wilderness and forest conservation, and sustainable landscape design for over twenty years, including a brief stint as gardeners for the queen of England in the Royal Gardens of Buckingham Palace. After casting about in the wrong direction, we selected Jeff Oldham, formerly the manager of our Renewable Energy Department, to be project manager. Jeff was familiar with the building trades and had just completed a large eco-design project, solarizing the Maho Bay Resort in the Virgin Islands. With our capable crew in place, we moved forward, selected a contractor, and began what would become the hardest task of all: keeping purity of vision while staying within the budget and the time line!

Probably the most exciting part of the project for me was seeing the vision come into action. I visited the site a minimum of two or three times per week. Progress seemed frustratingly slow in the beginning, but then, around the middle of 1995, began to accelerate rapidly. We made a conscious decision to buck the trend of most commercial projects in which the building is erected first and then the landscaping—which typically consists of a few trees and juniper bushes in the parking lot with some pansies thrown in for color—is done at the very end, when the budget is generally exhausted. We wanted our landscape finished first, so that when the grand opening rolled around, our customers would see meaningful growth and under stand the integration of landscape and building.

It was a challenge to stay pure. Our first thought was to build the building without a stick of wood, but this evolved into "not a stick of virgin wood that had been harvested unsustainably." We tried hard to use hemp wherever possible, but soon discovered that hemp plywood would cost us over $300 per 4- by 8-foot sheet (compared to $15 to $40 per sheet for conventional plywood). We committed to using rice-straw bales to highlight the necessity of decreasing our dependence on cutting down trees and to demonstrate a use for rice straw, which was creating an environmental nightmare for farmers in California who had to burn it in the fields. It took significant hand-holding and cajoling for the county building inspectors and planning department to accept our way of doing things, but in the end they gave us permits for what must have seemed like lunatic idiosyncracies to them.

As the project neared completion, my energies turned to the grand opening, scheduled for the Summer Solstice in 1996. We hoped the opening would become the largest gathering and promotion of Real Goods' customers in its nearly twenty-year history. We were fortunate to have Greenpeace as a partner who saw the Solar Living Center as an opportunity to accentuate positive examples of environmentalism rather than protesting about what is wrong with the environment. We assembled an array of notable speakers, including Amory

Vision Plan

A **Solar Bed-and-Breakfast** should be built with probably two to three bedrooms, a kitchen, a living room with pull-out couch, a bathroom, with the entire house built with recycled building materials, passive heating and cooling, using all of RG's products. The B&B can be rented to interested customers, shareowners, or members, for $100 per night or so. If it is for a potential customer, the price can be refunded upon purchase of a system. The living room can be used as a setting for strategic planning meetings. A pull-out couch could accommodate additional VIPs, shareowners, or RG lifetime members. Construction could be of straw bale walls and/or concrete material that Steve Heckeroth discussed. The materials that went into the Harmony Project in the Virgin Islands should all be considered in the construction. All powered by photovoltaics, a wind generator mounted outside, and if possible, a demonstration hydroelectric plant. Should use composting toilet, be outfitted with all the latest RG products and be a test bed for new products. The house could be used by technicians who are entertaining customers to show them how to live with solar. It can be used to entertain media and could also potentially act as our media reception room where we put our "Wall of Fame" with all

Continued on page 8

Lovins from the Rocky Mountain Institute, Wes Jackson from the Land Institute, Barbara Dudley, the executive director of Greenpeace, and Jeremy Leggett, the world's foremost authority on global warming. We had six workshops each day for three days, musicians, entertainers, and wonderful food. We drew over twelve thousand people to help us celebrate our completion of the project.

The highlight of the grand opening for me was the incredible "Sun Meets the Earth" dinner that Fetzer vineyards put together, featuring four outrageous chefs from around the country. At the end of the five-hour, seven-course, organically grown dinner, the chefs stood to speak about when they had planted the food that they served so that it would be ready for the dinner and about how proud each was to have taken part in such an inspirational grand opening. I realized that this night was the fruition of three years of planning and execution by an astoundingly dedicated and talented crew of true believers, all working toward a common vision.

Vision Plan

Continued from page 7

articles written about us, catalog covers framed, letters of commendation, etc. Will require a large living room. This house could also serve as a "model sustainable home" for potential developers to replicate in housing projects, and it is critical that it be beautiful, calming, creative, and spiritually uplifting. The dining room can double as a meeting place for managers' lunches, strategic planning meetings, and other RG events.

Restoration of the property should include plantings of native species of trees and vegetation and the restoration of the riparian canopy over Feliz Creek. Attempts will be made to involve local children in the plantings and to educate them in the history of the land. We need to encourage species diversity.

An extensive **Agricultural Endeavor** should take place on the floodway portion of the property. An area would be fenced and food would be grown with the latest technology in drip irrigation, double-digging gardening, testing solar tractors, and the new generation of wheel-hoes. This would be a demonstration garden/small farm through which we would lead guided walking tours to teach how it is being done. The food produced would be used in our restaurant, "Real Foods," and fed to employees and customers. The agricultural endeavor should have two or three demonstration gardens: Chadwick double-dig, traditional row, and raised bed. We can do research here and teach various methods. Maximum size: one acre.

An **Orchard** should be planted this winter to get the fruit trees started and should emphasize local varieties, apples, pears, Indian blood-red peaches, reestablishment of the viable grape vines, along with

Continued on page 11

John Schaeffer kicked off the grand opening celebration for the Solar Living Center on the Summer Solstice in 1996. Over twelve thousand people attended three days of workshops, listened to talks by notable speakers, enjoyed the "Sun Meets the Earth" organic dinner, and celebrated the completion of a project that demonstrates that the principles of sustainability really do work, even in a commercial enterprise of significant scope.

What we have constructed is so much more than just another commercial enterprise. It represents a ray of hope for the planet, a justification that we can really make a difference. Even though the U.S. Congress Office of Technology Assessment has declared that we are down to forty-one years of known oil reserves on the planet, we are not a minute closer to replacing them with renewable energy sources than we were ten years ago. We need to keep putting forth positive examples that will change our species' approach toward ensuring a sustainable future. The government just isn't going to do it. The utilities won't do it.

What we've tried to demonstrate with the Real Goods Solar Living Center is that the principles of sustainability really work. They are not an environmentalist's pipe dream. We

DAVID ARKIN

Like the wing of the eagle that foretold the success of John Schaeffer's vision, the curved shape of the Solar Living Center is aesthetic and symbolic as well as functional.

can build without cutting down trees; we can build with straw and earth, and we can use hemp and other plant fibers for a myriad of functions. We *can* build commercially without petroleum-laden asphalt parking lots. We *can* have businesses powered by electricity created from sunlight, with water pumped from sunlight, and without using one ounce of fossil fuels. We can have retail spaces as well lighted as any commercial building on the planet without using even one energy-hogging incandescent lightbulb. We can cool without artificial air conditioning and we can heat without guzzling electricity. We can create glorious landscapes without pesticides, producing enough organic food to feed our entire workforce. And we can demonstrate that sustainable building practices don't cost more; instead, they save in the long run, attracting more customers, bringing more business, making more profit, and keeping employees and customers alike motivated and inspired. It can be done and we all can do it. The eagle told us that we were right!

Vision Plan

Continued from page 8

some exotic varieties, and perhaps a hop patch with hop vines crawling on trellises (after all, this is Hopland!).

A large **Lake or Pond** can be dug on the floodway portion of the property, and natural plants and fish can be introduced to foster a healthy aquatic environment. This can be used recreationally by employees, shareowners, and members for swimming, fishing, or lounging. If we locate the lake that runs underneath the property, the lake can fill naturally or we can pump water from a well by solar water-pumping systems.

A beautiful **Sculpture** needs to be constructed that will eventually integrate into the property. The sculpture should be a monument to renewable energy, a sustainable lifestyle, and independent living. It should be an eye stopper and a head turner from both directions on Highway 101 in order to pique the interest of the thousands of car travelers every day. It could feature solar panels, a colored fountain with solar-pumped water, a giant sun that moves, a Stonehenge-type display, a solar tracking device, and many other possible ideas. By getting it installed soon, we can use the billboard aspect with something that says "Future Home of Real Goods" or "Welcome to the Solar Capital of the World." Or, create a simple billboard with a Windseeker wind generator mounted at each end and a couple of solar panels that charge batteries to light the sign at night. Those propellers spinning at each end of the billboard will get people's attention.

The **Oasis Atmosphere** should be maintained within the property. The goal is to make it alluring from Highway 101 so that people come and check it out. Parking should be tucked away where it is not highly visible. Walking, bicycling should be strongly encouraged; perhaps an electric shuttle can be present for elderly or handicapped people to tour. A gorgeous walking tour should be set up to tour all the elements of the 12-acre property.

Some kind of a **Children's Playground** and educational center should be constructed that teaches kids through hands-on experience how solar, wind, hydro, hydrogen, electric vehicles, and conservation work. Perhaps consult with Edwin Schlossberg (Caroline Kennedy's husband), visionary demo-educator in New York, if he isn't too expensive. This should be the definitive state-of-the-art anti–Ronald McDonald kids' play area, where parents from all over want to bring their kids to learn and experience solar and renewable energy. It should also be set up to cater to field trips from local schools and to encourage community participation.

Chapter 2

Getting Real: Real Goods and its Customers

Stephen Morris

Stephen Morris has been associated with Real Goods in a variety of capacities since 1980. He has helped shape many of the Real Goods customer communications. Currently the publisher at Chelsea Green, he also serves on the Real Goods Board of Directors.

Once you are Real you can't become unreal again. It lasts for always.
—*Margery Williams,* The Velveteen Rabbit

IT BEGAN WITH A PIECE OF DEAD, INERT ROCK called the Earth. The rock is similar to many other pieces of debris throughout the universe. What distinguishes it is a strong, stable relationship with a massive, gaseous sphere that is the only original source of energy in this solar system. It is called the Sun.

THE SUN'S LIGHT, through both its presence and its absence, creates temperature differences that stir movement, enabling the chance combination of elements. Over time—millions of years—the elements are reconfigured so that sunlight can be converted into energy. Life. And life begets life and more life and more life until there is a web of beings, plant and animal, interdependent upon each other.

Ecosystem. Civilization. California. Awesome!

Traced to its origins, each thin, intertwined strand of life has a tiny umbilical to the Sun. A sense of awe at our humble origins stirred in John Schaeffer when he beheld the plot of land in Hopland, California, that was to become the Solar Living Center. While most of us saw a flat and abused Highway Department dumping ground, John envisioned a place to pay homage to the original life source, the Sun.

The Myth

There is a Robin-Hood-and-his-Merry-Men quality to Real Goods and its customers (of course, this is almost the twenty-first century, so let's say Merry People). Look closely at the assemblage of people who follow the Real Goods flag and you will see that it consists of anarchists, outlaws, wild-eyed liberals, religious zealots, right-wing militiamen, tree huggers, conservative engineers, ranchers, and ex-hippies. Real Goods has always been a company (actually more of a "cause" than a company) that has been able to unite the extreme right and left beneath the same banner. If the company merchandise motto is "Everything Under the Sun," the customer motto might be ". . . And Everyone, Too."

The Setting

If John Schaeffer is the mythological Robin Hood, then Mendocino County is his Sherwood Forest. Mendocino is a big and rugged country, a meeting place for the manicured vineyards spilling over from Sonoma County and the ancient redwoods whose claim to the land predates human interlopers. Mendocino's rugged terrain runs directly into the Pacific Ocean. This is a beauty that intimidates, as anyone who has driven the sinuous road from Ukiah to Boonville can testify. You have to keep your attention on the road or you will experience the precipitous terrain in a way that is as brief as it is unpleasant. Only the bounteous Russian River Valley offers peaceful respite from the jagged hills and crashing waves of Mendocino.

Because of the terrain and the redwood forest, Mendocino is a great place to hide out, or even to get away entirely. It certainly seemed that way in the early 1970s to many young people who were weary of the strife that had been continuous since the bullet left Lee Harvey Oswald's gun, ending forever the days of Camelot and *Father Knows Best.* By the time we had extricated ourselves from Vietnam and chased Richard Nixon from office, the wounds were numerous and fresh. It was time to get away, to hang out, and let time work its magic cures. For many young ex-urbanites, Mendocino County became the sanctuary.

John Schaeffer, founder of Real Goods, had no ambition to become Robin Hood or even an outlaw. After graduating from the University of California at Berkeley, where he was exposed to every strand of the lunatic fringe, he moved to a commune called "Rainbow" between Philo and Elk, California, a 290-acre mountain community as picturesque as it was isolated. There he lived a life in pursuit of self-sufficiency.

It was a heady time, fueled by the sense that a revolution was at hand and populated by colorful characters who seemed equally at ease on either side of the law. This was

Mendocino, and it had its own laws and ethics. Not that these people were thieves, but they were refugees from a society run amok. They were unified only in their mistrust of institutions that had gotten us into a war, polluted our rivers, and cut down our virgin forests. They sought alternatives, different ways to satisfy the basic human needs of shelter, nourishment, and safety. You don't have to live in a suburban split-level; why not a geodesic dome in the redwood forest? You don't need red meat; you can thrive on vegetables and homemade bread. Your family doesn't need to be restricted to Mom, Dad, and baby sister; it can include all the people in the forest. Many of these "outlaw" attitudes were adopted by John Schaeffer and have been woven into the fabric of Real Goods.

Here's how the business happened:

Despite certain idyllic aspects of communal life, certain amenities were missing. (Remember, we're talking about a boy who was raised in Brentwood.) He didn't need a lot of money or power, but he did want some small amount to counterbalance the deprivation of communal life. Self-sufficiency, in other words, proved to be more challenging than it first appeared.

John found some 12-volt lightbulbs gathering dust on a back shelf of a Ukiah hardware store. Hmm. If these could operate off his car battery, then he could read at night. As long as he did not fall asleep with the lights on, he could renew his power supply the next day simply by driving his car to charge his batteries.

Knowing that he would be making the daily trek over the mountain to the big city, his friends would often ask him to buy supplies needed on the commune. As a conscientious, thrifty person, Schaeffer spent many hours combing the hardware stores and home centers of Ukiah, searching for the best deals on fertilizer, tools, rural amenities, and all manner of goods related to the communards' close-to-the-earth lifestyle. This became his graduate course in merchandising.

One day, while driving his Volvo station wagon (what else?) back to Boonville after a particularly vexing shopping trip, the thought occurred to him: "Wouldn't it be great if there was *one* store that sold all the products needed for independent living, the *real goods,* and sold them at fair prices?"

Real Goods was born.

THE GOODS

The merchandise focus of Real Goods has changed over the years. At various times in the company's history the hot product has been

- ZAP comic books
- Woodstoves made in Vermont from soapstone and cast iron
- Chicken wire and farm supplies
- Compact fluorescent lightbulbs
- Solar panels
- Creatures shaped out of dried dung
- Plastic gizmos that use solar power to repel mosquitoes
- Plastic disks that purport to replace the need for laundry detergent
- Books about houses made from straw bales
- Hats made of 100% hemp that say "Don't smoke this hat!"

These have all qualified as the "real goods."

The foundation of Real Goods is products that allow the generation and harvesting of energy. The company is the oldest and largest catalog firm devoted to the sale and service of renewable energy products. Do not think of the company as either old or large, however. The same principles that guided the buying decisions made by John Schaeffer for the commune govern the company merchants now—quality products at fair prices backed by thorough customer service.

Real Goods sells "everything under the sun," which means solar panels, 12-volt Christmas tree lights, water-conserving showerheads, and books on constructing your own pond. Look deeply enough into the lineage of every product, however, and you will see that each one is an alternative. That's what makes something the real goods. One of the company's great strengths has been its ability to adapt its merchandise premise to the public fancy without compromising its position as a company offering products of purpose and value.

While the specific merchandise has reflected changing, and sometimes chameleonlike consumer needs, what has remained rock solid has been the company's relationship with its customers. A love affair has developed between customers looking for "the real goods" and the company that provides them in so many forms and manifestations. As with all great love stories, there have been peaks and valleys, but ultimately this relationship qualifies as one of the most intense and enduring in the history of American business. The twin pillars upon which it has rested have been involvement and trust, a modern equivalent of "honor amongst thieves." The longtime supporters of Real Goods have made a pact. "Keep us entertained, don't cheat us, and try to do the right thing," they have said with their purchasing and investment dollars, "and we will be patient." This spirit prevails at Real Goods.

The Bottom Line

Growing businesses require capital. Real Goods was started on a shoestring, so there was precious little capital around. Moreover, those people with capital, such as banks, were loath to lend it to alternative upstarts whose business was with the lunatic fringers of the world.

John Schaeffer had an idea. It was so naive and outrageous he is probably embarrassed by it now that he has achieved a level of financial sophistication. He rolled out a proposition to his customers. Summarized, it was, "Banks are paying 8 percent interest and you have no idea what they do with your money. Here's an alternative. Send your money to Real Goods. We'll use it to grow the business and pay you 10 percent interest, better than you can do at the bank. Plus, you'll have the satisfaction of knowing that your money is benefitting a business that's trying to do the right things."

A quarter of a million dollars arrived in the mail from trusting customers. All of this money was eventually repaid, with interest. All involved apparently were satisfied with the transaction. It was not until years later, when Real Goods was dotting the i's and crossing the t's of its first public offering, that the company learned how non-traditional its original financial alliance with its customers had been. Indeed, the first pin-striped-suit–wearing advisor to hear of it nearly fell out of his overstuffed leather chair.

Real Goods has conducted two successful public offerings, raising over $4.6 million dollars of capital to fund the company's growth. It was this funding, in part, that enabled the construction of the Solar Living Center, which founder Schaeffer envisioned as the ultimate "return on investment" for Real Goods shareholders. Here is a place where people can see the products and practices of solar living, a living laboratory where the employees, owners, and customers can gather to joyfully experience the company philosophy in action.

Real Goods is now a real business, with Real Employees serving Real Customers, and even with Real Shareholders. This is "serious" business, as judged by the testaments of awards garnered along the way: the Corporate Conscience Award (from the Council on Economic Priorities), *INC.* magazine's inclusion of the company in their Top 500 Fastest-Growing Companies list, the Direct Marketing Association's Robert Rodale Award for environmental commitment (in 1996 and 1997), the Small Business Association's "Business of the Year"; and as attested to by news coverage in *Time, Fortune,* and *The Wall Street Journal,* and several thick scrapbooks full of press clippings. Has this gone to their heads?

Well ... sure. Shouldn't it?

Real Goods has been recognized by corporate associations and the media for its dedication to products and services for ecologically aware consumers, and to business principles consistent with its social and environmental mission. The company won the Direct Marketing Association's Robert Rodale Award for environmental commitment in both 1996 and 1997.

Real Goods has been so newsworthy because the company's decision makers have constantly challenged accepted ways of conducting business. The company's methods rarely represent the latest trend in business jargon. Instead, governed by a basic grasp of simple principles and an irrepressible urge to question authority, Real Goods does things in a way that the "straight" business world considers wildly innovative. This has not, repeat *not,* been the work of commercial gurus or public relations mavens, but rather the result of believing that business need not be so complicated that the average person cannot understand its workings.

The Vision

The company developed the motto "Knowledge is our most important product," and created the Real Goods Institute for Solar Living to give the company and its customers a chance to learn together interactively about all aspects of sustainable living. The Institute's first gathering was held in the company's cramped offices on Mazzoni Street in Ukiah with field trips to a nearby off-the-grid homestead. The setting was informal but charged with the energy and excitement of people gathering to share knowledge. One student, Rivers Brown, drove all the way from St. Francisville, Louisiana, and became so enamored with Real Goods that he became the largest purchaser of shares in the initial direct public offering. At the end of the weekend, everyone was infused with the exhilaration that comes only from the intoxicating mix of new friends and new knowledge. Upon reflection, this was the incident that gave rise to the vision of a Solar Living Center. Read this report from a vintage *Real Goods News:*

> In time, we plan the Institute to be a hallowed physical reality, with a completely off-the-grid campus that demonstrates the products, technologies, and techniques of the independent lifestyle. Landscaped with ecologically appropriate plants, needing minimal amounts of precious water or fertilization, the campus will be, at once, beautiful, while so environmentally compatible as to be nearly invisible. The professors will learn as much from the students as the students from the teachers. The products of Real Goods will be omnipresent—unobtrusive, yet essential in their functionality.
>
> Of course, it's a pipe dream!

This is the seed of the vision that found eventual expression in the Solar Living Center.

The current curriculum of the Institute includes courses and workshops on finding and buying land, shelter alternatives (domes, yurts, earth-bermed, straw bale), site orientation, water systems, solar, wind, and hydroelectric renewable power systems, organic gardening, and sustainable living in its infinite varieties. Instructors are technicians and staff of Real Goods, supplemented by a roster of guest speakers.

Finding new and interactive ways to involve customers became a company hallmark. A legendary customer interaction occurred with the advent of Off-the-Grid Day. The first "celebration of powerlessness" was held in 1991 to encourage people from coast to coast to flip off their breakers for one day. Pretentious for a small company in the hills of Mendocino to "declare" a national holiday? Of course, but it was expressly through such unhesitating self-aggrandizement that Robin and his Merry People could combat the very real, however intangible, Sheriffs of Nottingham such as global warming and the greenhouse effect.

The Billion Pound Goal, set in 1990 and being achieved in 1997, was another occasion for Real Goods and its legions to collectively slay a dragon. This time the enemy was global warming, and the battle was waged through the use of products that reduce the production of carbon dioxide, the most notorious "greenhouse gas." The Union of Concerned Scientists assisted with the development of formulas to translate the purchase and use of a certain item to a reduction in carbon dioxide emissions. Regular reports in company publications allowed customers to monitor their progress toward the goal of reducing those emissions by a billion pounds.

Beyond the company's interactive marketing programs, Real Goods uncovered the ultimate form of customer interaction by sharing ownership. Consistent with its other achievements, Real Goods went about selling stock by discovering alternative paths or, in some cases, forging new trails. Real Goods was the first company to attain a listing on the Pacific Stock Exchange (trading symbol RGT) and NASDAQ (RGTC) by successfully going

The Institute for Solar Living carries out Real Goods educational mission with a range of hands-on courses and workshops related to sustainability, such as classes on financing, designing, and building energy-efficient and self-sufficient homes, cooking with the sun, and restorative landscaping. Here, a class learns how to build using straw bale construction methods.

through a Direct Public Offering (DPO). In 1996, the company was the first approved by the Securities and Exchange Commission to launch its own trading marketplace on the Internet. You can buy or sell Real Goods stock "off the Wall Street grid" without paying a cent in broker commissions. The Web site is http://www.realgoods.com/.

The band of Merry People continues to grow. Sherwood Forest has been expanded across the land, with stakeholders in every state of the nation. The Solar Living Center is their long-awaited, tangible payback—a physical place, a sacred space, a sanctuary—a place that shows what the future might be.

The First Solstice Celebration

The road between vision and reality was neither straight nor smooth. There was still a growing company to run. There were still daily emergencies and crises of identity, but the vision did not fade. A giant step toward reality was taken when the company acquired the 12-acre parcel on the southern edge of Hopland. Like a kid with a new toy, John Schaeffer wanted to show off his acquisition, sharing a vision that was much further developed in his mind's eye than anywhere else.

On an otherwise gray and forgettable day in 1992, the Real Goods Board of Directors met to consider the company's future. John arranged for an elegant picnic on this ratty patch of ground that would four years hence become the Solar Living Center. (This particular November 9 was John's 43rd birthday.) At that time, no architects or landscapers had been contacted. The concept of "solar living" had not been articulated in a phrase, and therefore did not require a "center." Although the business folk shared the enthusiasm for a demonstration site of what was possible with the products of Real Goods, none but John could tangibly connect the aspiration to the dead earth, the dried-up creek bed, the passing cars on Highway 101, and the surrounding billboards.

It was a day without much sun, aside from the glow of the vision in John's mind's eye. The food was fresh and stylish, but the linkage was missing. The board members were awkward and quiet, squirming under the glare of passing truckers wondering why anyone would pick such an unlikely place for a repast. It wasn't an

The 12-acre site off Highway 101 outside of Hopland, California chosen for the Solar Living Center was once a dumping ground. At first only John Schaeffer could look at this bleak place and see the reality his dream could become. Fortunately, no one had the nerve to mention that the emperor was naked.

appropriate time to throw cold water on a dream, but the unspoken question on everyone's mind was, How do we get from here to there? There was a lot of silence.

The human animal's use of sunlight is indirect. We can't photosynthesize, so we consume vast amounts of stored sunlight as food. Within our bodies, the sunlight is combusted in a process remarkably similar to what happens to a stick of wood in a fire. The resulting conversion process creates warmth and energy. By the end of the picnic, spirits were slightly elevated. Although he was not saying so quite literally, what John was telling this group, as well as the employees and shareowners of Real Goods, was, "We need a place, somewhere we can celebrate the products of Real Goods, but also the practices of sustainable living. We need a place where we can celebrate the Sun."

Our protection comes from the Sun. Our clothing—whether derived from plant, animal, or fossil fuel—comes from the Sun. Our control of our interior environment comes from the Sun. We are, alas, a slash-and-burn species—not a slash-and-burn society, but

DAVID ARKIN

rather an entire species. It doesn't matter if we are living in the Stone Age in the remote Philippine hills or in luxurious decadence in Southern California, we slash and burn. Of course, as we sip our crisp Chablis and watch the sunset, we are insulated, much too insulated, from the consequences of our actions. With fossil fuels, we have simply learned to slash and burn vertically rather than horizontally. We take part of our planet, quite literally burn it, and put the wastes into the air and water.

"Okay, John," spoke the board in their collective, infinite wisdom. "We're not quite sure what it is that you're going to do, but your heart is in the right place. Real Goods as a business is at its best when you are following your passion, so go for it!"

The board members drank a toast to the future, saluting the dream, still feeling a little silly at their elaborately set folding table in the middle of a barren plain.

A time capsule was buried with great ceremony during the 1994 share-owner's meeting held on the site. Unfortunately, it was unearthed only two days later during construction excavation. Amidst jokes about California and instant gratification, the capsule was reinterred in a more fortuitous location and the project continued to move forward.

The ritual-tinged meeting was the first of several commemorative events that kept the Real Goods community focused on the dream of creating the business equivalent of a sacred place. At the shareowner's meeting in August of 1994, the attendees were given tours of the site, which by this time was a dusty series of contoured mounds surrounding two ponds. Rapt groups would listen to the descriptions of lush gardens, riparian canopies, and restored creek beds. Never once did someone raise a hand and say, "But all I see are dusty mounds."

A time capsule was created and buried amid great pomp and circumstance. Two days later, it was discovered to have been buried right where a construction excavation was required. The capsule found its way back into John Schaeffer's office and remained there for weeks, until eventually finding a more permanent home underground. Then it was the object of a bevy of retorts about how only in California would people use a time capsule as an agent of immediate gratification. This time capsule will be buried until . . . Tuesday! Why, we could even sell "instant time capsules" at the SLC.

Beneath the levity and the occasional blunder, however, the underlying sense of purpose to the project remained stable: to create a demonstration site for the products and practices of sustainable living. Toward that end, it was decided that the first Solstice Celebration would be held on December 21, 1994. By this time, the components of the solar calendar would be fully in place, and we could see whether or not this innovation actually worked.

As the season progressed toward the Winter Solstice, practical issues at the site of the Solar Living Center became urgent. What if it rains? What do you *do* at a Solstice Celebration?

By December 1 of every year, Sunny California, especially up north toward Mendocino, becomes Soggy California. The dry creeks (including Feliz Creek, which flows through the Hopland property) become sluices for the surrounding mountains and transform into raging torrents overnight. Relentless storms roll in off the Pacific, bringing walls of water, more drizzle than rain. With the water comes the flu, exotic new strains from the Far East, and for a few days before the holidays, the entire state is sniffling.

The activities for the first Winter Solstice Celebration were discussed at a management meeting. Drumming was deemed essential, in as many sizes and forms as possible. Swimming and streaking were ruled out as either inappropriate or insane. What else?

"We should ululate," suggested Douglas Bath, lead technician and manager of the renewable energy division.

"*Ululate*?" we all said in unison, the tone making apparent our collective ignorance.

"To ululate is to vocalize in a loud and random manner, often at a celestial object. It means exactly as it sounds: '*yule-you-late*.'"

It was thus decreed and passed by unanimous assent that ululation would be part of the Solstice Celebration. Within the halls of Real Goods there were many "ululation" jokes for the next few weeks.

To give a semblance of decorum to the proceeding, Scott Sherman, a local psychologist and shaman well versed in primitive and pagan rituals, agreed to conduct a nondenominational service.

True to form, the skies of California were gray and wet in the days preceding the first ever Real Goods Solar Living Center Solstice Celebration. It was looking fairly dismal. "I don't care if I'm the only one," said fearless leader Schaeffer, "I'm going down there at 4:21 P.M. and bang on a drum!"

And it came to pass that the day of the Solstice was the kind of day that only California can bestow on the world, even at the onset of winter. It was sunny, temperature in the fifties, with a lingering roundness to the air from the recent rain. (The rain would begin again the next day and continue, almost uninterrupted, into early January, resulting in widespread flooding and mudslides.)

A group of twenty or so hardy souls showed up for the ceremony, conducted by the aforementioned Mr. Sherman, who was brightly festooned for the occasion. The ceremony was equal parts educational and spiritual, giving us a more vivid impression of what it meant for ancient people to have a sense of their place in the cosmos. There was some chanting, some silence, some holding of hands. Then, at precisely the right moment when the predicted alignment of huge stones marked the lines of sight, the Sun, looking pale in the western sky, settled behind Duncan Peak, slid down the mountainside for a minute, then disappeared into a mystical notch.

Sunrises and sunsets provide inspiration to artists, lovers, and beach walkers. At the moment of sunset, we instinctively become still. Here is a moment when we can actually look at the Sun, connect with it directly, and share the universe. Words are unnecessary. We are renewed.

After the sacred nanosecond, the drumming and ululation began, foolish yet fulfilling. It continued for the next half hour, until the last flicker of light was gone. Exhilarated, exhausted, and exalted, we all knew that we had rediscovered something buried deeply within ourselves. A rebirth. A tradition.

The first Winter Solstice Celebration was held at the site on December 21, 1994, to test the newly installed Solar Calendar (see chapter 3). Despite inclement weather the preceding and following weeks, the day was sunny and warm. "At precisely the right moment when the predicted alignment of huge stones marked the lines of sight, the Sun settled behind Duncan Peak, slid down the mountainside for a minute, then disappeared into a mystical notch."

Real Goods Corporate Principles

PRINCIPLE 1. REAL GOODS IS A BUSINESS.

AND A BUSINESS IS, first and foremost, a financial institution. You can have the most noble social mission on the planet, but if you cannot maintain financial viability, you cease to exist, and so does your mission. In other words, sustainability must first be rigorously applied to economics. The survival instinct is very strong at Real Goods, and that reality governs many decisions. Anyone who thinks the company functions like a commune or worker's collective need not apply. A business with a strong mission but without financial stability will be short-lived and forgotten quickly. Real Goods has always maintained a healthy balance between vision, inspiration, and commonsense realism.

PRINCIPLE 2. KNOW YOUR STUFF.

OUR SOCIAL AND ENVIRONMENTAL MISSIONS are only as strong as the equipment that makes possible the independent lifestyle that forms the foundation of Real Goods. While the SLC demonstrates a particularly delightful (and somewhat futuristic) version of this lifestyle, it is the people who actually live off the grid who have pioneered the concepts. Solar, hydro, and wind technologies work, for sure, but require a degree of interaction between buyer and seller that has been almost forgotten during the national half-century binge on cheap power, when the definition of personalized service has become the greeter who says "Hello" when you enter Wal-Mart. Another way of saying this is that without the educational element of the business, there would be nothing to sell. The government and the media have conducted a concerted effort to convince the consuming public that renewable energy just doesn't work.

Real Goods sells equipment, but sells along with it the knowledge and service to ensure that what you buy performs to expectations. One of the keys to customer satisfaction is selection and installation of the right system to begin with. To assess your needs, capabilities, limitations, and working budget, Real Goods asks you to complete a worksheet that includes a complete list of potential energy needs, an inventory of desired appliances, site information, and potential for hydroelectric and wind development. A technical staff member is assigned to determine needs and to design an appropriate system. This person will order parts, assist with assembly, and work with you or your licensed contractor to assist with installation and troubleshooting.

For those more comfortable working with a local tradesman, Real Goods offers a no-charge referral program of "Local Pros." This is not an endorsement program, nor does it guarantee any degree of expertise provided via association with Real Goods. It is simply another way to accommodate the individual preferences of customers. The company recommends that you check references before using any installer.

Real Goods Corporate Principles

PRINCIPLE 3. GET INVOLVED!

THE LINES BETWEEN who owns the company, who works for it, and who benefits from it are intentionally fuzzy at Real Goods. The customers of Real Goods like to be involved too and have historically supported some highly unorthodox ways of doing business. One particularly unusual sequence of interactive events established the unabashed style for which Real Goods has become famous.

In 1991, in keeping with the intrepid spirit of our rebellious forebears, Real Goods (in partnership with some like-minded souls who organized the Solar Energy Expo and Rally) wrote and published a document called the Declaration of Energy Independence. Thousands of Real Goods customers and expo attendees signed.

A year later, the petitions were delivered to the White House, as promised, in an electric car. To add a little sex appeal, then-presidential candidate and former California Governor Jerry Brown drove the car. The event was filled with sound bites and photo ops; in fact, it was unabashed hype, but it did succeed in bringing the nation's energy situation to the attention of millions, making Real Goods a household word in the process. (Less than two years later, a Real Goods technician served on a committee of advisors to convert the White House into a model of energy efficiency.)

PRINCIPLE 4. TAKE A CHANCE, TAKE A STAND.

MANY BUSINESSES TREAT RISK as the financial equivalent of the Black Plague. This leads to the mealy-mouthed corporate jargon that has become synonymous with the term "public relations." Real Goods has made it its business to take stances consistent with the company's social and environmental mission. Occasionally, this practice goes awry, such as when owner John Schaeffer published his views on abortion in the *Real Goods News*. More typically, however, as long as the company has been honest enough to admit transgressions, Real Goods customers forgive and forget the rare misstep in their support of the company's efforts.

"Real Relief" was a program to provide discounts and priority shipping to those left without power in the aftermath of natural disasters in Florida (Hurricane Andrew), Hawaii (Hurricane Iniki), the Midwest (the floods of 1993), and Los Angeles (earthquakes, riots, mudslides). "Operation Desert Storm" offered soldiers in the combat zone the comforts of a solar shower or a battery-free source of music.

Off-the-Grid Day became a self-declared national holiday when consumers were encouraged to flip the breaker and experience the potential joys of powerlessness. The event was so successful that it spawned a National Tour of Independent Homes that for several years introduced tens of thousands of

Real Goods Corporate Principles

homeowners to the joys and realities of energy-independent life. The tour was eventually taken over by the American Solar Energy Society and continues to provide prospective off-the-gridders annually with their best opportunity to learn firsthand, by touring solar and energy-efficient houses all over the country, what it is like to cut the cord to the power company.

The tour was so successful that it led to the establishment in the spring of 1994 of a full-time network of demonstration homes. This program is designed for the homeowner or business owner who wants to make a serious personal commitment to solar and independent living.

The easiest way to become involved with the Real Goods community is to become a "Lifetime Member," that is, member of the company's preferred customer club. This group is the revenue lifeblood of Real Goods. Originally the program was called The Hard Corps in recognition of the willingness of the constituents to be militant in their protection of the Earth, but too many employees disliked any connection with the military or war, so the controversial moniker was replaced by a more palatable alternative. Lifetime Members receive the full roster of Real Goods publications, as well as a 5 percent discount on all purchases, including sale merchandise. Membership privileges continue indefinitely with annual renewal.

PRINCIPLE 5. IT'S OKAY TO HAVE FUN!

TECHNICAL LEAD "DOCTOR DOUG" PRATT ONCE OBSERVED, "Real Goods might not run the tightest ship in the business world, but we sure throw the best parties!" Real Goods has discovered that you can have fun doing business.

Celebration is a regular part of the company marketing plan. Grand openings, shareowner meetings, groundbreakings, and Solstices are occasions to gather the employees, shareowners, and Lifetime Members to eat, drink, and be merry, and in all likelihood, to sell a fair amount of product in the process.

The vigor of Real Goods' customers' collective willingness to participate is a source of continual amazement. Tales abound that testify to their loyalty. Shareowners routinely drive hundreds of miles for annual meetings to see how their $100 investment is faring. When Lifetime Members were invited to submit lists of songs that had the Sun as a theme, hundreds responded, some with lists of up to eight hundred songs, representing hours of painstaking research. More astonishing, this effort was to win a prize that was billed as "some piece of junk from our warehouse."

Stephanie Kotin and **Christopher Tebbutt** are the principals of Land & Place, a design/build company based in Boonville, California, with over twenty years garden-making experience in both hemispheres and in a wide range of climates and approaches. They draw upon apprenticeships in classic horticulture under Alan Chadwick at the Round Valley Garden Project, training in botanical horticulture at the Royal Botanic Gardens, Edinburgh, and the Crown Estate Gardens, Windsor Great Park, and an ongoing exploration into the nature of restorative landscape design, both here and abroad. Fundamental to their approach is an environmental ethic that has translated into forestry reform efforts, stream-bank stabilization projects, and extensive travel studying endangered plants in their native habitats throughout the temperate world.

Chapter 3

The Landscape Plan: A Place Study

Stephanie Kotin and Christopher Tebbutt

The more one immerses oneself in the complexity of the familiar, the more one can attain the simplicity of life.—*Gene Logsdon*

Living as we do in Anderson Valley, along Anderson Creek, part of the grand Navarro River watershed, we are familiar with flood plains and remnant riparian forests that cling precariously to the banks of our valley's stream and river systems. On the opposite slope of the same coastal hills, only a stone's throw from the head-waters of our own Anderson Creek, Feliz Creek commences. By the time it flows past the Solar Living Center, it is close to its confluence with the Russian River.

A Watershed Approach

Our preferred nonhighway route to Hopland, "the slow route," is via the well-known Mountain House Road. As we travel up to the southern edge of the Navarro watershed, we leave behind the redwood and Douglas fir of the north and west slopes and, with some altitude on the southern and eastern exposures, enter rich oak woodlands consisting of three species of deciduous and two of evergreen oak mixed with alder, big-leaf maple, Oregon ash, and the odd "Wolf Tree," or rogue Douglas fir. We have done this journey so many times now that we can watch the progress of the year in our favorite familiar trees.

The dryness at the end of the year brings the first color to the Oregon ash. As we turn eastward, inland toward Hopland, we quickly descend into hot rain-shadow country of great beauty, the climate defined by the trees and the soil. Blue oak appears suddenly, along with foothills pine on the serpentine soils. The distance between the foothills pine and the last redwood may be only a few miles, yet between them lies a vast change, almost night and day, of aspect and orientation toward the Sun. These are the lowland foothills of great heat,

where spring comes early and is brief. We have left behind the "coolth" of the coast with its frequent fog and moisture-laden dark forests, for the openness and aridity of the smoky-blue pine hills studded with slow-growing oaks.

Mountain House Road is more famous in California for its wildflowers: acres of goldfields and blue lupine, Chinese houses and larkspur on the road banks, even whole sweeps of shooting stars at the tail end of winter. And late in the growing year, when the pink of summer's darling *(Clarkia amoena)* is finishing, the golden cups of the mariposa lily can be found, singly, in the long, now-dry grass. The serpen-

Looking west across the barren site toward Duncan Peak on the Summer Solstice in 1994, Stephanie Kotin and Chris Tebbutt needed vivid imaginations to clothe the barren flood plain by the dry Feliz Creek with gardens and orchards and ponds. Their landscaping works with nature's own tools—water, sunlight, native and adaptive plants—to restore a blighted place to productivity and health.

tine soil inhibits European weeds such as oat grass (the great choker of native annuals), permitting the wildflowers to grow prolifically along this rural road.

We describe these hills in detail because they are a fundamental part of the "borrowed landscape" of the Solar Living Center and provide context and constant inspiration. Duncan Peak is the site's Magic Mountain. The landscape pays homage to its beauty and dominance by facing and actively engaging it at pivotal points in the garden.

The State of the Site

We stopped at a pull-out above Hopland's Sanel Valley and looked down on the Real Goods site near the Feliz Creek bridge one particular June day in 1994. We could see the Russian River, defined by its canopy of riparian trees dominated by the Fremont poplar against the flat pattern of one-dimensional grapes and acres of pears. There was nothing growing on the site save the garishness of billboards and a lone juvenile valley oak. It could have been Anywhere, USA: a freeway dump site.

A glance back. Before the CalTrans dump site of bric-a-brac, debris of slides and slips, broken concrete and piles of weed-growing gravel; before the head-trained vineyard (probably Zinfandel); before the hops plantations; before any early agricultural endeavors, this

DAVID ARKIN

flood plain was once a part of the immense riparian woodlands of the Russian River, a climax forest of pre-European proportions. The three benches that make up this complex plant community are still recognizable. On the banks of the creek itself were once the willows—Pacific, arroyo, red, and sandbar—growing among white alder. On the second bench, box elder, Oregon ash, and black walnut were predominated by cottonwood, with perhaps big-leaf maple giving way to western sycamore. And on the upper bench, in the more stable, loamy soils, grew valley oak, beautifully spaced and festooned with wild grape, rich with wildflowers and herbaceous perennials. A forested flood plain is among the richest of lands, the most dynamic, and always in a state of flux, hence the apt description "a plant community designed by catastrophe."

Initially, we had an aversion to the site. The place was a fishbowl full of highway noise and fumes, debris, and star thistle. All of this changed on June 22—the Summer Solstice. We had come in the semidarkness to stand in the rubble in the center of the imagined courtyard. This was to become the central axis point of the fountain, the pool, the spiral, the solar calendar, indeed of the entire garden. With compass and 300-foot measuring tapes, we marked the spot and waited for the dawn on this, the longest day of the year. In the semi-darkness, the edges of the valley bowl were lit up, the road was quiet. We waited for the morning star to fade.

5:37 A.M.: Horizon sunrise
5:50 A.M.: Sun gilds top of Duncan Peak
6:14 A.M.: Sun clears the ridge

In the near dark, we sensed a certain wildness in the surrounding hills. The ancient geomorphology of the place bespoke its origins, dominated by the shadow of Duncan Peak. And we wondered, what was its real name?

We returned that evening for the sunset, 8:25 P.M. on the lower ridge and 8:37 P.M. at the horizon.

How much easier it is in the hours around dawn and twilight to gloss over all of the many shortcomings of such a raw site. But it was all the hours "in between," day in and day out, in the full blaze of sun and dust, that we would have to mitigate. Yet we had already begun to leaf out its barrenness in our mind's eye.

SOME THOUGHTS ON RESTORATION *OR* A FACE ONLY A MOTHER COULD LOVE

This generation may either be the last to exist in any semblance of a civilized world or it will be the first to have the vision, the bearing, and the greatness to say, "I will have nothing more to do with this destruction of life. I will play no more part in this devastation of the land. I am determined to live and work for peaceful reconstruction for I am morally responsible for the world today and the generations of tomorrow."

—*Richard St. Barbe Baker**

THERE'S NO ESCAPING IT. Anyone who is even remotely tuned in today, whether via the Internet or their local radio station, feels a sense of heightened concern, even anguish, over the fate of the natural world. The imperative of what Edward Goldsmith calls "the Great U-Turn," which must occur in our culture, is as much a result of action and creative work as it is the product of those technological means necessary to accomplish it (*The Great U-Turn*. Devon, England: Green Books, 1988). The complex questions of right livelihood and quality of life remain paramount, as the "development age" comes to an end and we approach the biophysical limits of nature's largesse. The rapid advent of a solar culture and the ongoing work of restoration are two of the imperatives embodied in the Great U-Turn.

There are always difficulties in allying ecological forces to the framework of the marketplace, just as there are inherent contradictions for a for-profit company that advocates knowledge as its most valuable commodity. How do you do all this and still make a profit at the end of the day without bastardizing the whole thing? By starting with a property that no one would touch, with little intrinsic value on that self-same marketplace. Or, as Rivers Brown of Louisiana, original Real Goods shareholder and first graduate of the Institute for Solar Living, said upon first viewing the site, "This place has a face that only a mother could love."

Sandwiched as it is between a sewage treatment plant and Interstate 101, surely this dump was tailor-made for Real Goods!

True to form for "a plant community designed by catastrophe," the flood plain here is an active site geologically, accruing new soil, in the form of silt as well as debris, in major flood events. Since garden construction began in the fall of 1994, the Solar Living Center has already sustained three such events, all considered at least of a twenty-five-year

*See Karen Gridley's *Man of the Trees: Selected Writings of Richard St. Barbe Baker* (Willits, California: Ecology Action, 1989).

The Hopland site has sustained "twenty-five year" floods several times since construction began. The building and grounds were bermed and designed to withstand such flooding, and even to take advantage of the rich soil and fish stocks washed in by the river.

magnitude, further proof that this site and its environs are in a state of disrepair. However, as these gardens were designed to be flood prone, such incidents become biological opportunities. Where else can one capture one's upland neighbors' soil, and even sort and recycle their garbage for them? Situated as we are on this volatile river system, the concept of private property rights is regularly turned on its ear.

For the ponds and the proposed wetland, these floods are the highlight of an ongoing reclamation project that nature is conducting. One example of many: The ponds were built behind a twenty-five-year-event levee, now the main access road, to conform to a Department of Fish and Game requirement to prevent migration of exotic fish species (we had none proposed) into the once-famous salmon and steelhead runs of the Russian River. However, the opposite occurred. In the first winter, the floods arrived and, as predictably as the Nile carrying her baskets of silt and debris, the river stocked the ponds for us with blue gill and other fish.

Landscape and pond construction commenced before the building, providing the massive amounts of fill needed to raise the straw bale structure well above the hundred-year flood plain. In this way, the garden and habitat restoration give life to the building both figuratively and literally. But it was not until the highway was bermed and screened, even partially, that we could begin to rebuild a sense of atmosphere, the very foundation of an "achieved" place.

Landscaping was begun before building construction so that the gardens and trees could begin their long process of restoring life to the place. The fill scooped from the ponds went into the berm that raises the building above flood levels.

JEFF OLDHAM

AN OASIS

As barren as this land may have appeared, it had one tremendous, overriding asset: the presence of an abundant and high water table. This will be clearly manifest when the hundreds of trees now planted on the site find their feet in that underground flow, resulting in a proliferation of growth and signaling the return to a native expression of the place.

Perhaps it is no accident that the Solar Living Center is situated next to Hopland's Sewerage Treatment Plant. At first consideration, this would seem to be a negative and a limitation on the site. Yet here is an opportunity to extend the goals of restoration into the community at large. Taking our cues from the City of Arcata's Water Reclamation Project, for example, by putting the regenerative power of water plants to work cleaning and absorbing heavy metals and toxic substances, we can export the alchemy of turning foul water to sweet.

LAWRENCE WATSON

This cleansing of the water is analogous to the constant, daily renewal by the plant kingdom of our oxygen-rich atmosphere. What plants can do for air, they do with equal grace for water.

Fundamental to a restorative landscape is an independence from the petrochemical grip upon our so-called modern agricultural and horticultural practices. "Off-the-grid" applies to more than just the power companies. The SLC, from day one, has been off the chemical grid as well. An immediate illustration of this lies at our feet, where we have put to work the plants' ability to garner nitrogen from the atmosphere through the use of prostrate clover and alfalfa as a key landscape ingredient. In so doing, we bypass the number one user of chemical fertilizers and poisons in the United States today: the deceptively innocent Great American Lawn.

Ehrenfried Pfeiffer has written, "People must again become conscious that expenditures for beauty and integration into the landscape are not a luxury but a necessity for the health and indeed for the moral firmness of the population" (*The Earth's Face*, Rodale Press, 1947). Is it not time to make a prerequisite of beauty key to the goals of "second generation" organic culture? How else can we inspire, move, and reach people without the artificial pheromones of a Disneyland or a Madison Avenue? We may live in a place, physically, yet it is the way in which we imaginatively take possession of places on the Earth, whether in the act of garden-making, home-making, or place-making, that defines our sense of belonging. (If one is a city-dweller, it is the relationship to the tree outside the window, perhaps, or to the wilderness of the night sky.) Is the Earth alive or do we view it as a machine to satisfy our own needs? "Either all the world's a miracle or there are no miracles" (Albert Einstein).

It was Jonathan Porritt who wrote, "Humankind's greatest priority is to reintegrate with the natural world" (*Save the Earth*, Turner, 1991). If we expand the meaning of our habitation to include knowledge of and commitment to our watersheds, to the physical folds of our landscape, the character of its soil and its flora—from forest to wildflowers—then this is our reintegration. How else can we engender and spread the necessary "biophilia," the love of life, such that restoration, like the Great U-Turn, becomes inevitable?

By beginning with the reality of the Solar Living Center site, which is a flood plain, and extending water throughout as the unifying garden feature, we not only create diverse oases, but re-create the meaning of this place: garden making and habitat restoration at the same time. Human-made ponds, reclaimed by nature as constructed wetlands, gradually take the site back to what it once was. Water becomes the vehicle for a theme and variation between wild and built landscapes, origin and culture.

Water, the cardinal directions, and solar orientation provide the underlying structure for the landscape plan.

LAWRENCE WATSON

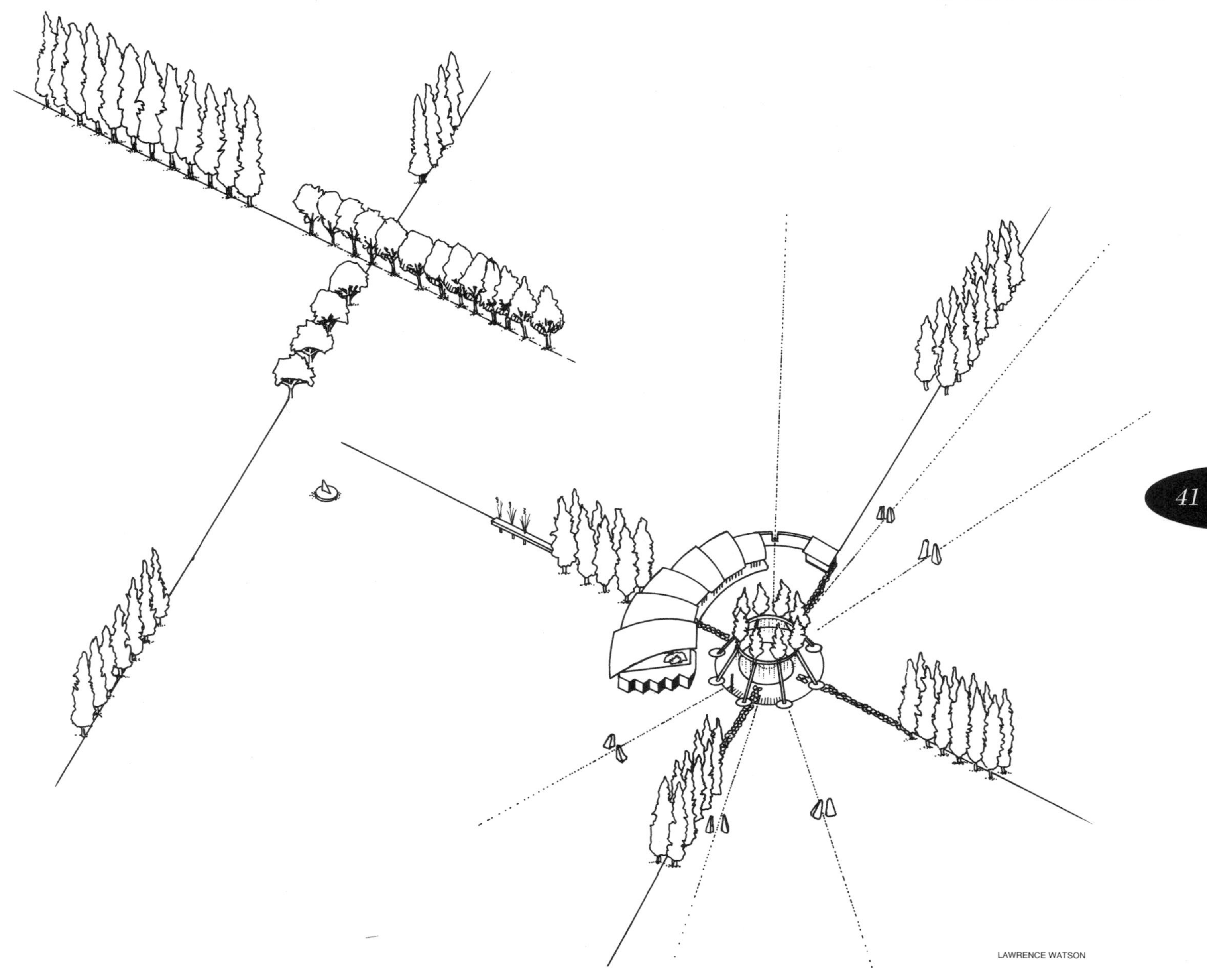
LAWRENCE WATSON

Rethinking the Landscape

Even before the access road off Interstate 101 to the Solar Living Center site was staked out (or conceived of, for that matter), the approaches to the project witnessed a huge metaphorical pileup. All of the aspirations, expectations, and projections for this very public endeavor collided at the south end of Hopland. Sifting through the rubble with our 100-mesh screens, we managed to separate the seed from the chaff and, as the project's landscape designers, came up initially with the following objectives:

- resource efficiency
- demonstration of alternative methodologies for cultivation, fertilization, irrigation
- practice of aspects of a home-based garden economy
- congruence with the project's native place
- harmonious marriage between built and natural spaces
- education and productivity
- practicality as well as beauty
- interactive living displays/rooms
- use of water as a unifying garden feature

Also the following wish list:

- forested groves as managed habitat for heat mitigation
- alternative lawns/meadows
- ornamental orchard
- herb garden featuring native and non-native medicinal and culinary herbs
- soft fruit production
- compost/recycled greenwaste niche
- nut-tree copse
- native California dry scree garden
- natural rock formation/river-washed boulders/flowforms
- stream as biological filter
- sacred lotus and water lilies
- lowland marsh habitat garden
- demonstration "kitchen garden"

With these working tools before us, we asked, What is the context of this garden (a marriage between commercialism and the demonstration and promotion of sustainable living) from its vantage point in the Sanel Valley and the town of Hopland? We drew the context from the meander of the flood plain and its associated flora, local agriculture, and its pronounced grid and regular rhythm, and from a certain wildness present in the surrounding hills. In addition to these local patterns, we defined three human themes that are both a simile for and the product of the site's long-term potential:

inspiration: memory, story, ritual
production: fertility, abundance, the craft of horticulture, self-sufficiency
restoration: commitment, reintegration, responses to the question: "What kind of currency grows in these new deserts? These brand new flood plains?"*

Inspiration, production, restoration. These elements represent the full field of endeavor for anyone seeking to integrate human needs with those of the natural world. Taken alone, any one of these themes could have been magnified across the site. The whole site could have been devoted to productivity. Or returned to entirely native vegetation. Or, the total site could have been a representation of the landscape of imagination.

However, we chose what it is today: a union of all three themes, richer, more complete, an expression of this time and place.

We designed the central Courtyard as a gathering place of inspiration. The former valley oak zone would become a place of high biological productivity and complexity. Native habitat restoration would take the form of a constructed wetland.

The immeasurable pre-European dignity of this little patch of earth along Feliz Creek was reduced to the degradation of an abandoned, star-thistled wasteland, dry and exposed, an appropriate metaphor for the marginalized piece of Earth most people inherit today. By listening to the narrative of our native context, it is possible to turn, again, and begin to reestablish the qualities that make up *place.*

A zone of productivity

At first glance, the landscape garden looks like a modified flood plain, as it is only a few years old and still showing the bones of its initial construction. The trees have yet to close canopy and the understory to mass up and soften the pronounced lines of the underlying grid. A central, elevated circular courtyard sweeps from curving berm to curving building and round to berm again, marrying earthen wall and sloping bank to the same radius. By necessity, the passive-solar showroom has turned its back on the north, where a majority of the property lies. We searched for a way to unite the two.

*From Bruce Cockburn's song, "If a Tree Falls," Golden Mountain Music Corp. (SOCAN), 1988. Reproduced pursuant to express license from Sony Music Special Products, Sony Music Entertainment, Inc.

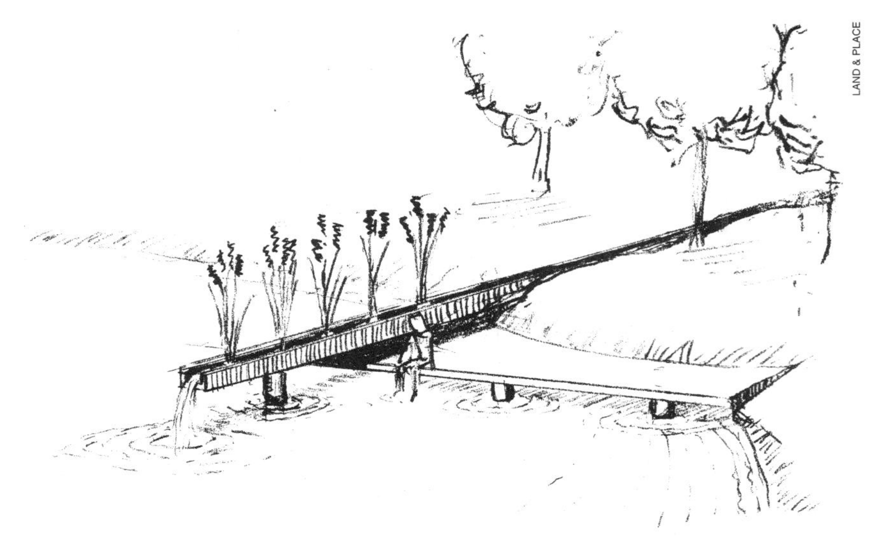

Taking our cue from the building (always a curved bird's wing in our mind's eye), we chose a spiral to project the central oasis out into the landscape at large. It is bisected by the traditional agricultural grid, realigned to honor the cardinal directions: north, south, east, west.

Out of the dominant spiral descends a sloping path with the main water course as its guide. The water course disappears into a "room" of timber bamboo (dubbed the Bamboo Pyramid) and re-emerges to follow a rustic water chute that turns the course toward due north and, at child's height, cantilevers out into the first of the ponds. A 3-foot drop provides the source of health and renewal universal to all water bodies, oxygenation. This upper pond sits at the original grade of the third bench in the flood plain of the past, where a riparian forest once grew with giant valley oaks *(Quercus lobata)*.

Flowing water serves as a symbolic device and a necessary ingredient in the Solar Living Center landscape. The water is oxygenated as it bubbles through flowforms and channels into the ponds; in turn, it cools the atmosphere, nourishes the plants, teaches and entertains the children and adult visitors, and provides a home for the micro- and macroinvertebrates, fish, birds, and animals that share the created and restored habitats.

A floating dock near the splash and spray of the water chute gives access to a more circular view of this bench—the region of productivity—bounded to the north and east by the entry drive. Here, all four zones are represented: woodland, wetland, dryland, and grassland. Beginning with a forest planting in the northeast corner, these zones flow to the center, where water is the abundant element, and where wild stock becomes the graft upon which the cultivated crops reflect the abundance and fertility of a home-based garden economy.

The hot, extended, and dry summer, temperate winter, high water table, and valley-bottom soils make the Sanel Valley suitable habitat for plants from a broad cross section of the temperate world. Pomegranate, fig, and apricot, with the blue-flowered chaste tree for a honey-flow in midsummer and alstroemeria for spring; loquat and persimmon among *Rosa rugosa* (the finest producer of rose hips); black currant and gooseberry, red currant and jostaberry, in beds of agastache, oregano, and wild dianthus; mulberry trees and raspberry beds; plum, peach, and nectarine amid narcissus, chicory, and blue-eyed grass; Asian pear and aromatic quince-pineapple, Smyrna and orange; feijoa and olive; hops and grape; representatives of the great nut crops of the world: black walnut, Spanish sweet chestnut, buartnut and heartnut, pecan (the native and her cultivars), the Turkish hazel and the

American hickory; new, heat-hardy varieties of blueberry; Siberian almond and wild apricot with maximillian sunflower . . . the zone of productivity, where sound horticultural practices maximize a site's potential.

This is the role of biologically productive gardening: the magnification of the potentialities of nature. At the height of the French fruit culture, there were over six hundred varieties of pears. The Inca peoples perfected hundreds of varieties of potato. Farmers in southern India have developed, over generations, a different variety of rice for every day of the year. The art and craft of horticulture create a Royal Gala apple from a wild crab, a Sugarsnap from a wild pea. This "graft" is the marriage between the wild rootstock and the scion that is our human imagination. Is this not the true definition of economy?

A canal connects the upper and lower ponds (with a mere 8 inches of fall) knitted by torrent sedge and water iris. Hop across the canal to find bold plants of great architectural beauty: wachendorfia and angels' fishing rod from South Africa, sages from Mexico, fountainesque grasses from Japan.

LAND & PLACE

On the isthmus between the upper and lower ponds, a sundial planted in thyme requires a human gnomon to chart the Sun's course.

LIVING STRUCTURES

SEVEN "LIVING STRUCTURES" serve as dominant features in the landscape of the SLC. Most of them are a play and variation on the theme we began with the Tree-Sculpted Fountain. They contain a minimum of physical structure that plants are coaxed around, within, or among to express a familiar human gesture: a single room, a single roof, a tunnel, an exclamation point. Constructed from inexpensive, mostly off-the-shelf materials, these living structures are fun and oddly familiar, lightening the tenor of the landscape plan as a whole. An additional goal was to minimize the use of wood. Why mimic the function of a tree to define a place of shade and shelter with the end-product of its life—timber—when we can induce the living plant, in all its varied forms, to do the same?

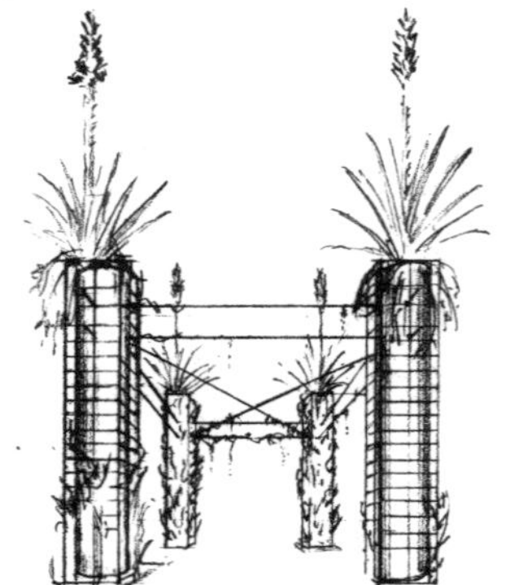

AGAVE COOLING TOWER

Stepping out of your car on a summer day in Hopland can feel like stepping into a blast furnace. Our first requirement for a welcoming entry portal, here, was its capacity to cool. The first of the living structures, the Agave Cooling Tower,

But to sit between the ponds, we must continue out onto the isthmus proper. Here it is possible to imagine a native scree, a secluded backwater outwash of gravel, boulders, penstemon, and deer grass, enlivened by hummingbirds working the desert willow, the local green-backed heron on the hunt, and the native water chinquapin in a shallow pool. Here, the visitor becomes a life-sized gnomon in a sundial built to human scale, bringing back solar orientation and aspect, solar time, solar "reality." The sundial, planted in different varieties of *Thymus,* is laid out with the hours of the day set in thirteen round birdbaths. By standing on the line of solar noon, with one's head touching the gnomon, one casts a shadow across the time of day.

Across the footbridge at the narrow of the pond, the kitchen garden sits at the northwest corner of this rich zone, complete with nut trees, heirloom apples and espaliered pears, soft fruit and stone fruit, perennial vegetables, herbs, and annual vegetable beds prepared in the French intensive, double-dug manner. Independent from the rest of the garden and separated from it by the lower pond, this garden is self-contained in its raison d'être: intensive cultivation for the table.

From the kitchen garden, we can reorient our internal compass by following the axis line that runs west to east, from Turkish upright poplar to ornamental pear. Near the northeast apex of this productivity zone, find a water lily pool, a crisscross fountain, and an open terrace for educational displays, stargazing, and respite. Dominated on two sides by the strong north-south, east-west lines of fastigiate pear and bounded by the arcs of feijoa and dwarf olive hedges, this lily-laden pool serves as one of the most important focal points in the garden (and the site of the only existing tree on the place when we began: the small, solitary valley oak). Across the drive stands the northeast forest of redwood, box elder, alder, incense cedar, bigleaf maple, western sycamore, sequoia, and ash. Just in front, the paulownia grove is gaining girth and height

LAND & PLACE

The northeast corner of the garden supports a broad range of plants from the temperate world, including woodland, wetland, dryland, and grassland species. The designers of these gardens sought to magnify the site's potential, merging the themes of inspiration, production, and restoration.

at a phenomenal rate. This tree mass will eventually join into one great, mixed canopy and then precipitously stop all of a sudden, on the cardinal axis lines, creating a sheltering quadrant of concentrated, south-facing solar intensity and aspect.

This northeast corner of the garden is transformed into a play of opposites by the presence of the cooling, reflective lily pool. Here, the large, round leaf of a tropical water lily provides a great analogy. This most extravagant producer of life-giving chloro-

LIVING STRUCTURES

provides an introduction to the theme of water in the form of cooling atomized mist. We constructed a 12-foot, green-columned retreat of upended culverts filled with soil and planted with honeysuckle, agave, and giant New Zealand flax.

TREE-SCULPTED FOUNTAIN

The Tree-Sculpted Fountain is the only living structure designed within a "serious" symbolic theme. Although planted with fast-growing tree species, it will take about ten years to assume its imagined form, a densely shaded grotto.

BAMBOO PYRAMID

We outlined the proportions of a pyramid with thick steel cable and a central post. Rather than serve as a structure that plants grow upon or clamber among, the volume of this thinnest of outer skeletons is filled by timber bamboo. Once a year after the rapid spring growth, we prune and thin the stems to fill the lofty geometric form and create an open space within this grove of the world's most vigorous member of the grass family. The

Continued on page 51

LAND & PLACE

The shores of the pond are flanked by scent gardens of lavender, germander, rosemary, and Jerusalem sage. To the west, Duncan Peak keeps watch over the Solar Living Center.

phyll bears close resemblance to the human-fashioned producer of electricity, the photovoltaic solar cell. (Peter Russell somewhat arrogantly asserted in his book *The Awakening Earth* [Routledge and Kegan Paul, 1982] that the invention of the solar cell "represents an evolutionary development as significant as that of photosynthesis 3.5 billion years ago"!)

A single Italian cypress on the terrace serves as figurative gnomon. The lavender, germander, rosemary, and Jerusalem sage of the Mediterranean chaparral flanking both sides of the pool turn hot sun into scent. But the real magnetism of this spot lies outside the boundaries of the Solar Living Center. For here the view crosses the water and an array of flowering plants, leaps the clover lawn, rolls over the northwest berm and its mixed trees, and ascends into the surrounding hills with one destination—Duncan Peak.

Duncan Peak stands as the dominant feature in the native landscape, ultimate inspiration throughout the cycles and the seasons, guardian of this valley. A good place to tip one's hat to wild nature.

Wherever valley oaks grew, in this case on the third, most stable bench of the flood plain, it indicated, in the words of Donald Peattie, "arable land, level for the plough and tractor, the richest soil and a high water table." The American beech *(Fagus grandiflora)* fulfilled a similar role on the East Coast; hence the current scarcity of both species. Riparian groves of valley oak are rare in California today. The current wealth of California's agriculture is primarily due to these forests, where this tree was literally the "stately lord" of the woods. Imagine: at least twenty million years of soil building, which we have cashed in for a brief one hundred and fifty years of profligate wealth. Millions of acres of valley-oak–dominated riparian forestlands are today in the hands of agribusiness, where biological impoverishment is clearly visible. We have transformed millions of acres of a mature, complex ecosystem to a perverse degree, to grow monocultures that, without the use of chemical inputs, would quickly collapse, effete and overhybridized. On such lands, one can travel for miles without seeing a single human being.

These lost riparian forests once held the highest plant species diversity, the highest bird and mammal diversity, and the choicest home for the native peoples. The forests covered millions of acres, but by 1848 only 800,000 acres remained. By 1972, a mere 12,000 acres remained (see Winthrop A. Stiles, *Valley Riparian Forests of California,* Santa Clara Valley Water District, 1978). The valley oak grew to over one hundred feet in height, lived for half a millenia, and provided over 70 percent of the total plant species canopy coverage in these forests.

Although our landscape design may employ a rich variety of texture, form, and color, nothing comes close to this tree's legacy, to its almost Edenesque qualities. The specter and profile of this one tree still dominates the site, even though its time passed away 150 years ago.

Only one juvenile specimen of valley oak remains today on the site of the Solar Living Center. To meet the needs of Real Goods on this site, it would not have been appropriate to replicate the forest, as much as we relished the thought. The scale is vast, the time frame in centuries. What existed before European colonization was a mature "permaculture," with a wealth of productivity that rendered agriculture redundant. It was stable and infinitely renewable. The inspiration for us, now, is to honor this zone of high biological productivity and be conscious of the shadow and pattern of its once great ecosystem.

By planting this zone in food crops, mainly cultivars that have traveled here in European hands, we have swapped the biological diversity of this native place for that of our present culture. However, it is incumbent upon us to maintain a high biological productivity, not just for human needs, but for birds, insects, moths. . . . Born of wildflowers, grasses, herbs, flowering shrubs, and ornamental and fruiting trees, such diversity brings a sense of abundance and fertility to the created atmosphere of a mature garden.

Restored native habitat

The overflow spillway for the lower pond runs under the entry drive and out into a shallow wetland of considerable size. This wetland will be restored in a second phase of the project and will represent the return to a completely native habitat. The water, which has traveled the length and breadth of the garden, having been solar-pumped with the ease and independence of an artesian well through a score of water features, now finds itself at the end of its visible water cycle. From here, it returns down into the water table after one final gesture—

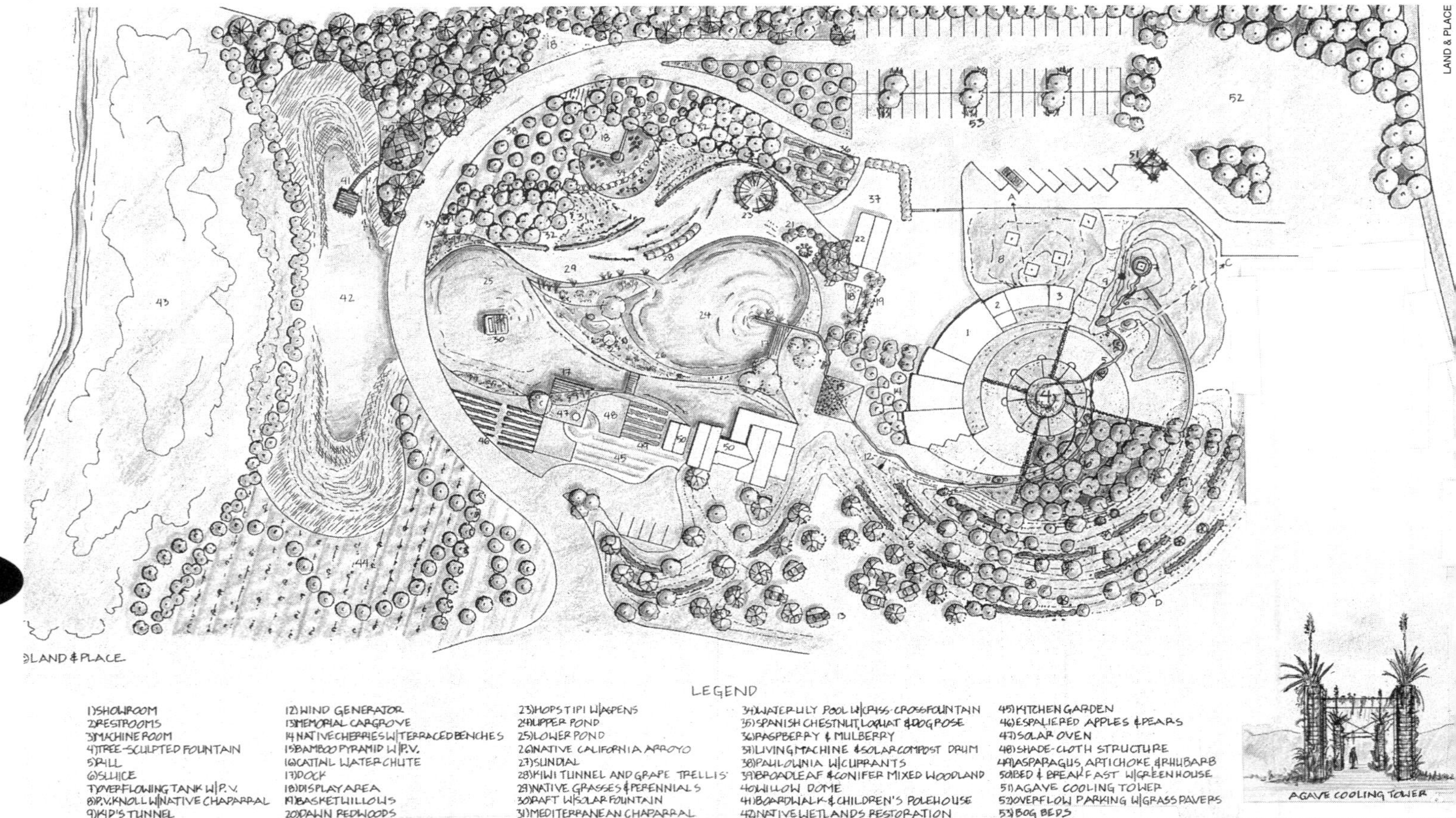

providing for a diversity of native species that thrive in a fluctuating water level. From floating and submerged aquatics to species resident in the highly seasonable vernal pool conditions, the wetlands will provide for a diversity of aquatic life in a variety of ecological niches. Permanent clear water, deep marsh, shallow marsh, wet meadow . . . each will be planted in native flora garnered from within a 50-mile radius of Hopland. Waterfowl, frogs, salamanders, dragonflies, and numerous aquatic insects find a home in these niches in addition to the numerous bird species known to use our local wetlands and their riparian margins. Vernal pools, in particular, undoubtedly once existed on this site. We have an obligation to restore them and provide homes for their highly specialized inhabitants, such as the endangered fairy shrimp. A boardwalk will traverse the eastern section, commencing at the Willow Dome and leading to a children's pole house and viewing platform for this zone of restoration, a biologically rich and productive return, if only on a remnant scale, to what once may have been.

A gathering place for inspiration

Situated on the highest point at the Solar Living Center atop the Southeast Knoll, and elevated above a broad basin filled with cobblestones, sits an old redwood tank. Through all weathers and times of day, this tank serves as the first working display of solar technology that visitors encounter. Designed to demonstrate a literal connection between the intensity of the Sun and the production of electricity, the leaky tank becomes an immediate, visceral lesson in solar potentialities. It serves also as the original wellhead of the first ingredient of the Courtyard: water. It also lies at the point of the winter solstice sunrise as seen from the central fountain, and is therefore a representation of rebirth.

Just moments after sunrise, the quiet is broken, imperceptibly, by the first signs of a solar tracker in motion. What begins as a trickle and broken droplets, by noon becomes a circular water wall with water cascading over the brim of the tank at a rate of 3,000 gallons per hour (see chapter 5 for more technical detail about this solar-powered pump). The cobbled basin quickly fills and overflows into a water chute that falls directly into the sculptural piece renowned for its water-regenerative properties: the flowform.

Winding our way up between the Southeast Knoll on the left and PV Knoll on the right, with hum-

LIVING STRUCTURES

Continued from page 47

water rill with its blue-flowered pickerelweed, torrent sedge, and Anemonopsis runs on the diagonal through what will eventually become a secluded place.

HOPS TIPI

More a hybrid between a rondavel and a tipi, this structure lifts its dimensions from the central fountain. A 5-foot-high, soil-filled wall encircles a 30-foot space planted with dwarf olive and hops vines. Twelve thin steel trusses create the shape of a tipi, projecting 20 feet into the air, stopping shy of a circular opening at its peak. When fully grown in, this "shade house" will provide a completely private space, a useful teaching circle whose built-in benches can accommodate up to forty people. Hops is a perennial that can put on as much as 20 feet of growth in a single season, dying down to its crown in winter, when the structure is returned to its naked form.

KIWI TUNNEL

Shade! There is no end to the shade requirements in this climate. We joined a curved series of metal hoops to create a light, sturdy structure, high enough for a vigorous climbing vine. Providing shade in the central lawn area, it is the mere tracery of a tunnel in winter, but in summer comes to life with the luxuriant, velvety foliage of *Actinidia chinensis*, the kiwi vine, otherwise known as Chinese gooseberry. The fruit will hang from the top of the tunnel and ripen in late

Continued on page 52

LIVING STRUCTURES

November, when the first frosts defoliate the structure.

WILLOW DOME

A single willow provided the cuttings from which the thirty individual trees grew that we wove together for this living structure. Our ability to contain the vigor of this large timber willow will be temporary. After a few years of training, it will be too high and too "wild" for any further manipulation. At that point, it will have grafted the woven stems of itself into a single entity, literally a huge upside-down willow "basket." From there, it will take off into a multi-trunked circular tree of great induced character and shade-bearing bounty. Appropriately, we must pass through this friendly thicket of willow to reach the wetland beyond.

LAND & PLACE

Pumped from the solar-powered redwood tank, through flowforms, past the childen's play area, over rocks, and among reeds, water flows into the main rill in rhythms determined by the daily patterns of the Sun.

mingbirds whizzing between California fuschia and apricot monkey flower, our ascent runs in tandem with the descending water. By the time we pass the entry to the kid's tunnel (a secret route through the heart of the knoll to the children's area), the flowform has deposited its rhythmic water in one final oscillation into the main water rill of the Courtyard.

This solar event, and its relationship to light and shadow, are expressed in the pattern of the day; as the day lengthens toward sunset and evens out, the water slows, recedes and pulses, finally, like an ebb tide in miniature.

And here we find ourselves in the Courtyard.

If this were midday, the circular space would be filled with the sounds and reverberations of water. Water splashing over flat dishes of rock, around boulders, and among rushes and reeds, water diverted into the play area by children with a hand pump, water circling round toward a small weir. At the weir, a diversion takes a portion of the flow, so that the rill is divided. The diverted portion flows across the main apron and finds its spiral path to the center of the fountain with an eagerness born of water's familiarity with traveling in the lure of a vortex.

Rhythmic water jets pulsing from four quadrants (corresponding to the cardinal directions) are natural magnets to children in the heat of the day, and the circumference of the main pool becomes an exuberant arena. From this pool rim, they can touch a circular curtain of water. High overhead, the drip ring, an exact mirror image of the pool below, rains down droplets that are transformed into glistening beads of light as they fall, held aloft long enough to become a vertical enclosure of light-filled water. "A monkey's wedding and

"In a few years' time, the height of the building will be surpassed by the height of the fountain trees. The Courtyard's substance and expression will change to a green architecture: upright trees, horizontal planes of vines, circular flowering berms, all held by the spiral of shaded lawn, decomposed granite, and sanded concrete."

LAND & PLACE

LIVING STRUCTURES

MEMORIAL CAR GROVE

This controversial structure has taken on a life of its own. It has been red-tagged by the county Building Department, faced hearings before the local Board of Supervisors debating whether it is art or "junk," and made the front page of all the local newspapers.

Five large, 1950s-vintage gas guzzlers have indented themselves into the landscape on the highway side of the Solar Living Center. A grove of trees "happens" to grow out of the rusted hulks of these car bodies. An experiment, perhaps, for determining how long the iron of these vessels of combustion will take to reappear, fully dissolved, in the green pigment of the trees that have settled there?

We took our inspiration for the Memorial Car Grove from the now passé practice of incorporating car bodies into eroded creek banks as a substitute for riprap. After a few seasons of nature's catastrophic change, a car body, now filled with silt and gravel, can be found sprouting all manner of native vegetation. Symbolizing nature's power of regeneration, the Memorial Car Grove reminds us who bats last, and serves as a public recycling of this overt icon of the American Dream. Highly visible even at 55 miles per hour, living sculpture inadvertently becomes living billboard! A fitting monument for a business whose mission is the elimination of fossil fuels.

a fox's dance," goes the old East African saying to describe the ineffable moment when sun shines through falling rain.

This spectacle of the play of light and water—like a child's energy released on contact with water, like the volume, velocity, and sound emanating from the overflowing water tank—is directly proportional to the epochal movement and intensity of the Sun, the second ingredient of the Courtyard. We have used solar energy to power the ameliorating magic that is moving water. The very harshest element of the site thereby becomes the perennial source of its rejuvenation.

The Courtyard is a gathering place for inspiration. It is a positive shape, an open space, a large and capacious room. When fully grown, it aspires to be an oasis: a fertile center in a desert or a waste place. Outwardly, it presents a composition where nothing changes—simply green grass, shade, sunlight, and the glinting surface of moving water. Children play. Birds drink. We can enjoy it at a glance on our way to the showroom and never suppose that it is a complex timepiece, a solar calendar, the full reading of which might connect the imagination to the mathematics of the year and our four seasons.

If we sit on the low bench against the sheltering arc of the showroom and its red-ochre soil cement walls that make up a full quarter of the circumference of the Courtyard, we sense a dialogue between the interior and the exterior. This earthen building desires to be covered in living canopy all around, and even be patched in lichen and moss. The Courtyard responds with a broad framework of luxuriant foliage, made up of native grape (*Vitis californica* var. Rodger's red) and glory vine (*Vitis cognetiae*). Deciduous and open to the full winter sun, a full canopy of living green in summer, and suffusing light to brilliant crimson in autumn, the native grape marks a symbolic return to the time when the giant valley oak was festooned with this rampant climber.

From this vantage, protected by the berms and their massed plantings, one can sense the roundness of this elevated space within the roundness of the Sanel Valley itself. Duncan Peak, aligned with the top of the drip ring, is again the dominant presence.

Trees are the natural architecture of this place-in-the-making, and the third ingredient of the Courtyard. Eight gray poplars (*Populus canescens* var. *macrophylla,* a natural cross between poplar and aspen) planted on the cardinal directions and their intermediaries, surround the central pool of the Tree-Sculpted Fountain. The trees are trained on angle toward the center to form an intensely shaded grotto, much the way they lean out to find light where they grow in steep canyons and gorges in their native habitat. The elevated Courtyard was built from compacted material excavated from the ponds and salvaged from CalTrans rubble heaps. To plant the gray poplars, we dug 10-foot-deep by 3-foot-wide holes

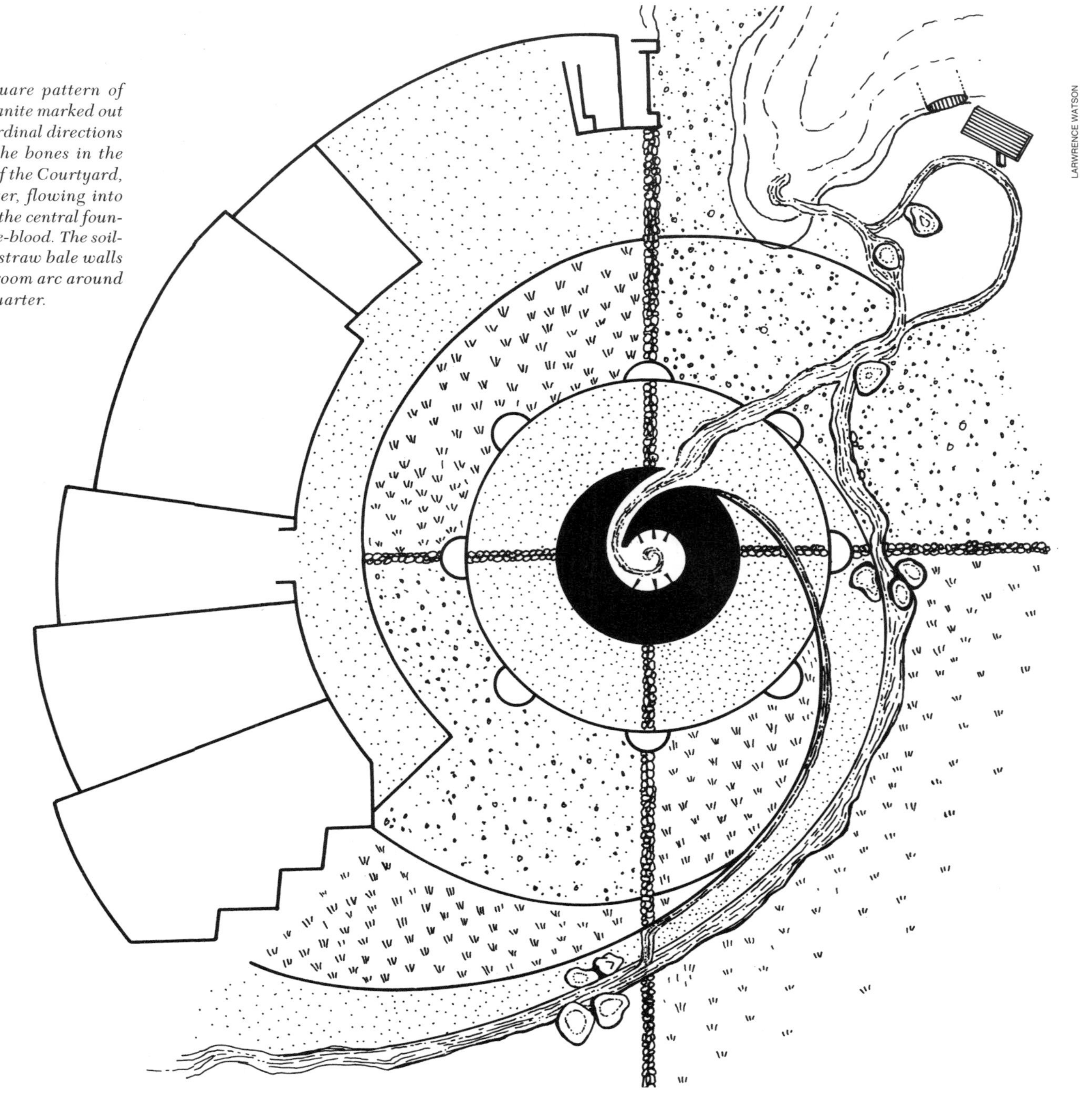

The four-square pattern of lawn and granite marked out along the cardinal directions represents the bones in the "anatomy" of the Courtyard, and the water, flowing into the spiral of the central fountain, is its life-blood. The soil-cement and straw bale walls of the showroom arc around the north quarter.

LARWRENCE WATSON

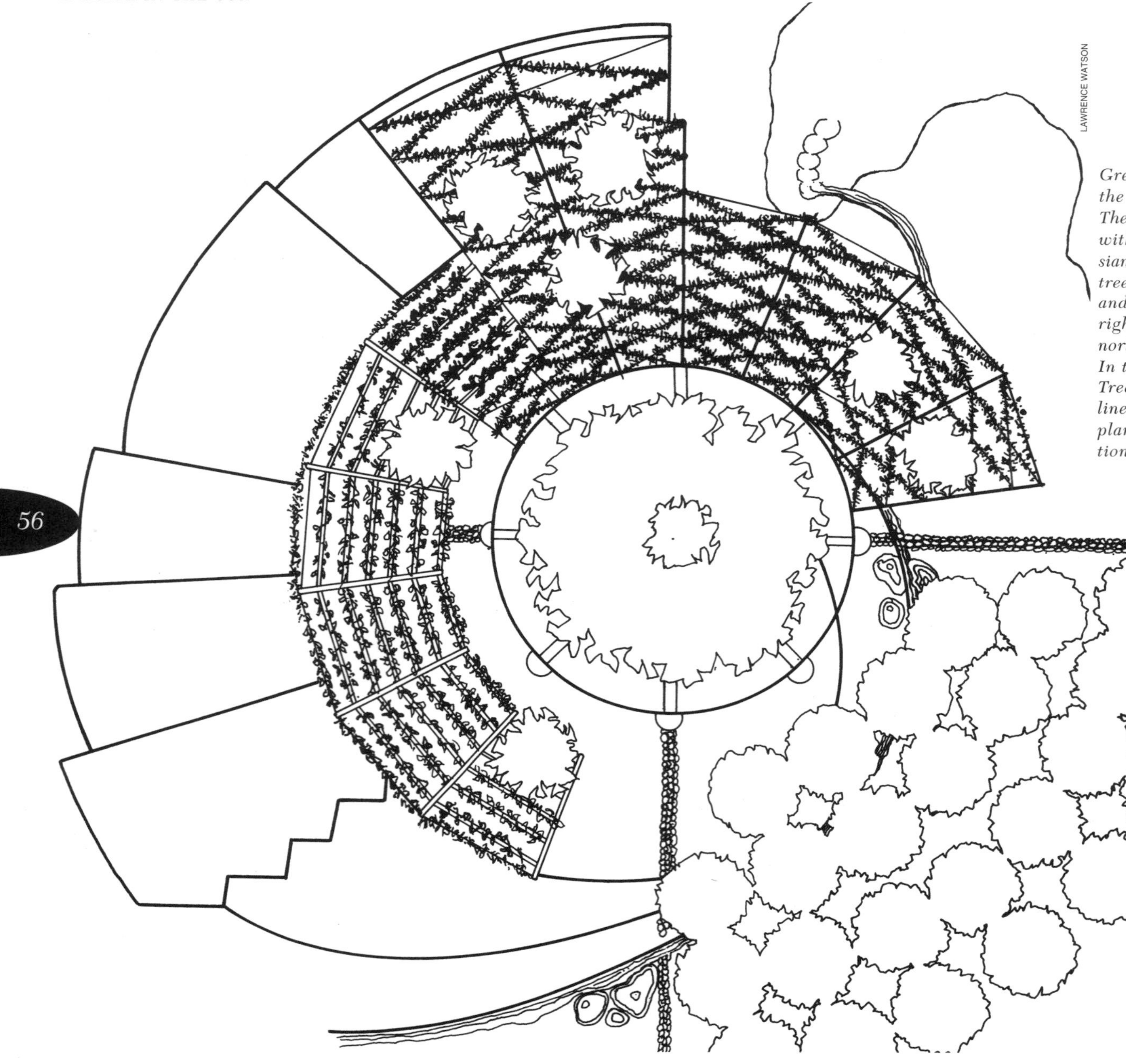

LAWRENCE WATSON

Green architecture fleshes out the skeleton of the Courtyard. The southwest quadrant is filled with a grove of olive and Russian olive. Seven Texas umbrella trees stand amidst native grape and glory vine. Avenues of upright poplars lead in along the north-south and east-west axes. In the center, the spiral of the Tree-Sculpted Fountain is delineated by eight gray poplars planted on the cardinal directions and intermediaries.

Visitors' view of Duncan Peak from the seats under the grape trellis along the southern wall of the showroom will eventually be obscured by the plantings around the Central Courtyard.

and refilled them with sandy loam so that this riparian species could have a "straight run" to the natural grade below and the abundant water table of the Russian River.

In a few years' time, the height of the building will be surpassed by the height of the fountain trees. The Courtyard's substance and expression will change to a green architecture: upright trees, horizontal planes of vines, circular flowering berms, all held by the spiral of shaded lawn, decomposed granite, and sanded concrete.

The grove, the umbrella, and the avenue define the other distinctive spaces in the Courtyard.

The southwest quadrant of the Courtyard, the hottest and driest aspect, is taken up by the oldest of all garden features, the grove. A massed planting of olive and Russian olive (the latter a nitrogen fixer where the fill soil and drainage is poor) have been placed for fruit, scent, and shade. These silver-leafed trees make up the foreground of an entire planting of arid-climate, heat-tolerant species, best represented on the berm by foothills pine, red bud, palo verde, yucca, and matilija poppy.

Seven Texas umbrella trees (*Melia azadarach umbractiformis*), known for their ability to withstand great heat, great drought, and hideous soils, provide intermittent places for individual repose. Along with the fountain trees and grape vines, these *Melia* are happy recipients of all the graywater produced on the site.

Avenues have been used since antiquity to represent power and authority. However, their intended use here is as a passageway. These tree-lined pathways lead us in, much like the lights of a harbor entrance. For it is within these corridors that the different qualities of the cardinal directions—the fourth ingredient of the Courtyard—find their way into the center of the circle. Likewise, these double avenues of upright poplars, unmistakable in their bearing, help project the circle out into the landscape at large. Marking the east-west axis down in the parking lot, traversing the main berm between the highway and the Courtyard, picking up where the cobbled pathways end, these avenues even lift up and over intercepting landscape features. The north line from the center of the fountain projects right through the showroom to become the colorful Solar Noon Calendar (described later in this chapter), then picks up again as avenue out the back door, where it merges with the water chute that feeds the upper pond.

From the photovoltaic modules on their trackers to the sheltering arc of the showroom to every cultivated inch of the garden, solar alignment, aspect, and orientation become theme and symbol. Ultimately, the garden is one huge sundial, reflecting not so much the time of day, but the Sun's journey through the seasons.

No matter where we are standing in this garden, we will know our compass orientation. The upright poplars, chosen for the speed with which they will dominate all the other plantings, become a highly visible magnetic needle. The experience of the four directions is as diverse and personal as the world's ecosystems and the cultures that people them. For us, due north invokes red-tailed hawk over red fir *(Abies magnifica)* on Snow Mountain (the closest wilderness to Hopland); west is marbled murrelet nesting in the mossy branches of old-growth Douglas fir in the Sinkyone; south becomes, for us, foothills pine, manzanita, and hummingbird along Mountain House Road; and east is meadowlark, valley oak, and carpets of lupines on the edges of the Sanel Valley.

East. Sunrise. Moments later the quiet is broken. The old redwood tank begins to overflow. To experience this garden, simply follow the water, having placed yourself within the solar day.

The Narrative of the Solar Calendar: The Circle, the Spiral, and the Great U-Turn

The three great inspirations are the inspiration to learn, the inspiration to meet, and the inspiration for well-being. They all serve, really, the will to be, to express.—*Louis Kahn**

The Courtyard grew organically from a central theme which originated in the vision statement and which gained in dimension as it was laid out. This central theme was born out of the meaning of a spiral, and the spiral served the need to express a place where water is manifest in its many forms and inherent vortical laws. What better symbol of inspiration than a spiral? For a spiral, in this case set in motion by water, is much like our own imaginations kept in motion through a continual revisiting of basic principles that provide an ever

*See John Lobell's *Between Silence and Light: Spirit in the Architecture of Louis I. Kahn* (Shambala, 1985).

deeper and broader perspective. The spiral is also the most profound image of the movement of time, and therefore the foundation of the solar calendar. To read it we must stand at the center of the spiral vortex.

The Courtyard became a place on two levels: a place to simply be, listening to the reverberations of water, watching children play, sitting on the grass under a tree. Through collaboration with David Arkin and Baile Oakes, the entire Courtyard also became a solar calendar for deepening and broadening our perspective in space and time. The reflection of this calendar is to be found in many features of the Courtyard, including the water spiral, the living circle of trees, and the daily, weekly, and seasonal calendars.

The sensibility of the solar calendar can also be found in intangibles:

- the cycle of return: Sun, Earth, place, time
- the ritual of return: the shortest day, the longest day
- the circle, the spiral, and the Great U-Turn

In Latin, the word *radicalis* means "having roots." As Terry Tempest Williams has said, the most radical thing a person can do today is to stay put. To live in "the particular" is to live in a definite place where one can experience time as a cycle of returns within that place. Time, as it is too often read today, as a one-way linear path flowing into the future, becomes a rejected concept. The nebulousness of our modern culture is also partially due to our concept of "space" as the same everywhere, as divorced from "place." The context of no context. Wilfrido Tinoco, one of the two gardeners at the SLC and a principal contributor to its current incarnation, remarked upon leaving for Buena Vista de Zapata, Mexico, to work on his own homestead for the winter, "Time, here, goes very fast. So fast. But in Mexico, the time, she goes really slow. You can see the plants grow."

When we separate our "inspiration for well-being" from one-dimensional linear time, from time-as-money, from the commodification of time, then we can leave the disconnected modern world behind and enter the world of total interdependency and, perhaps, "timelessness." The time when the tree frogs begin to sing: January. The time when the manzanita flowers in the hills: February. The time when swallows return to the ponds and creek: mid-March. The time when the valley oak leafs out: April. The endless cycles of return. Time becomes relative to a place, just as a place spirals out in its context to its bioregion and beyond. A defined place is found in the shape of the Earth's surface, in her latitude, slope, aspect, and elevation. In the nature of her thin mantle of topsoil. It is in her canopy cover and closure, capacity to conserve moisture and absorb radiant energy, light and heat, cold and dry. It is found in her frost and fog and proximity to the ocean. In her annual rainfall. The place where the serpentine soils grow unique wildflowers. The place where the Sitka spruce meets the redwood. The place where the blue bunchgrass grows among white oak. The place where the coho salmon still spawns. The cycles experienced on a mountainside in south-facing chaparral, compared to those same cycles on the valley floor in deep rich soil among valley oaks, are as different as night and day.

LAND & PLACE

The gray poplars that form the Tree-Sculpted Fountain are trained to grow into a single dense canopy over the drip ring, creating a cool, shady room filled with the sound of running water and the magic of sunlight reflected through falling droplets.

We may refer to the solar calendar, the solar year, the breathing of the landscape, the stillness of a foggy morning, the heat of noon, the afternoon breeze, the evening out of the day into night, a particular sunset. Yet in reality we are referring to the Earth's rotation, the Earth's orbit around the Sun, and the magical tilt of the Earth that is the pendulum of our seasons. The solar calendar is as much about the Earth as it is about the Sun. It is as much about place as it is about time. It is a circle, and it is an upward and returning spiral.

The Earth with her tilt bears a cocked expression of attentive listening . . . a listening-out for planetary influence. Likewise, stand in the center of the water spiral and listen, connect, and begin to draw lines between distant points that express the arc of the Sun and the rotation of the Earth. In so doing, open the door onto the dynamics of the moment, the day, the week, the seasons, the solar year, and the four elements that combine to create energy and life. But first, we must build a living and symbolic space around this place beneath the unique presence of Duncan Peak.

The living symbolism of the central fountain, heart of the solar calendar, happens in the combination of the four elements and in the alchemy of moving water as it meets the "fire" of solar energy: sun and wind, light and shadow, warmth and evaporative cooling. It is in the movement of the outer circle of trees, leaning in toward the inner circle of water. It is in the human gesture of those eight trees trained to eventually become one, forming a round house of the sky as eight leaning trunks return to upright upon reaching the high drip ring.

There is a pool of sky (defined by the circular drip ring) above, and a pool of water below. Between the two is the constant conversation of falling water droplets. Beyond the central spiral, the circle of water, and the trees, we can sense the open pathways of the cardinal directions as their diverse energies enter along the cobblestones from north, south, east, and west, and join to become part of the circle. The inclusiveness of the circle becomes the meeting place of opposites and a gathering place of inspiration. Yet the individual can fully experience the solar calendar only by crossing through the threshold of water and following a low-relief sculptural spiral, inwardly slanting and flowing toward the central vortex. The center of the spiral is the center of the solar calendar, the realm of living water, a vortex of the imagination.

As the fountain trees find the water table of the river below, grow to about 60 feet in height, and become the "round house of the sky," they become the one individual created out of the unification of the four cardinal directions. They raise the circle on the ground to create an elevated circle in the air. It is to these trees that we look to engage the Sun as its arc travels to its zenith, reaching an intensity that becomes, for us, almost poisonous. A tree of many trunks, as broad as it is high, which will represent the gesture of the tree, all trees, the archetypal tree that has lived for two hundred million years, rooted in the Earth but projected high into the light and air: the green plant that is "the light breather," harnessing the energy of the Sun, assimilating carbon and creating sweet atmosphere, the fruits of green chlorophyll. The most noble of timekeepers, trees impart the qualities of age, absorbed and expressed in their living permanence. What we need to proliferate today are examples and symbols such as this of how the Earth is alive. The epochal insight of our century (known by all native peoples from the beginning) is that the entire life of Earth, through its atmosphere, forests, and oceans, functions effectively as one self-regulating organism, Gaia; that life, in her carbon, energy, and water cycles is always complete and unbroken; that it is only we who stand outside the circle with one-dimensional

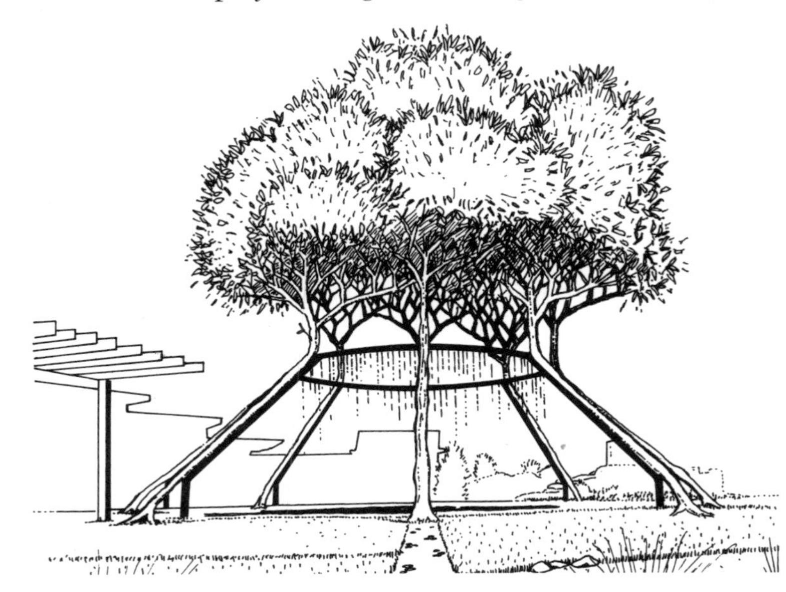

thinking and linear time. Inside the circle, one escapes, for a moment, this gridlock and experiences the 70 percent of Earth that is water . . . above, below, and all around. Gerbert Grahmann has written, in his book *The Plant* (Rudolf Steiner Press, 1974):

> Water brings equilibrium to opposing principles. It is a mediator, both in general and in the life of individual plants. During rainfall and when the moisture rises again into the atmosphere, water acts as mediator between cosmos and Earth. It gives life to the plant and connects flower with root—the mirror image of cosmos and Earth. It creates the leaves and makes them spread wide. Observe the luxuriant leaf growth developed by plants in wet places and see how water counteracts the form-giving influences of light.

The reflection of the moment

May we not call water nature's central organ, "its heart," the pulsing oscillating drop that lets the whole cosmos pass through it?
—Theodore Schwenk, from Sensitive Chaos *(Rudolf Steiner Press, 1976)*

How do we join the complex mathematics of the multiple cycles of the years (Sun, Moon, Earth) to that of the individual? Through the reflection of the moment! Within the current of the solar year, a moment of pulsing water finds its metaphor in the individual human heartbeat. The flowforms, which carry the water from the overflowing tank to the water rill itself, tie the circulation of the Courtyard to our own bloodstream. By observing the flowforms on even a partially sunny day, we can see reflected in the rhythm and pulse of the water, pumped by solar power and now coursing through the flowform's five basins, a connection between these two rhythmical waters.

When the Sun comes out, this stopwatch of the solar calendar begins to tick, initiated by photovoltaic energy. A gentle rhythmical swishing of water from side to side begins in the basins at about 12 gallons per minute. By the time the Sun is high enough to pump 45 gallons per minute (optimum rate for this size flowform), a rhythmical pulsation of water creates a completely formed double spiral . . . a full figure eight. This moment-to-moment pattern within the flowform corresponds with the full cycle of the solar year. (At over 60 gallons per minute, which occurs when the water table is very close to the surface, the flowforms begin to exhibit an "arrhythmia." The vessel is overwhelmed, the water spills, the motion becomes chaotic. This "rapid heart rate" is remedied by turning the valve down.)

Flow-forms, designed by Skylark, Inc., are proportioned and calibrated to mimic the rhythms of naturally flowing water, and to refresh and rejuvenate the water that passes through them.

LAND & PLACE

The solar year, in "the sum of its days," is also a double spiral and symbol of infinity, the figure eight. In his sculpture *Sunlight Convergence Solar Burn: The Equinoxial Year,* Charles Ross burnt the Sun's rays through a lens for 366 days onto a wood surface. He found, in the end, the image of the double cycle of return, the double spiral of the Sun's journey through the year. (See his book, *Sunlight Convergence Solar Burn,* University of Utah Press, 1976.)

Stamped into each pulsation of the flowform is the very shape of the multiple cycles of return, from the pulsation of the moment to the sum of its days: one calendar year. Of course, the reflection of the moment also occurs on any sunny day (the hotter the better) when children come into contact with the sound, pulse, and rhythms of the various water elements of the Courtyard (not to mention wetness!). Combustion occurs: light and energy are released!

It is in the random pulse of the water jets set at each cardinal direction around the central pool. It is in wind and water creating myriad beads of light that scatter and spray on the pool surface.

The daily calendar

Two polished brass staffs on either side of the pool mark the position of the sunrise and sunset. From the spiral's center, we can project from these two markers to the horizon and, by drawing an arc

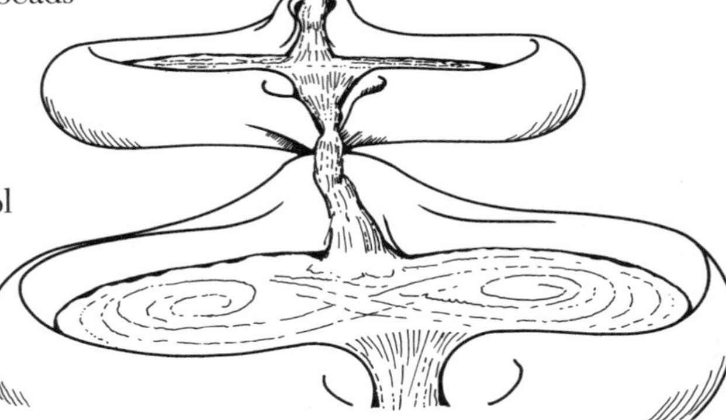

in the sky, complete the shape of the day. The huge solar panels on the trackers also follow the arc of the Sun, realigning themselves almost minute to minute. They are an integral part of the landscape of the solar calendar as they harness the daily energy and convert it into the life of the Courtyard. The ebb and flow of solar energy production, like a daily tide, is reflected in the sound and velocity of the water rill, with a definite morning, noon, and evening. On partially sunny days, cloud shadows accompany quiet pauses in the water rill, contrasting with sudden wakenings as the Sun breaks through. The Sun has a voice in the Courtyard and sets a tone that mirrors the nature of the day.

BAILE OAKES

Through the long hours of the day, water flows along the spiral to its central vortex and down into the pool below, then it follows the overflow spiral on its orbit around the Courtyard and out into the garden. All of this ceases at sundown, as the Sun's energy wanes and the last drops fall from the drip ring, the jets in the cardinal axes cease to pulsate, and the flowform slows to a trickle. Within the center of the vortex, a hidden fountain jet, timed to run 365 days of the year, spouts just as the Sun sets. On clear evenings, the low angle of the last rays pass through the Courtyard and strike the water column, a final exclamation mark to the passage of the day, signaling another cycle of return, this time to nightfall.

The weekly calendar

The sun pushes and the moon pulls.—*Alan Chadwick*

EVEN THOSE WHO STILL LIVE WITH THE IMPERATIVES OF THE EARTH'S TIMINGS, sowing seed in sync with the inclination of the Sun and Moon, even those living within the agricultural year, will be surprised by the weekly calendar. For it is not until you see it laid out on the ground, week by week, that this phenomenal aspect of the Sun's cycles becomes clear. The

The pattern laid out on the ground by the two brass staffs that mark the weekly sunrise and sunset positions from the Courtyard's center reveal a secret of the Sun's cycle. Like a pendulum, the swing of the Sun slows at the Winter and Summer Solstices as the days lengthen and shorten slowly. At the bottom of the pendulum's swing, at the Equinoxes, the change in the length of the day hastens, with dramatic movement of the Sun's position against the horizon.

Sun's twenty-six weekly loci (half a year) are marked on either side of the pool by dated plaques. These double as a housing for the two polished brass staffs, transferred weekly to the new position specific to the Solar Living Center and the ever-shifting sunrise and sunset. The pattern created by these markers can best be expressed by the nature and speed of a pendulum. On the two "far sides" of the year (winter and summer) lies a dormancy period when the Sun's movement is hardly perceptible. Yet toward the center of the pendulum, the Sun's change is dramatic. Indeed, a one-week shift at the bottom of the swing is equivalent to three to four weeks of movement in the "dormancies." Revealed in this great swing is something gardeners know all about: that the equinoxial periods are the heart and soul of the solar year. The big festivals of Winter Solstice and June's longest day are easy to understand. It takes a lifetime to fully comprehend the meaning of the equinox. Imagine the accelerating pendulum of the weekly calendar. Then weave through it waves of lunar influence, waxing or waning every two weeks. It is the inclinations of the Sun and the Moon in tandem, together with the equinox, which create the tidal wave that is spring. Either we catch this wave, or we are merely swept along, reluctant travelers trying to figure out what all of the commotion is about. The birth of the year? The resurrection of the year? Easter? Or Persephone returning to her mother? The myths and legends are endless as humankind has endeavored to comprehend this rapid acceleration within the living cycles of the Earth. Then, twenty-six weeks later, the cycle returns again; this time in the opposite direction. And this time, opposite emotions are engendered as one is mollified, satiated by the abundance and finality that is the harvest Equinox.

The calendar of the seasons

From the cycles of the day and the breathing of the landscape we have come to the all-encompassing major rhythms of the year. This "sea change" of the seasons affects the larger breathing of the continents. The Pacific high-pressure systems follow in the wake of the Sun's traverse;

LAND & PLACE

Pairs of standing stones along the perimeter of the circle formed by the building and the raised berm provide the sight lines from the center of the spiral to the horizon.

the high- and low-pressure zones mix the continental and oceanic influences in seasonal rhythms accompanied by waves of frontal systems (such as our west coast "Pineapple Express"); and complex habitats and ecosystems are arrayed along the north-south lines of the Sun's trajectory and arrayed as well at different elevations created by changes in altitude. Imagine, for example, the richest temperate forest in the world, stretching along the Pacific coast from Big Sur to Sitka, Alaska: In pre-European times this was one single, unbroken forest, with a diversity unimaginable today. This breathing of landscapes and continents affects all weather and determines the nature of our biosphere. These are the literal connections that stitch our woods and tall evergreen forests to the fogs, cloud formations, and rainfall that signify our region.

Six pairs of upright stone apertures (one is actually a cleft in the wall) are situated on the outer radius of the circle that unites the curved building to the tops of the berms and knolls. These are the outer reaches of the visible calendar. These apertures mark corridors that travel from the center of the vortex, through the stone columns and on to the horizon line, and vice versa.

These six intangible lines radiate from the center of the six horizon points on the very position of sunrise and sunset for each Solstice and Equinox. Like spokes of a wheel, these invisible sight lines become the avenues along which the cycles of return travel back into the central vortex. At sunset on the Summer Solstice, this intangible avenue aligns with that festival's apertures to become a tangible ephemeral corridor of light. The nearly horizontal sunlight is captured, if only briefly, by the vertical column of water at the center of the vortex, to signal the end of the longest day and of the twenty-six weeks that make up the Sun's northbound journey.

From the lowest point of the year, the Sun's turnabout and ascent to spring:
December 21 to March 21.
From the equator to the tropic of Cancer, the Sun's ascent to its zenith:
March 21 to June 21.
From the tropic of Cancer to the equator again, the Sun's descent into autumn:
June 21 to September 23.
From the equator to the tropic of Capricorn, the Sun's final descent into deepest winter:
September 23 to December 21.

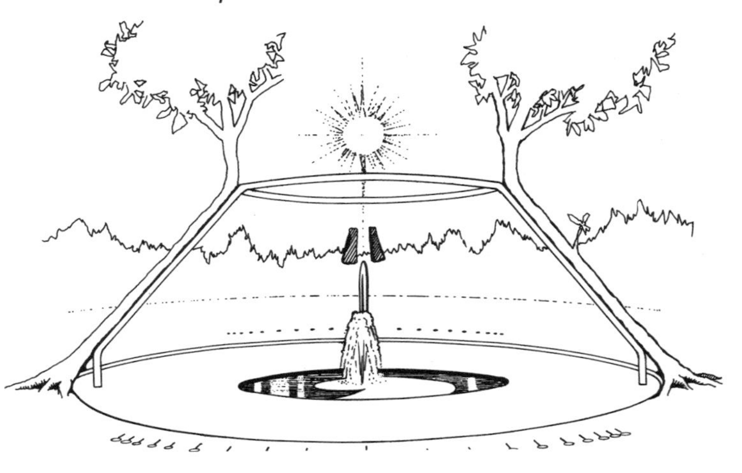

"At sunset on the Summer Solstice, the nearly horizontal sunlight is captured, if only briefly, by the vertical column of water at the center of the vortex, to signal the end of the longest day and of the twenty-six weeks that make up the Sun's northbound journey."

On the equator, sunrise and sunset are rapid and decisive. Sunset is almost due west. Align yourself with the cardinal directions within the Courtyard and look due east. You can imagine the arc of an equatorial sun: straight up to its zenith and then straight down again like a shot, due west and with no lingering about on the horizon. However, here we are at 39 degrees north in the Sanel Valley, looking toward sunset on the longest day. The distance between due west and the stone column aperture that marks the Summer Solstice sunset is a direct expression of the magical tilt of the Earth; the ultimate source of the endless diversity found in the more than ten million species of life on the planet (the actual tilt is one quarter of the angle between the equator and the poles, 23.5 degrees). That tilt is also the very source of the cycle of return we call the four seasons.

The solar year

The cycle of return known as the solar year is found in "the sum of its days." It is possible to take one cycle only, out of the 365, and find the macrocosm within the microcosm. The simplest image of the yearly cycle of return is reflected in the four cardinal directions that bisect the central pool. From the central vortex, draw three arcs: the familiar arc of the day along the east-west axis, defining the side of the dawn and that of the evening; the arc of the Sun's inclination on the morning side of the pool, in which the Sun travels from south to north; and, finally, the arc of the declination of the Sun that is on the evening side of the pool, where the Sun travels from north to south. One can observe the cycles of the Earth's twenty-four-hour day as a mirror image of the cycles of the one solar year by simply rotating from axis line to axis line.

The light and dark of the twenty-four-hour day is a model of the light and dark of the year. To know the Sun's pendulum is to know the play of opposites. That winter is born in midsummer and that summer is born in its opposite—midwinter; that the dawn of the day is the Equinox of spring; that noon correlates to the longest day, sunset to the Autumn Equinox and midnight to the "birth of the light"—the Winter Solstice.

The gestures of two weeds sum up the two impulses of the year:

Chicory *(Chicorium intybrus)* is a flower of the morning, a deep-rooted wayside European weed whose intense blue reflects an unsullied morning sky. By noon the flowers have closed up tight, to become nearly invisible.

Soap plant *(Chlorogalum pomeridianum)* is the local wildflower of the evening. After sundown, it opens its pale white flowers like a string of stars on 6-foot wiry stems. By morning, the flowers have disappeared.

From the circle and the spiral we come to the Great U-Turn: The entire westernized arm of our species must follow a complete reversal of its destructive course. It is only a question of when and in what manner. But to be like water and flow over the coming obstacles with ease, the individual may prefer the spiral as a symbol upon which to go gently a few steps back to metaphorically pick up the old track. Here on this site, we are beginning to follow through on the central theme of the landscape, to arrive at a place of inspiration, a zone of productivity, and an act of restoration. The solar calendar and the gardens themselves, under the prospect of Duncan Peak, represent a realignment to *living* time and a revaluing of native place, two of the pathmarkers of that long-overdue cycle of return known as the Great U-Turn.

RICHARD BARNES

"What we've tried to demonstrate with the Real Goods Solar Living Center is that the principles of sustainability really work.

By April, the gardens at the Solar Living Center are filled with color and scent, but the grape trellis on the southern facade will not be fully leafed out for two months, when it will be needed to shade the interior from the hot, bright summer sun. Choosing a vine whose growth matches the seasonal shading needs of the building is an example of the sensitivity to climate, geography, and biology taken at every step in the evolution of the project.

They are not an environmentalist's pipe dream.

The team of innovative designers, landscapers, artists, engineers, and builders used every tool at hand—from climate analyses and computer modeling, to carpooling and tracking gas mileage; from passive and renewable energy systems to feng shui—to ensure that both the construction and the operation of the SLC minimize environmental impacts and maximize the productivity and health of the site for people and other living things.

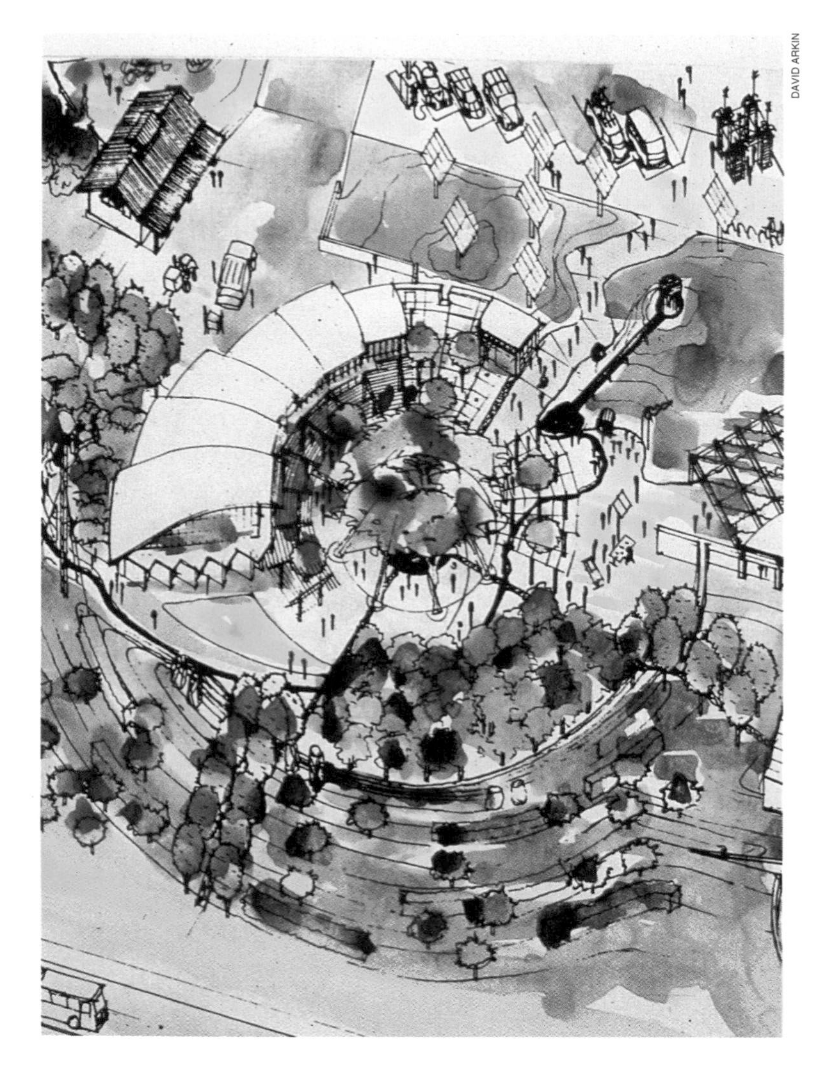

DAVID ARKIN

DAVID ARKIN

We can build without cutting down trees; we can build with straw and earth.

Rice-straw bales finished with PISE™ form walls that are highly insulating and provide a thermal-mass cooling effect. Rice straw is an agricultural byproduct, while the finish is derived from surplus soil quarried for another local building project. Utilizing appropriate recycled and local materials was a priority in building construction.

We *can* have businesses powered by electricity created from sunlight,...

Even the electrical room is a straw bale building, which naturally maintains temperatures for the equipment. The SLC generates virtually all of its own power with photovoltaics and wind, and maintains an intertie with the local utility, PG&E, to purchase any shortfall and to sell excess electricity.

RICHARD BARNES

RICHARD BARNES

...with water pumped from sunlight, and without using one ounce of fossil fuels.

A solar-powered pump provides irrigation for the landscaping and gardens. Water overflows from this recycled redwood tank, and is aerated as it passes through flowforms designed to mimic natural streambeds. Native and adaptive plantings such as California fuscia and monkeyflower attract pollinating insects, birds, and human visitors.

RICHARD BARNES

We can have retail spaces as well lighted as any commercial building on the planet without using even one energy-hogging incandescent lightbulb.

The climate-response systems designed into the showroom fulfill more than one need simultaneously. For example, the curved, east-facing clerestories formed by the stepped, faceted roof assist in daylighting the interior without causing glare or overheating in summer. At the same time, opening these windows overnight permits natural ventilation of the building, as wind blowing across the stepped roof draws out hot air and cools the thermal mass of the building so it may absorb the next day's heat.

RICHARD BARNES

We can cool without artificial air conditioning and we can heat without guzzling electricity.

Even outside, the Sun is recruited to combat its own heating power. The Agave Cooling Tower is a shady oasis that functions like a "swamp cooler." The PV-direct pump system pipes mist through the tower, cooling by evaporation.

We can create glorious landscapes without pesticides,...

The SLC is a work-in-progress. When fully grown out, the Bamboo Pyramid will be filled with timber bamboo, a member of the grass family. The living structure echoes the shape of Duncan Peak, the most impressive natural feature of the landscape.

RICHARD BARNES

LAND & PLACE

...producing enough organic food to feed our entire workforce.

In this view south across the main pond, note the low profile of the showroom building, designed to provide protection from winter winds. The north quadrant of the site is planted with productive gardens, including fruit and nut trees, berry bushes, perennial vegetables, herbs, and annual vegetable beds, all grown organically using innovative methods to preserve and restore the soil.

And we can demonstrate that sustainable building practices don't cost more;...

Double rows of upright poplars form avenues along the cardinal directions. Here, the young poplars guide the visitor from the pond through the north door of the showroom, out the front of the building, and into the Solar Calendar in the Courtyard.

JEFF OLDHAM

LAND & PLACE

...instead they save in the long run, attracting more customers, bringing more business, making more profit,...

Several hundred thousand people visit annually to shop for renewable energy and conservation products, attend workshops, and enjoy Solar Living first-hand. At sunset on the Summer Solstice, a fountain emerges from the center of the spiral in the Courtyard. Other elements of the Solar Calendar teach visitors about the rhythms and cycles of the Sun and the Earth.

…and keeping employees and customers alike motivated and inspired.

Like the Solar Calendar in the Courtyard, the Rainbow Solar Noon Calendar charts the course of the day and the course of the year within the showroom. Another multi-functional design feature shown here is the light shelves along the southern wall, which help distribute light evenly throughout the interior, and which can be rotated vertically to enhance insulation on cold winter nights.

DAVID ARKIN

DAVID ARKIN

It can be done and we all can do it."
—John Schaeffer

John Schaeffer, president and founder of Real Goods Trading Company, and Jeff Oldham, project manager for the SLC, bask in the rainbow rays of the Solar Noon Calendar. The Sun provides heat, light, power, and the raw energy that plants convert into green life. The Real Goods Solar Living Center is a source for the products, technologies, and training we need to make the power of the Sun work for us.

The Solar Calendar

Baile Oakes

Memory is one of the strongest forces in Nature, it guides action. When memory is broken, as is happening today, we slide into chaos. —*Dr. Jonas Salk, January, 1995*

MY LIFE IS DEDICATED TO THE EXPLORATION AND DISCOVERY OF WAYS TO USE VISUAL LANGUAGE to help bring our culture to a fuller understanding of our place within the living systems of the Earth. Madison Avenue has shown us the power of art and design to transform needs, wants, and belief systems. Icons are very powerful, and it is well past time that we dedicate the design of our public spaces to forms of expression that speak to us of our interrelationship with the natural world. However, public design reflects public beliefs—we have a chicken and egg situation here. And yet slowly but surely images and design are moving into a public dialogue with Nature, as those who commission public works begin to appreciate the need to transform our built environment into one that is more in balance with a healthy ecosystem. With the vision of John Schaeffer, Real Goods Trading Company has created a singular example of a healthy and balanced development.

I would like you to consider that all of us are very ill today. And I believe that this illness is primarily caused by a remarkable fact: as a culture, we are having an "out-of-body experience." We do not understand ourselves to be—and therefore do not perceive ourselves to be—part of the living "body" of the Earth. Our cultural perception has us understand ourselves as entities separate from, and even superior to, the life systems that create our very existence. We are presently experiencing a crisis of perception that goes to the very core of our spirit.

One of the first steps to healing is to diagnose the dis-ease, and to comprehend the cause of imbalance in the system. Even those of us who profess to be ecologically conscious citizens are still in a state of denial about our own addiction to lifestyles that we intellectually know to be harmful. Merely assess your lifestyle, transportation mode, or refrigeration needs, and then ask yourself if every person on Earth followed your example, what type of vibrant life would be left on our planet. We are all addicted to speed. The relatively cheap power of gasoline for transportation has addicted us all to lifestyles which are dependent upon quick, wasteful energy that is catastrophic to the health of the ecosystem and of our health as well.

What is needed in our culture is a spiritual transformation. Most spiritual philosophies are based on the concept of the infinite nature of the spirit. Therefore, it must follow that the nature of time is intimately connected to our perceptions of our spirit, our world, our consciousness.

Baile Oakes lives with his wife and three children near Westport on the Mendocino Coast of California. He has been working for over twenty years to incorporate reminders of our intimate connection with the natural world into public art and design. He has taught courses in ecologically conscious public art and design, curated two exhibitions featuring public artists whose work is concerned with ecological design; and authored *Sculpting with the Environment: A Natural Dialogue* (Van Nostrand Reinhold, 1995).

Today, we have become totally out of sync with the natural time of the Earth, the sense of time within which we evolved as a species. We are presently living in an accelerated time frame within which we are moving incredibly fast, with an equal increase in our stress level but still feeling that we do not have enough time to do what we need. In the age of the computer, many of us are living our lives within the framework of nanoseconds. How can we truly perceive and understand natural systems if we are living in a totally separate time frame? I personally tend to begin with transformation by looking at the bottom line, the origin of the Universe or what we share with all of creation: our relationship to the life-giving energy of the Sun—the energy that creates and moderates all life on our planet.

Ancient peoples based their creation myths on celestial phenomena, many contemporary religions speak of "God who dwells in the heavens," and scientists today search the cosmos with ever more powerful telescopes seeking information about the origin of the universe.

However, artificial lighting has severed the connection to the celestial bodies for people in cities around the world. As we become isolated from the rest of the universe, we lose our roots, a basis of the meaning of our lives and a connection to each other.

Before the advent of electricity, it was common knowledge that the Moon rose approximately an hour later each evening and that the full Moon rose at sunset. Today, few people in developed countries are aware of this essential phenomenon. We understand that some of the ways in which we produce electricity cause pollution of the air, ground, and water; but few of us realize that light pollution is robbing us of our connection to our heritage, myths, and spirit.

Past cultures integrated light and shadow events into the everyday structures that sustained their communities and lives, in order to mark the consistency of the cosmic order. In our culture, the solstice for the most part goes unnoticed. The day that marks the resurgence of the life-giving power of the Sun has been adopted by different religions as one of those special events that are the foundation of their respective belief systems. While the specific rituals of celebration may be various, all of these religious events make a singular reference to the return of the light.

The Rebirth of the Sun

My work with the Solar Living Center included the design of solar calendar elements throughout the central courtyard, children's area, and the entrance to the showroom. The Solar Calendar concerns itself with slowing down our perception of time, in order to help us understand the framework of time within which all life is created. We desperately need to reconnect with the cycles of life and it is virtually impossible to do so while we are living in a parallel universe of accelerated time. The integration of the Solar Calendar was the result of an intense collaboration between myself, Chris Tebbutt and Stephanie Kotin of Land & Place, and David Arkin of the Ecological Design Institute.

Like Stonehenge, Machu Picchu, and the Imperial Palace in Peking, the Solar Living Center celebrates in its art and architecture the life-giving solar year. Visitors can feel this connection as they enter the central dais of the oasis pool in front of the showroom. From this central point, they can begin to perceive the design of the entire central oasis as a working weekly and seasonal calendar that works in accord with the consistent order of the Earth's relationship to the Sun.

Our yearly calendar starts at the birth of the Sun—the Winter Solstice. By wonderful chance, the corner of the central oasis that Chris and Stephanie had allocated for a children's play area was in visual alignment with the Winter Solstice sunrise as viewed from the central dais. Since the calendar concerns itself with rebirth, I felt that it was important to recognize the children, our rebirth, as part of this cosmic dance.

Therefore several gestures were designed into the children's area. We placed a softly rounded boulder in the water course that defines the children's area, directly aligned with the Winter Solstice sunrise. The children use this boulder as a gathering place and island. A river-stone sighting tower serves as the center piece of the play area. Designed for climbing, the tower has a number of holes through which the child's gaze is directed to landmarks around the Solar Living Center and locations of the solstice and equinox

JEFF OLDHAM

Holes in the stone gnomon in the play area direct a child's gaze to landmarks around the Solar Living Center and locations of the solstice and equinox sunsets.

LAND & PLACE

During the solstice and equinox sunsets, the drain is closed and a fountain emerges from the center of the spiral. The water overflows through the triangular copper inlays toward the six major solar directions.

sunrises and sunsets. It also serves as a seasonal solar gnomon. The shadow it casts at sunset on the solstices and equinoxes will be marked over the years upon the aqueduct. It will become another gentle reminder for the children of the order and balance of our seasonal relationship to the Sun.

A small stream of water diverted from the rill follows the Winter Solstice sunrise alignment into the spiral dais, metaphorically merging the life-giving properties of water with the mineral bed of the stream and the birth of the energy of the Sun. Walking from the direction of the Winter Solstice sunrise, visitors following the spiral flow of water onto the pool's central dais will find six copper inlays. Each inlay directs the view to stone monuments on the surrounding berms that define the oasis. These stone monuments mark the location of the solstice and equinox sunrises and sunsets on the local horizon.

The copper inlays also serve a ceremonial purpose. During the sunsets of the solstices and equinoxes, the drain in the dais is closed while a fountain of water emerges from the center. The pool of water created by the fountain overflows the dais through these six major solar directions, celebrating the local sunset and the defining moment of the seasons of the year.

This fountain was intended to emerge from the central dais to celebrate the end of each day as the setting Sun energizes the life of the water with its golden light, completing the life-confirming cycle of the gift of water and sunlight. However, for the time being, the Solar Living Center will need to wait for a better computer to program this moment for the

BAILE OAKES

Near the solstices, the copper sleeves that hold the brass staffs marking the weekly position of the sunrise and sunset are very close together, illustrating that the Sun changes position against the Earth's horizon slowly at the turn of winter and summer. At the Spring and Fall Equinoxes, the brass staff is moved more than a foot each week.

LAND & PLACE

By standing in the center of the spiral, visitors can observe the weekly sunrise and sunset locations by aligning the brass staffs on each side of the pool with stone markers set into the surrounding berm.

central fountain, or rely on the diligence of a sunset watcher to manually control this event.

To bring to the visitor a greater sense of the seasonal relationship between the Earth and the Sun, we designed a weekly calendar also focused from the central dais in the pool. The true horizon defines the weekly locations of sunrise and sunset. In this way, the visitor can perceive the beautifully balanced relationship of the dance of the Earth and Sun. The markers that indicate the weekly position of the staff are very close together as we approach the solstices and more than a foot apart at the time of the equinox.

Copper sleeves set into the outside perimeter of the surrounding concrete apron of the pool support a movable brass staff. Each of these sleeves is sealed with a copper cap engraved with an image of the Sun and the dates during the year when the Sun is setting in this location as viewed from the dais. Each week, a new sleeve is uncapped and the seven-foot tall polished brass staff is moved to its new location. Visitors standing in the center of the dais can observe the sunrise and sunset location for the week by aligning themselves to this tall brass staff from the central dais.

Rainbow Solar Noon Calendar

The Rainbow is a very deep memory for humans. It has been coded into our genetic material over millions of years. Seeing a rainbow restores our connection to Nature—it restores our physical and psychic functions.

—Dr. Jonas Salk

The effects of the outdoor Solar Calendar were continued into the showroom by means of a collaborative work with artist Peter Erskine, who also co-authored this section. Erskine designed a solar-prism skylight that reveals the wondrous beauty of the full spectrum. Four flat prisms precisely aligned in a skylight surround a solar oculus or lens. The movement of this arrangement is powered by the rotation of the Earth and its changing seasonal tilt toward the Sun. The rainbow-haloed solar disk moves the distance of its own diameter of six inches in less than thirty seconds. The resulting projected image and spectrum is first seen in the morning along the west wall of the showroom, and over the course of the day gradually flows over to the eastern end of the showroom.

The landscape and architectural plan of the Solar Living Center are oriented upon a true north/south axis, with the long dimension of the building and site parallel to the path of the Sun. The front and back doors of the showroom are precisely aligned so that a north-south line arrives through the southern entrance of the building and exits through the north-side doors. Along this north-south line, we articulated a visible solar zenith/solar noon calendar. This Solar Noon Calendar is a 2-foot wide line inlaid into the floor. At exactly solar noon, the disk of white light projected through the solar oculus by the sun crosses the center of this calendar line. On June 21st, the Summer Solstice in the northern hemisphere, the Sun reaches its highest point in the sky at solar noon. The Sun's image is projected by the oculus upon the calendar line at the southern end of the calendar. On the Winter Solstice, December 21st, the Sun is at its lowest angle in the sky at solar noon and its image is projected upon the calendar line at the farthest north position on the noon line.

One of the first discoveries made by visitors is that the "noon" as defined by the Solar Noon Calendar will not match the noon on their watches. The Center's time piece expresses the actual time of Nature, one not restricted and controlled by time zones and daylight savings time.

Over the year, the Sun's zenith position as it relates to the Solar Living Center will continually redefine the calendar. This is a work in progress; each week, we mark a wooden template placed along the north-south line with the Sun's projected image, which marks a pattern corresponding to the dates of the weekly horizon calendar that is indicated by the oasis in the front of the showroom. When a full record for the Sun's journey from northerly arc to southerly arc has been recorded on the template, the wood will be removed and used to inscribe an accurate calendar line in an archival material. In the years to come, this record of the Sun's passage will underscore the Solar Living Center's intimate sense of place, an ongoing connection between the showroom and the Earth and the heavens.

The Rainbow Solar Noon Calendar at the Solar Living Center is the first walk-in solar time piece in the world that tells time with a natural rainbow!

Main Entry Doors/A Sense of Place

The front doors to the showroom act as a point of reference, an architectural gesture intended to establish in the visitor a genuine sense of place. The lower portion of these doors is comprised of a detailed wood carving that visually locates the Solar Living Center within its watershed. The glass panels in the upper portion of the doors acquaint the visitor with a sense of this place on a global scale. There are eight different views of the location of the Solar Living Center etched into the glass. Each view is perceptually centered from the vantage point of the dais, and the shift in perspective among the eight views progresses in each instance by a power of ten.

For example, since the dais is 8 feet wide, the next view is of an 80-foot wide area of the site, the next view shows an 800-foot wide area, and so on until the last view, which shows a view of the planet centered upon the location of the Solar Living Center. The images etched into the glass panels progress as follows: the central dais; the central oasis; the Solar Living Center; Hopland, California; the regional vicinity of Hopland; Northern California; the Western United

States; and the Earth. The images in the glass are very accurate but also subtle, with only sandblasted carving to define the mapping. This design is intended to provide a source of discovery for the inquisitive mind.

It is my hope that those who control the infrastructure development in our world will be convinced of the educational and inspirational role of visual art in helping us reestablish a balance within the living systems of our planet. The Solar Living Center represents understanding that art and design can and should be used as a tool to bring us closer to our planet, to help us look at the Earth and see ourselves. It is time we empower our artistic resources, and renew our dialogue with the Earth.

Sim Van der Ryn is president of the Ecological Design Institute, the architectural firm that designed the site and structures of the Solar Living Center. A former California State Architect and Professor Emeritus of Architecture at the University of California, he has been a proponent of sustainable design and building practices for more than forty years.

CHAPTER 4

Design: Manifesting the Vision

Sim Van der Ryn

Form follows flow. —*Sim Van der Ryn*

FROM THE OUTSET, there was a very good fit between John Schaeffer's vision for the Solar Living Center and Van der Ryn Architects' philosophy and work. I have always preached to students that great architecture takes great clients. In our practice, we spend as much time interviewing potential clients to see whether there is a good fit in values and working styles as we do selling our services. It is hard to bring good buildings into being; it is impossible if client and architect are not in alignment. I knew of Real Goods for many years, and John knew of my work as California State Architect and as founder of Farallones Institute, the predecessor to the Ecological Design Institute, the nonprofit education and research affiliate of Van der Ryn Architects.

THE COMPETITION ENTRY: WHAT WORKED AND WHAT DIDN'T

Real Goods invited six architects to compete in preparing concept plans for their proposed Solar Living Center, from which they would select an architect. Although they offered a very small honorarium, suggesting a low valuation of architects and what they do, I found John Schaeffer's vision statement intriguing and closely aligned with my own values. I had no choice but to accept the invitation.

I visited the site with my associate, David Arkin. The site is bounded on the west by Highway 101 (the major route north, but not yet a freeway). To the east is the town's sewage treatment plant. To the south, a neglected vineyard awaits development. To the north runs Feliz Creek, tributary to the Russian River, the major drainage in the area, and just beyond it the town of Hopland, including two favorite stops, the Fetzer Winery tasting room and Mendocino Brewing Company, one of the region's first microbreweries (incidentally, founded by a former student of mine). The highway features a steady stream of trucks shifting down to climb the grade to the south. There are wonderful views to the west of the coastal range, including the local promontory Duncan's Peak, and to the east to the range that separates the Ukiah Valley from the great Central Valley of California. The bad news was that the site was flat, treeless, a flood plain with few memorable features. The good

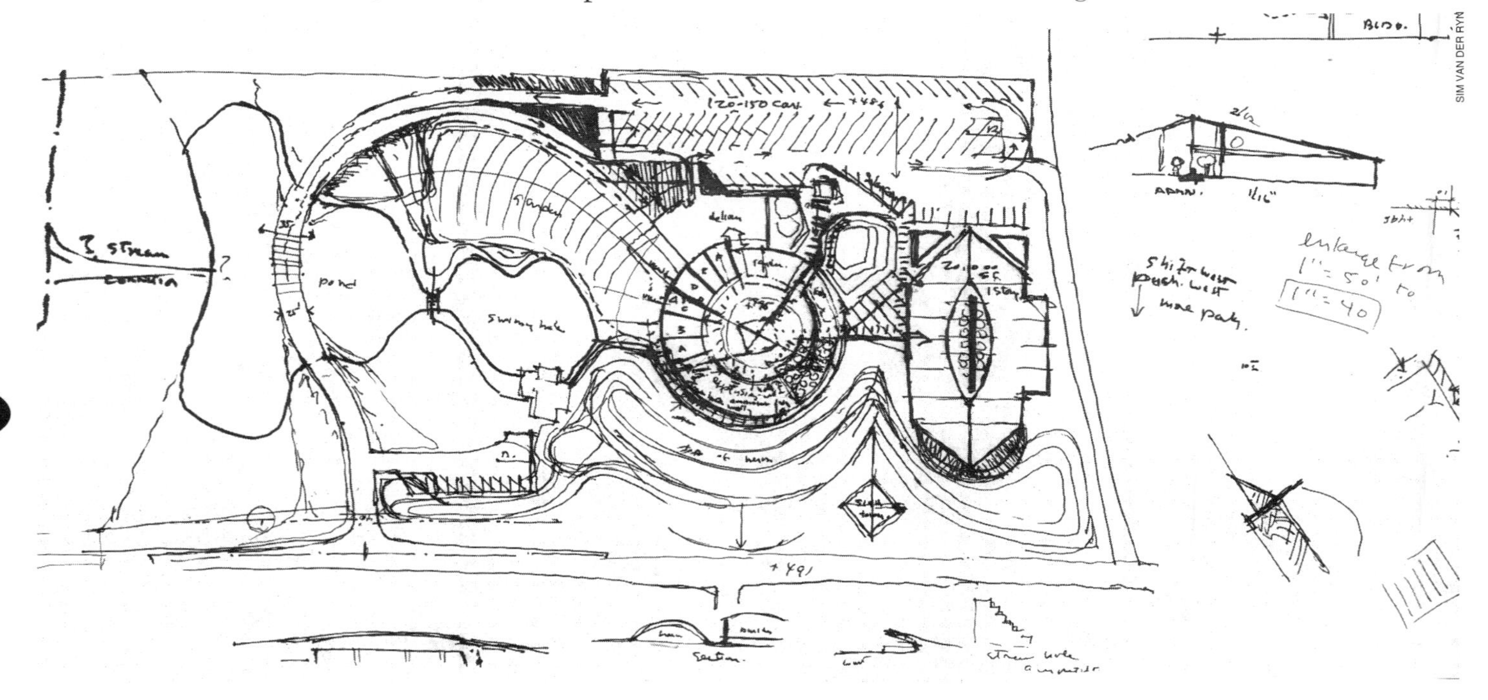

SIM VAN DER RYN

news was that it had full solar access, good views, and felt like a place waiting to be enhanced by thoughtful, creative design.

I sat for a while, then pulled out my everpresent watercolor kit. I start every project by doing a watercolor on-site and letting the site speak to me through the process. For forty years, I have watercolored landscapes all over the world. It is a form of meditation, a way to get quiet and become aware of the subtleties of place: colors, forms, and patterns, sounds and spaces, how the light changes. Watercolor helps me to actually see fully, not just with

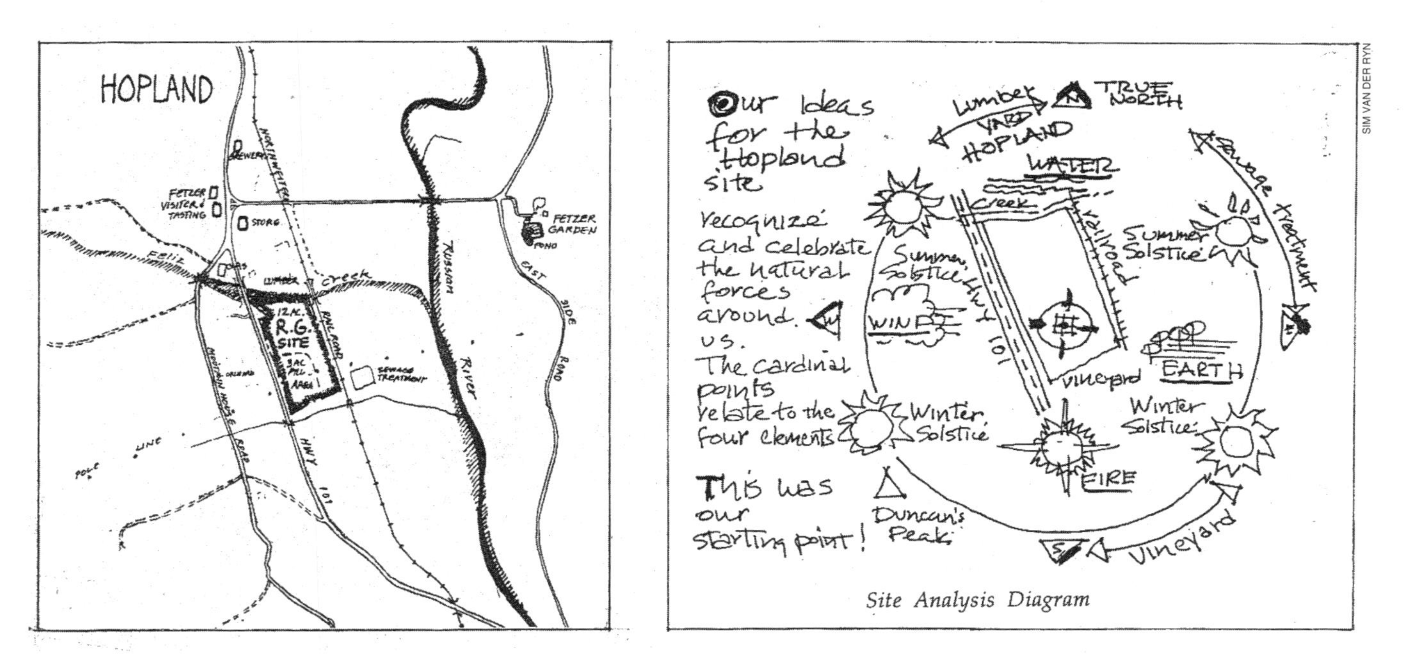

Site Analysis Diagram

SIM VAN DER RYN

Sim Van der Ryn was one of six architects invited by Real Goods to prepare concept plans for the proposed Solar Living Center. He visited the site to watercolor and sketch, letting the site teach him what was necessary and possible. The shape of the landscape, climate, solar access, and compass orientation must all work together in the ecological design process.

the eyes and brain, but with my whole being. Its the difference between merely *looking*, which is a passive involvement in place, and *seeing*, which is active involvement.

After painting, I started sketching. The topographic map we were given showed a slight mound at the south end of the site. This highest point, offering protection from flooding, was where the building had to be. As I sat there for several hours, the noise from the highway became increasingly irritating. Why not scoop out part of the site to create the ponds and water elements that John's vision statement mentioned, and use the excavated material to create a berm or earth mound to screen the building from the highway's noise and view? If the Solar Living Center was truly to be an oasis, then it should not be like most commercial highway structures that insist on being seen from the road. Instead, we would partially hide it and create a series of ecological cues announcing that something interesting and fascinating was around the bend.

Within the rounded berm, I sketched the building itself as a south-facing curve. Why not make the building truly invisible, as well as adapted to the hot summers, by using a sod

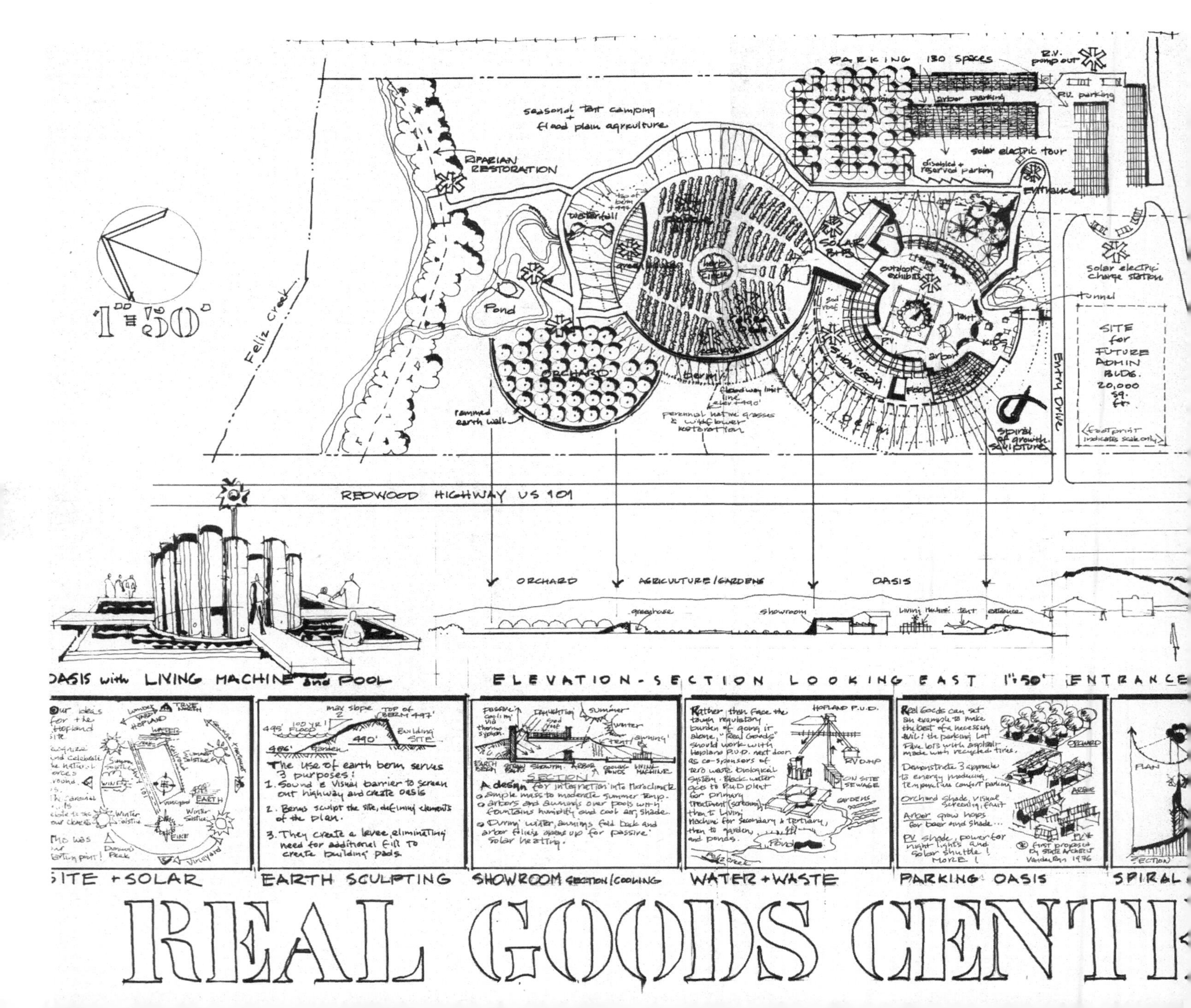
PARKING 130 SPACES
R.V. pump out
R.V. parking
orchard parking
arbor parking
seasonal tent camping + flood plain agriculture
RIPARIAN RESTORATION
solar electric tour
disabled + reserved parking
ENTRANCE
waterfall
Solar electric charge station
tunnel
outdoor exhibits
tent
KIDS
arbor
FOOD
SHOWROOM
Pond
ORCHARD
berm
Feliz Creek
1"=50'
rammed earth wall
floodway limit line
perennial native grasses & wildflower restoration
SITE for FUTURE ADMIN BLDG. 20,000 sq. ft.
(footprint indicates scale only)
Entry Drive
spiral of growth sculpture
REDWOOD HIGHWAY US 101
ORCHARD
AGRICULTURE/GARDENS
OASIS
greenhouse
showroom
Living Machine
tent
entrance
OASIS with LIVING MACHINE and POOL
ELEVATION-SECTION LOOKING EAST 1"=50'
ENTRANCE
max slope 2
TOP of BERM 497'
495' 100 YR FLOOD
490'
486'
Garden
Building SITE
The use of earth berm serves 3 purposes:
1. Sound & Visual barrier to screen out highway and create oasis
2. Berms sculpt the site, defining elements of the plan.
3. They create a levee, eliminating need for additional fill to create building pads.
EARTH SCULPTING
Passive cooling via thermo syphon.
Daylighting
Sod roof
summer
winter
tent/awning
EARTH BERM
STRAW BALES
SHOWRM.
ARBOR
COOLING PONDS
LIVING MACHINE
SECTION
A design for integration into Microclimate
o simple mass to moderate summer temp.
o arbors and awnings over pools with fountains humidify and cool air; shade.
o During winter, awnings fold back and arbor foliage opens up for passive solar heating.
SHOWROOM SECTION/COOLING
Rather than face the tough regulatory burden of going it alone, "Real Goods" should work with Hopland P.U.D. next door as co-sponsors of zero waste biological system. Black water goes to P.U.D plant for primary treatment (screening), then to Living Machine for secondary & tertiary, then to garden and ponds.
HOPLAND P.U.D.
RV DUMP
ON SITE SEWAGE
GARDENS
Pond
Feliz Creek
WATER + WASTE
Real Goods can set an example to make the best of a necessary evil! the parking lot
Pave lots with asphalt made with recycled tires.
Demonstrate 3 approaches to energy producing, temperature comfort parking
Orchard shade, visual screening, fruit
Arbor grow hops for beer and shade...
PV shade, power for night lights and solar shuttle! MORE!
ORCHARD
ARBOR
PV
first proposed by State Architect Van der Ryn 1976
PARKING OASIS
SITE + SOLAR
SPIRAL
PLAN
SECTION
REAL GOODS CENT

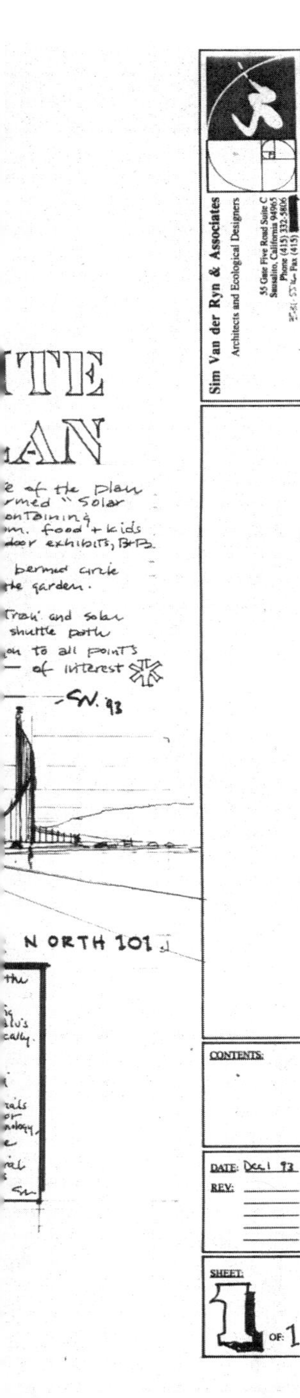

roof, arbors along the south facade, and a mass wall into the berm to the north? Why not have the building open onto a central meeting space marked by a shallow round pond and sundial? The pond would provide natural cooling in summer. The sundial would always mark the Sun's path—something that many of today's architects do not take into account when designing. To the north, I located the experimental gardens and orchards that John's program mentioned. And as a signpost near the entry, I sketched a hundred-foot-high, three-dimensional spiral with the center as its highest point, a sculptural expression of growth, a symbol of an ecologically evolving civilization.

That weekend, David and I developed the competition drawing based on my sketches. As another meditation, I spent a day carefully preparing the finished drawing and sent it off to Real Goods. We later went to Ukiah to present our design and answer questions. And then we waited and then waited some more. Finally I heard from John: "You got the job."

The Design Process: The Eco-Logic Design Curve

Sustainable design is a "front-loaded process": Only through careful planning at the beginning can you expect to reap rewards at the end. Eco-Logic is Van der Ryn Architects' name for the design process we follow, which adds value in its special attention to sustainable design opportunities. Eco-Logic provides the logical, inclusive, step-by-step process needed to achieve results in a high-risk, innovative situation where the caveat "design in haste, repent at leisure" is too often the reality.

We used our Eco-Logic design process in the design of the Solar Living Center. The Eco-Logic design process includes seven steps (see diagram on following page). The left side of the process curve begins with (1) Creating Program Scenarios, then moves to (2) Analyzing the Site and Ecological Resources, followed by (3) Investigating Renewable and Sustainable Materials and Systems. Then comes the critical turn, when facts and data combine with creativity, experience, and intuition: (4) Designing the Vision. The righthand side of the curve completes the process with three integrative steps: (5) Developing and Integrating Systems, (6) Completing the Detailed Design, and (7) Facilitating Construction.

We have found a number of design benefits in using the Eco-Logic process. First, we lower life-cycle costs. Over its life, operation and maintenance of the typical commercial building cost three times as much as initial construction. Under Governor Jerry Brown in the 1970s, I developed and managed a program to build over a million square feet of new, energy-efficient office space. We were able to reduce energy costs by as much as 80 percent through careful climate-responsive design. In the SLC, careful design not only created a net

ECO - LOGIC DESIGN PROCESS

THE BENEFITS OF ECO-LOGIC DESIGN

1. LOWER LIFE CYCLE COSTS
Over a 30-year period, the operations and maintenance of a typical commercial building equal three times the construction costs. Van der Ryn designed buildings, employing sustainable methods and materials, have reduced these costs significantly.

2. HIGHER PRODUCTIVITY
Personnel costs represent 92 percent of typical facility operations. Worker productivity, health, and satisfaction contribute to higher efficiency in Eco-Logic buildings.

3. HEALTHIER PLACES
Tranquility, peace of mind, comfort qualities attributed to thick wall, passive solar buildings. Eco-Logic creates healthier work places, living spaces, and communities.

1. PROGRAM SCENARIOS
- establish an interactive partnership with our client to give voice to their values
- match the vision and values with criteria for sustainability
- determine functional requirements, phasing priorities, and schedules
- establish budgets which balance the vision, values, and intentions

2. ANALYZE THE SITE AND ECOLOGICAL RESOURCES
- understand the site context, ecology, spirit, health, and restorative possibilities
- overlay mapping of the resources inventory including soils, geology, topography, vegetation, hydrology, watershed, solar, and microclimate
- summary map of opportunities/ constraints and site potential

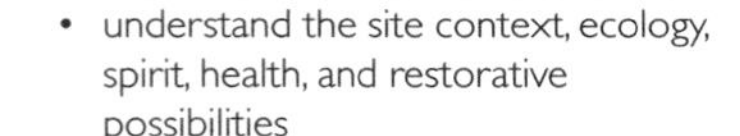

3. INVESTIGATE RENEWABLE AND SUSTAINABLE SYSTEMS AND MATERIALS
- analyze renewable, non-toxic, and regenerative sources
- research material alternatives—renewable, natural, reclaimed, and/or recycled
- create building ecology through analysis of energy flow, materials, methods, and money

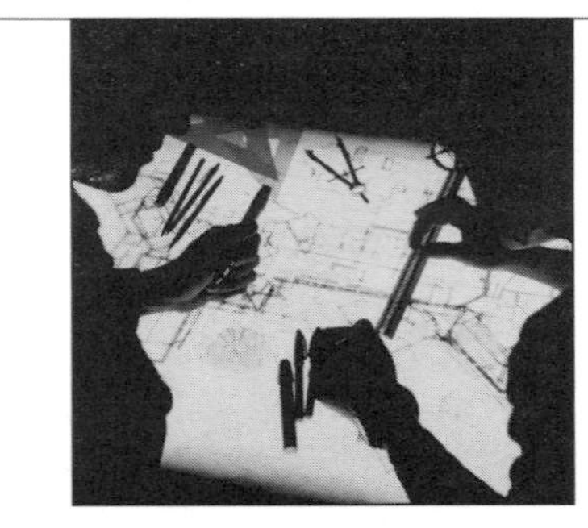

4. DESIGN THE VISION
- design synthesis of the program, site, resources, systems, materials, and budget
- present the vision
- evaluate and evolve design in collaboration with client

7. **FACILITATE CONSTRUCTION**
- secure approvals
- establish contractor team
- monitor budget and schedule
- develop and supervise test program

4. **INCREASED IMAGE AND MARKETABILITY**
Commercial structures designed by the firm command attention, attract interest, and exceed proforma. Homes in Eco-Logic communities command 10–20 percent premiums.

6. **COMPLETE DETAILED DESIGN**
- communicate design vision and intent
- write specifications with sustainability criteria, methods, and materials
- complete analytical reports to support decisions

5. **REDUCED ENVIRONMENTAL IMPACTS**
Eco-Logic buildings and communities take less from the earth by reducing waste and pollution toxicity, and by preserving natural resources.

5. **DEVELOP AND INTEGRATE SYSTEMS**
- establish the materials palette through qualitative and quantitative analysis
- test materials and systems
- computer model the systems, resources, and flows
- validate and coordinate sequencing
- establish the foundation for completion of design

surplus of electrical energy, it also eliminated the need for mechanical heating or cooling, a savings in both life-cycle costs and operating expenses.

A second benefit of the process is reduced environmental impact. By tracing the footprint or lineage of every material used in the building (a special kind of architectural detective work), we avoid the destruction of virgin forests, the pollution of faraway places, and global warming. Eco-Logic buildings are designed to reduce waste, pollution, and toxicity not only in their immediate environments but in the whole biosphere.

A third benefit of our brand of ecological design is that users and owners of our buildings experience higher productivity, satisfaction, sales, and value. This has certainly been true of the SLC. Sales have exceeded the early optimistic projections. The center and site have become a regional attraction, with people clamoring for more information, which is leading to a new project: an on-site education center. People are amazed at how comfortable and comforting the building is. Kept warm in winter and cool in summer by the sun and wind, it is exactly the oasis that John Schaeffer envisioned. This is not an accident or the sheer inspiration of a lone artistic genius. It is the result of teamwork, partnership, and a unique design process.

Step 1. Creating Program Scenarios

Good buildings don't get made by handing the architect a laundry list. John's vision statement was a valuable beginning. This is the best starting point for any project: a sense of the qualities, feeling, character, and performance attributes that would make a successful project from the client's point of view. This is supplemented by descriptions of functions, activities, spaces—the more quantitative data that, together with budget, time line, and team, make up a program.

The weakest part of John's program was a lack of recognition of the design and building process and the team required to make it happen. This is a common weakness among clients who are first-time builders. It is an area where architects are called upon to help clients understand the design/construction process and its requirements.

Entering the process as a competition winner short-circuited the program development step, where ideas are thoroughly explored before solutions are proposed. This is the phase when communication paths and patterns are developed. In the design process, skipping a step generally means repeating it later with greater difficulty.

An analysis of the site included inventories of soils and geology, topography, vegetation, hydrology and watershed, solar access, and microclimate. The ecological design process gives new meaning to that business mantra: "Location, location, location."

Step 2. Analyzing the Site and Ecological Resources

The second step in our Eco-Logic process is to analyze the site and its ecological resources, including its native ecology, spirit, health, and restorative possibilities. We create resource overlay maps through inventory of soils and geology, topography, vegetation, hydrology and watershed, solar access, and microclimate. The most critical factors turned out to be the site's flood-plain location and its microclimate. Test wells indicated that the site is perched on a gravel-base aquifer that provides copious water. This permitted to us to design major water elements and also guaranteed a steady source of water for the gardens. Excess water percolates back down into the aquifer, providing a natural water-recycling system.

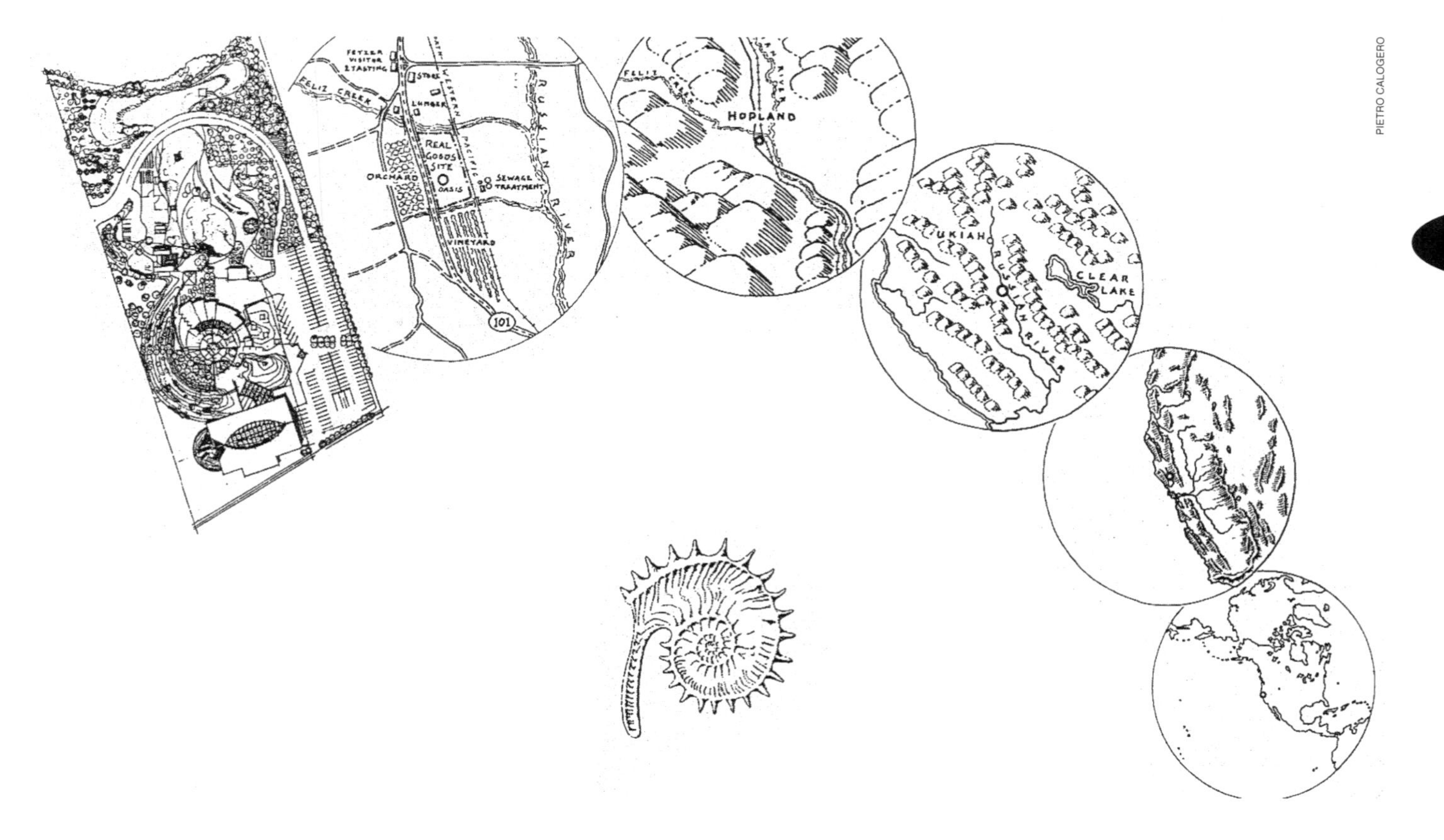

PIETRO CALOGERO

JEFF OLDHAM

Understanding the microclimate of the site is the key to climate-responsive design. The Solar Living Center has excellent solar access. With its hot, dry summers, and mild winters, cooling is more of a factor than heating in the Hopland area. Shading, evaporative cooling, and nighttime ventilation were strategies Van der Ryn Architects considered essential to the project design from the start.

A detailed analysis and understanding of microclimate is a key to climate-responsive design. Hopland lies in a valley 50 miles inland, separated from the coast by rugged, hilly terrain. Average rainfall is 39 inches per year, mostly falling in the winter months, with extremely dry, hot summers. Annual mean wind is 6 miles per hour, generally insufficient to operate wind electric generators (but see chapter 5). There are no significant horizon obstructions to solar access at the SLC site. Solar access is often impaired by foggy winter mornings, but the rest of the year is clear with good potential solar gain.

The analysis led to some conclusions regarding design strategies. Heating is not as big a factor as cooling, since winter days tend to be mild and the building would have daytime occupancy, suggesting that direct solar gain could provide necessary winter heating. The need for summer shading is crucial, with temperatures reaching 110 degrees Fahrenheit, sometimes for days in a row. Low summer humidity suggested the potential for evaporative cooling. Cool summer nights offered an opportunity for nighttime ventilation.

Step 3. Investigating Renewable and Sustainable Materials and Systems

The Eco-Logic design process outlines a systematic investigation of the materials and ecology necessary for the project's construction and operation, including:

- performing systems analysis of renewable, nontoxic, and regenerative sources for opportunities, needs, and compatibility;
- researching material alternatives—renewable, natural, nontoxic, reclaimed, and/or recycled resources—that are effective, appropriate, and affordable;
- creating a building ecology with preliminary analysis of flows of energy, materials, methods, and money.

"Real Goods wanted a building that takes less from the Earth and gives back more to people." Among the innovative materials and methods employed in the Solar Living Center, the use of straw bale walls is perhaps the most significant. Not only are the bales an effective, fire-resistant insulation, but rice straw is an agricultural waste product that was formerly burned in the field, creating greenhouse gas and particulate pollution. Sustainability means making decisions that solve more than one problem.

DAVID ARKIN

In the SLC project, all of these points were a high priority to Real Goods and to us.

Real Goods wanted a building that takes less from the Earth and gives back more to people. Important objectives were to select materials and systems that used recycled and waste materials; were low in embodied energy (the energy required to manufacture and transport them); used local sources wherever possible; reduced the use of new wood and used only certified sustainably harvested new wood; were nontoxic; and were reasonably priced. The other important objective was that the building be a net producer of electrical energy and have absolutely no need for mechanical heating and cooling fueled by imported fuels.

The results of our ecological accounting brought us to the following decisions:

- Substitute fly ash (a byproduct of power plant combustion) for some percentage of cement in the concrete. Recent tests show that the use of up to 25 percent fly ash in concrete actually increases its strength, durability, and resistance to water penetration and spalling. A win-win decision!
- Use rice-straw bales for the north wall. Rice straw is a high-silica-content agricultural waste product that was previously burned. Baled, it has an

R-value of over 56, is highly fire resistant, and is not subject to rodent or insect infestation. Another win-win decision!

- Use sprayed earth veneer rather than cement stucco over the straw bales. We invented a new technology for spraying quarry waste directly over the straw bales with gunite equipment, for a soft, earthy finish that is proving to be durable as well. Chalk up another win!
- Use glu-lam (glued and laminated) beams made out of recycled and local, sustainably harvested woods.
- Use other straw-based materials for finishes, including a lightweight board and panel material.
- Supply all electrical energy from renewable sources using photovoltaic arrays. The building maintains thermal comfort summer and winter without the use of a centralized mechanical system. Wood stoves provide backup heating, and solar-powered evaporative coolers provide summer backup cooling (which has yet to be used, since the passive cooling and ventilating techniques are working so well).

Step 4. Designing the Vision

The next step integrates aspects of the design into presentable form:

- perform a design synthesis of the program, site and resources, systems, materials, and budget;
- present the vision graphically and physically;
- evaluate and evolve the design through active teamwork between the client and Van der Ryn Architects.

The starting point for this step was the design developed in the competition with a minimum of input from client or consultants. The sod roof solution was discarded because the store's requirements for clear spans and ceiling height, added to the heavy weight of 18 inches of soil, would require massive concrete column structures in the earthquake-prone location. Our hope was to be able to rely on daylight to illuminate the store during daytime hours. Adam Jackaway, our daylighting consultant, suggested the curved roof form in section for its elegant efficiency in evenly distributing daylight. A light shelf was added to the south wall to provide additional efficiency in reflecting daylight onto the ceiling. The curved roof section fit beautifully with the curved plan in our model. To further enhance natural light, we "staircased" the plan so that each segment became wider as it moved to the west,

creating a window to the east. Having done this in plan, we then decided to do the same thing in section, with the curved roof segments rising as they moved west, creating high east-facing windows or clerestories between each segment of roof.

Engineer Bruce King then developed a structural plan with cantilevered concrete columns and glu-lam beams. A search began for other materials that met our criteria for energy efficiency, sourcing, and other factors.

An early feature discarded during the design process was the sod roof proposed for the building. Given the high, open ceilings required in the retail store, the weight of the soil would require a massive support structure. The new curved roof design was superior to an earlier "bunker" option in permitting natural daylighting illumination of the store.

Chris Tebbutt and Stephanie Kotin, the two finest landscape designers and horticulturists I've ever run into, were Real Goods' choice to develop and install the landscaping. Chris and Stephanie worked with us on the site and landscape plan. John wanted the ponds enlarged. Together we developed a beautiful reflective layout with two ponds and intricate gardens between. The straight road in my early sketch was moved north and became a gentle meandering introduction to the site. We eliminated the berm enclosing the north wall of the building and raised the building on a pad above the hundred-year-flood line. Key decisions were in place.

This model shows the integration of the curved roof with the bird's-wing shape of the building. The plan is "staircased," with segments rising and becoming wider as they move to the west, creating high east-facing windows between each segment.

Working with Stephanie Kotin and Chris Tebbut, Sim made important changes to the site and landscape plan. The straight road in an earlier sketch became a meandering curve to the north. Enlarged ponds and intricate gardens surround the building. The berm intended to enclose the north wall and protect against flooding was replaced by a raised pad constructed of fill excavated during landscaping.

DAVID ARKIN

Step 5. Developing and Integrating Systems

Next, the Eco-Logic process demands extensive modeling and testing of all project materials and systems, including:

- establishing materials palette through re-evaluation and qualitative and quantitative decision making, and applying it to the design;
- testing materials and systems;
- running computer models of systems, resources, and flows;
- understanding, rationalizing, and coordinating sequencing;
- establishing a solid foundation for completing the design.

The analytic tools and knowledge available for ecological designing have grown in number and sophistication in the last generation. We were able to take advantage of many new techniques and software programs in this critical and fascinating phase of the work. We used both physical models and computer models in our analysis.

Evaluating and predicting daylight effects is one area where physical models work very well, because daylight doesn't change regardless of scale. We built a large-scale section of

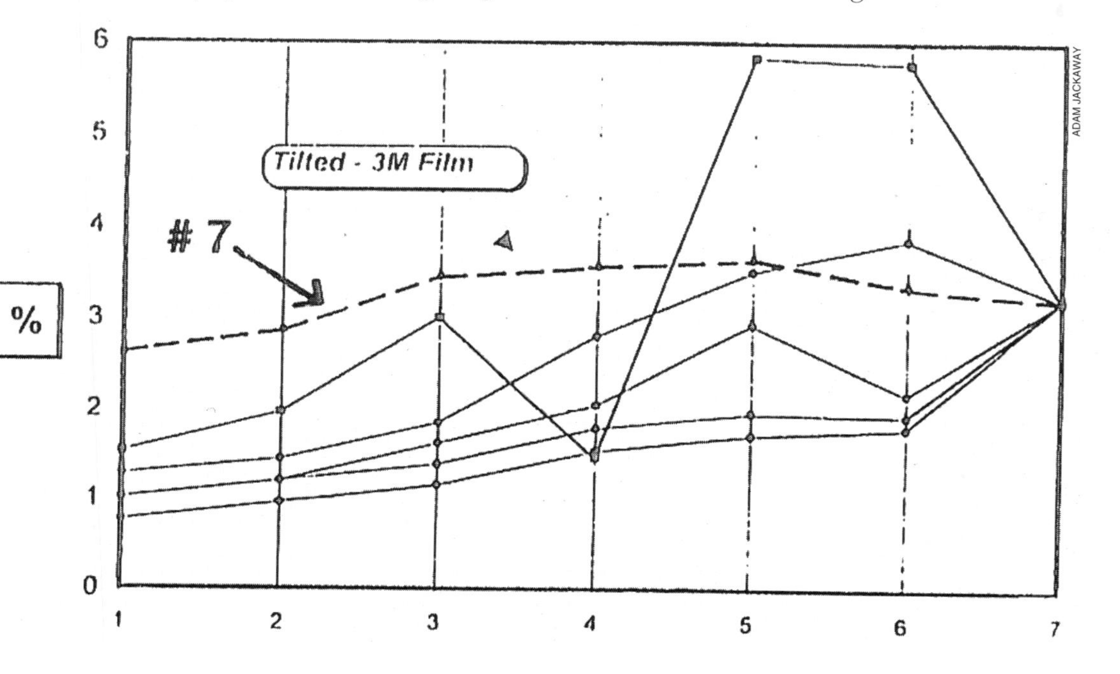

The extensive analysis and testing required by the Eco-Logic design process includes the use of both computer and physical modeling. Studies by climate-responsive design specialist Adam Jackaway included his daylight factor graph produced with a large-scale model tested at the Sky Dome simulator at UC-Berkeley. This graph shows that a highly reflective film on a tilted shelf in the ceiling produces the most even distribution of daylight in the building.

ADAM JACKAWAY

Wind tunnel tests with the building model showed that the east-facing clerestory windows could be used for venting. The physical model was also tested on the Heliodon at the PG&E Energy Center in San Francisco to film solar penetration into the space. A videotape recording of the lighting changes in the building as the Sun moves through the sky prompted John Schaeffer to exclaim, "Hey, everyone will want to be at work by five-thirty in the morning just to experience the light show!"

one of the bays and tested several options for the distribution of light in the Sky Dome simulator at UC-Berkeley. Seven Licor Photometric sensors wired to a Campbell Scientific Datalogger produced the daylight factor graph on the previous page. The seventh test, using a highly reflective film on a tilted shelf, produced the most even light. For the final design, at the recommendation of Pacific Energy Center staff, these shelves were designed as curves to account for the constantly changing sun angle during the day.

To model solar controls, we used a physical model of the building on the Heliodon at the Pacific Energy Center in San Francisco. The Heliodon is a mechanical device that simulates the position of the Sun at any time of the day or year for any location. A video camera equipped with a fiber optic lens is mounted inside the model to film solar penetration into the space, creating a time-lapse videotape recording of the Sun moving through the sky to simulate maximum and minimum sunlight at such critical times as the equinoxes and solstices. The videotape, in addition to its value as an analytic tool to design sunlight control, turned out to be an exciting teaser for John and the Real Goods team to experience the building to come. When he saw the summer sunrise coming through the high east windows, John exclaimed, "Hey, everyone will want to be at work by five-thirty in the morning just to experience the light show!"

We also performed wind tunnel tests using the building model. With the wind tunnel set to produce prevailing northwest winds, the model was filled with smoke. We had assumed we would need venting windows high in the south wall, but these tests revealed that the roof configuration produced areas of low pressure at each roof step, making it practical to use the east-facing windows to provide additional warm-weather venting.

The building became a test bed for the use of recycled woods and waste-straw products. Glu-lams were made of recycled Douglas fir from an old lumber mill. Suppliers of manufactured truss joists and sheathing were contacted to see if hemp and straw products could be substituted for the now widely used oriented strandboard (OSB), typically made of new wood.

Step 6. Completing the Detailed Design

This step encompasses the preparation of construction drawings and specifications that are used to obtain bids and permits and to guide all phases of the construction:

- produce graphics communicating design, vision, and intent;
- write specifications incorporating sustainability criteria of methods and materials;
- complete analytical reports to support decisions;
- produce documents that are simple, coherent, and buildable.

For the SLC project, the final design package included twenty-five 3- by 4-foot sheets of drawings densely packed with information. These drawings included fourteen sheets of architectural drawings, five of structural engineering, three electrical and mechanical, and three landscape sheets. These construction drawings are the "software" and operating system required to create the "hardware" constituting a finished building.

Step 7. Facilitating Construction

The last step in the Eco-Logic process carries through the construction of the project. Essential aspects of the designer's responsibility during construction include the need to

- gain necessary approvals through public dialogue and processes;
- foster early partnering with the builder to establish a team spirit that respects the integrity of the design, vision, and values;
- monitor conformance to budgets and schedules;
- develop and supervise testing programs.

DAVID ARKIN

Chapter 6 provides a detailed description of the construction process. I'd like to comment on some issues that are unique to pioneering projects such as the SLC. First, the question of dealing with planning and building bureaucracies: Having been both a highly visible "outlaw" builder and California's highest-level building official, I have experienced both perspectives. Planning and building codes are, first and foremost, political and cultural documents; truth, justice, and science are secondary. Building-code officials in California raised required railing heights from 36 to 42 inches in honor of a tall comrade who pitched over a railing in a drunken stupor at the annual convention of building officials. The code is built piece by piece out of experiences, anecdotes, political pressures, plain prejudices, the catastrophic evidence events such as earthquakes produce, and—sometimes—common sense.

The career health or building official probably has a civil service job because he or she is not a risk taker, and is not interested in sticking his or her neck out in defense of the new or untested, no matter how noble or rational the cause. Cover Your Ass (CYA) is the golden rule of bureaucracies. I am not saying these are bad or stupid people, and to treat them as if they are is the worst stupidity of all. But there comes a time in the life of an innovator, after you are told one too many times, "You can't do that," when you smile and do it anyway. Such was the case at the SLC when we had the idea of finishing the straw bale walls with earth. The plans showed a cement gunite finish. We told the building official we intended to use earth as the final finish. The building official demanded calculations and tests even though the earth finish had no structural function and health and safety issues were not involved. We told him as much. He threatened to stop the job. I declared, "Let us spray." We sprayed. He didn't stop the job. The walls are there and everybody loves them.

A decision to use sprayed earth veneer rather than cement stucco over the straw bales raised questions from local building officials. Since the finish has no structural function and health and safety issues were not involved (the earth was sprayed using standard gunite equipment), Sim approved the spraying. The soft-toned, earthy finish, made from quarry waste from a nearby construction project, is proving to be durable as well as economical.

Let me add a few words about early partnering. Real Goods, having never managed a major building project, hired two local designers/builders to manage the project for them. This seemed a reasonable move. But "Rough and Tough," as I nicknamed them, had never heard of partnering. They were from the old school of adversarial management where to look good and make it seem like you are in charge, you never listen, bark a lot, make 'em sweat, and kiss the boss's butt while kicking the guy below. It didn't work for long and soon they were gone, replaced by Jeff Oldham, Real Goods' manager of technical services and a member of the Building Committee. Jeff was a hardworking team player: competent, practical, and decisive, but a listener and always open to ideas. Together with contractor Tom Myers and his superintendent, Steve Gresham, and Van der Ryn Architects' project architect David Arkin, a solid partnership evolved that deserves credit for carrying the project into solid reality.

The Five Ecological Design Principles and Their Application

THE INVITED COMPETITION FOR THE DESIGN OF THE SOLAR LIVING CENTER was held in December of 1993, and we began our work on the project early in 1994. At the same time, I began work on another project, a book called *Ecological Design* (co-authored by Stuart Cowan, Island Press, 1996). The book was not intended as a how-to book. I wanted to present my vision of how we could build a new kind of partnership between nature and technology through design grounded in ecological principles and applications. The types of design I had in mind were not limited to architecture and urban planning. I was thinking of agriculture, the design of chemical molecules, toothbrushes, toilets, dams, clothing, computers, anything. The design of the modern environment occurs at all levels of scale from DNA to huge regional projects. None of them are connected through conscious design intelligence. Thus their effect is to disrupt the exquisitely nested scales of pattern and process that form the great living support systems of our biosphere, a biosphere increasingly endangered by human activities.

As I was writing the book, we were designing the Solar Living Center, and each process informed the other. The second half of the book, "The Ecological Design Process," is built around what I found to be five fundamental themes or principles. The book was completed about the same time as the SLC. During these simultaneous projects, I noticed that the SLC was literally a textbook example of the principles in practice. While some of these principles overlap the Eco-Logic process already discussed, I present the five principles as they apply to the Solar Living Center.

The Five Ecological Design Principles and Their Application

PRINCIPLE 1. THE BEST SOLUTIONS START FROM PAYING ATTENTION TO THE UNIQUE QUALITIES OF PLACE.

THIS PRINCIPLE AND THOSE THAT FOLLOW MAY SEEM SO COMMONSENSICAL that you may wonder why they need to be stated at all. An anecdote from my early solar days may be illuminating. I received a call from a hotel in Fiji that had installed solar hot water collectors that didn't seem to be working. After troubleshooting on the phone for an hour, I discovered that they had carefully followed the North American manufacturer's instruction manual—and installed the collectors on a south-facing roof. It helps to know what hemisphere you live in.

Under step two of the Eco-Logic process above, I discussed the many technical factors relating to site that we studied and how they affected the nature of the solution. This first principle touches on the more subtle and perhaps mysterious nature of site, the spirit of place, and its relation to design. My approach to design is both eclectic and pragmatic. I tend to shy away from any rigid dogma, whether scientismic or mystical. I avoid the fallacy of misplaced concreteness, of putting undue faith in numbers and quantification, just as I look with great skepticism on many ethereal New Age claims. What I do know is that when I become fully present and engaged with the qualities of a place, it will influence the quality and form of what I do, sometimes outside of my conscious awareness.

For example, it was not obvious to us until we photographed a model of the building on the site that the different faces of the building mirror the surrounding views. For example, the north profile of the building echoes Duncan Peak behind it, the western view reflects the rolling hills to the east, and the whole building resembles the wing of the eagle that John Schaeffer took to be an initial propitious sign.

The Five Ecological Design Principles and Their Application

PRINCIPLE 2. TRACE THE DIRECT AND INDIRECT ENVIRONMENTAL COSTS OF DESIGN DECISIONS: USE ECOLOGICAL ACCOUNTING, OR "ENVIRONOMICS."

ALL ECONOMIC DECISIONS HAVE DIRECT AND INDIRECT EFFECTS on the social and environmental health of the community. The costs of these decisions need to be part of the economy/ecology equation, a process I've labeled "environomics." Green buildings are proving to make economic as well as ecologic sense as a sure way to "get rich slow." The examples I've given in this chapter show how environomics was an essential tool in the design of the SLC.

PRINCIPLE 3. MIMIC NATURE'S PROCESSES IN DESIGN, SO THAT YOUR DESIGN FITS NATURE.

FOUR KEY "LAWS" OF ECOLOGICAL SYSTEMS ARE: (1) nature lives off solar income as captured in food webs; (2) all wastes are recycled as food for other processes; (3) biodiversity promotes stability; and (4) networks of relationships are maintained through feedback.

These natural laws are built into the Solar Living Center site and building design in many ways. The site plan enhances biodiversity through its designed aquatic and terrestrial systems. Major components of the building are made of reprocessed wastes. Direct solar income powers the building, and through a climate-responsive design, the building modulates the climate to capture and store heat in winter and provide summer cooling. The entire complex is designed so that people become part of the feedback loop, particularly through features whereby the Sun's path—an elemental rhythm of life—becomes integral to one's experience of place. The movement and flow of water supplies another elemental feedback medium, as do seasonal breezes. The cycle of plant growth provides the last elemental rhythm, repeated throughout the garden area.

PRINCIPLE 4. HONOR EVERY VOICE IN THE DESIGN PROCESS.

PROFESSIONAL TRAINING IN ARCHITECTURE, as in other fields such as medicine, tends to denigrate nonprofessional local knowledge. Our work over the years has been shaped very often by insights from unlikely sources: local residents who know the history of a site; local builders with knowledge of local materials and techniques; building occupants and users; and especially janitors and maintenance people, who can tell you the unworkable peculiarities of an award-winning building, a point made well in Stewart

The Five Ecological Design Principles and Their Application

JEFF OLDHAM

Brand's book *How Buildings Learn: What Happens After They're Built* (Viking, 1994). Besides good clients, creating a good building takes committed and skilled construction people, the unsung workers who seldom get credit for their work. At the Solar Living Center, as in all our projects, we brought the work team into the process, rather than treating them as expendable, interchangeable automatons. We explained the whole project and the rationale for its design to the team. Primed by this understanding and invitation to participate, the work team accepted the unconventional nature of the design as a challenge rather than as a nuisance requiring extra mindfulness.

A 1/16-inch scale model of the complete Solar Living Center with mature landscaping was displayed at the temporary showroom in Hopland to help educate members of the local community and invite their participation in the design process.

The Five Ecological Design Principles and Their Application

PRINCIPLE 5. MAKING NATURE VISIBLE THROUGH DESIGN TRANSFORMS BOTH MAKERS AND USERS.

In today's urbanized culture, the everyday processes, cycles, and flows of the natural environment are rarely visible. No amount of technology or culture can substitute in an environment deprived of the direct experience of nature. School curricula attempt to teach ecology in classrooms cut off from the out-of-doors. Environmental education programs provide valuable outdoor experiences for kids to supplement ecologically arid curricula, but it's not enough. We need learning places whose design *is* environmental education. We need workplaces where the daily routine is enriched by the Sun's path, the sound of birds, the fragrance and patterns of plants, the musical sound of water. That is the message of the Solar Living Center: Commerce and nature are synergistic. When consumers feel good about where they are, they'll stay longer and spend more!

This principle also implies that when we follow all of the above principles with our hearts as well as our minds, not only will the environment be changed for the better, so will we. When we work to heal social and environmental wounds, we are healed as well.

Adam Jackaway is a climate analyst and building science specialist. He was especially influential in shaping the design of the showroom at the Solar Living Center.

Jeff Oldham is the lead technician at Real Goods, and for more than a year spent his time as project manager for the Solar Living Center. Jeff has contributed to the designs of solar installations worldwide and served as a member of the presidential "Greening of the White House" Committee. He lives off-the-grid with his wife, Vicki, and children in Potter Valley, California.

CHAPTER 5

Power Systems and Climate Response Systems

Jeff Oldham and Adam Jackaway

When you turn to face the sun, all shadows are behind you.—*African proverb*

ENERGY SELF-SUFFICIENCY IS A KEY PRINCIPLE OF SUSTAINABILITY. To embrace sustainability, we must first identify and minimize every use of energy. Then we need to figure out how to generate on-site as much as possible of the required energy ourselves, in order not to be dependent on external sources such as the utilities.

REAL GOODS HAS ALWAYS PREACHED THE GLORIES AND ROMANCE OF BEING OFF-THE-GRID. Building the Solar Living Center was our golden opportunity to create the lifestyle we had always advocated, but had not yet been able to practice. As a young start-up business, Real Goods had never been able to afford anything but low-rent workspaces built without a single thought of energy efficiency. Working in these energy hogs while preaching the wonders of renewable energy was hard on everyone's morale. The Solar Living Center, as a project that epitomizes energy responsibility and the use of innovative, nontoxic materials, finally gave Real Goods employees the joyful experience of harvesting energy and inspiration from the Sun.

The first question when evaluating energy sources is what resources are available at the site. Each site is unique (which is why prefabricated housing is by definition usually an energy abomination, unless designed to be customized in place). The wind-study data from the Ukiah airport, 15 miles to the north, was not indicative of the conditions at the Solar Living Center site in Hopland. The data from Ukiah showed only an inconsistent wind source; however, when I stood on the site and looked to the northwest, where the prevailing winds come from, I saw that Feliz Creek Canyon funnels air currents to produce higher pressures and gusting wind. Despite what the meteorological data told us, we would have a very good wind site here. During the construction, especially while grading, giant dust storms and wind devils confirmed the wind potential. There is not enough terrain variation for hydroelectric, so wind and solar were our on-site energy sources.

Although the wind potential was impressive, wind patterns were too unreliable to be our primary source of energy, so we based our system on energy from the Sun. Our site has some of the best solar exposure in Mendocino County. The east and west horizons are relatively low, meaning a full day of sun. As we created the landscaping, we located trees carefully to avoid obstructing this exposure.

While evaluating energy sources for the Solar Living Center, Jeff Oldham observed that Feliz Creek Canyon functions as a funnel, producing higher pressures and gusting winds. Although data from the Ukiah airport just 15 miles north show inadequate wind for power generation, the site has its own microclimate. Wind patterns are somewhat unreliable, so wind power serves as a backup for the more extensive and predictable solar energy production. A primary goal was to make the Solar Living Center energy self-sufficient.

JEFF OLDHAM

Designing the Active Power Systems

Once all potential sources of natural energy have been evaluated and included in the site plan, the next step with any energy supply system is to perform a load analysis to quantify the present and future energy needs. We approached this task with the Solar Living Center in the same way we do with our customers. I began by examining utility bills from previous years to measure energy consumption in our existing facilities. Gotta start somewhere! Then I projected future growth. The crystal ball at Real Goods, as everywhere, is foggy. Even our best guesses often have turned out too low. So we planned to be wrong again, and installed plenty of unfinished "stub-outs" for future expansions from the electrical room. This way, we gave ourselves the option to increase capacity if growth warrants, but did not incur the costs of oversizing for our current needs.

We went to great extremes to reduce energy consumption of the building. In the load analysis, we scrutinized lighting, plugloads, equipment loads, and the heating, ventilation, and air conditioning (HVAC) systems. We eliminated power requirements whenever possible, because conservation is definitely the most cost-effective form of power generation.

In our point-of-sales area, we use computers that carry the Environmental Protection Agency's Energy-Star label, certifying that they are substantially more frugal than is "standard." Plugloads in the building are virtually nonexistent, other than in our compact fluorescent lighting display.

Compact fluorescent lights, while initially more expensive, use far less power and operate more economically than conventional, incandescent lights. The new compact fluorescents do not flicker or buzz as earlier versions usually did, and warm colors (as well as full-spectrum bulbs) have replaced that cold blue effect. In the main showroom area, we used the new (and slimmer) T-8s with electronic ballasts and automatic daylight-dimming systems. We chose a similarly efficient bulb for the back wall wash-lights (32-watt compact fluorescent), and the lights underneath the light shelves on the front curtain wall are 27-watt compact fluorescents. With the extraordinary daylighting design of the building, however, we do not need supplemental lighting very often. Our calculations indicate that additional lighting will be needed for only two hundred hours per year maximum, compared to a standard retail or commercial building, which typically uses supplemental lighting for more than 3,000 hours per year.

Nighttime exterior and security lighting uses compact fluorescents, spaced at maximum distances to minimize the number needed. Even the exterior sign on the west side of the building is lit by a single 13-watt compact fluorescent lightbulb.

Because the Real Goods' product line emphasizes appliances and devices that promote a healthy environment, we wanted the Solar Living Center to showcase nontoxic products, while capturing that intangible quality that makes living in a home surrounded by natural materials so pleasant. An increasing number of Americans are realizing that luxury, comfort, and cost are not the only considerations for the products we use every day. How a product interacts with an environment in terms of healthfulness is a top priority. What is beautiful about a carpet that fouls the air by emitting the noxious chemicals used in its manufacture? We must look beneath the surface to understand how a product is made, and what the consequences of its full life cycle will be in terms of environmental impact.

We minimized electromagnetic fields (EMFs) by twisting all wire with a cordless drill before placing it in conduits. Twisting the wires together results in "wave cancellation," much like the flat spot created on the water's surface when the circles of ripples from two stones dropped into the water intersect. Although the scientific community is divided about the

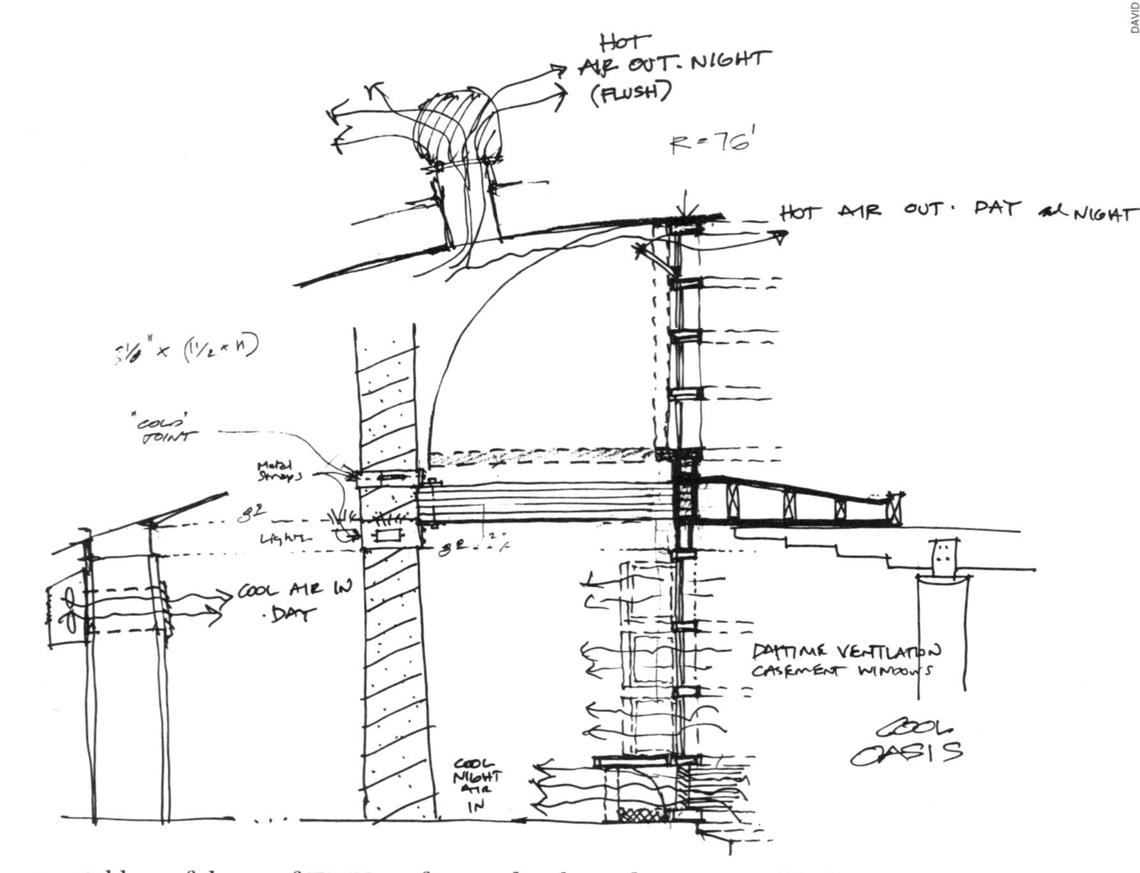

DAVID ARKIN

The showroom does not have a centralized heating, ventilation, and air conditioning system. Most heating and cooling needs are met passively, and the small evaporative coolers originally installed in the building were never used during the first year of operation. Several solar-powered ceiling fans provide nighttime flushing during the hottest days of the summer, cooling the mass of the building itself, so that this mass can absorb the next day's heat. One visitor criticized Real Goods for setting the air conditioning too low, and was astonished to learn that the building cooled itself naturally.

potential harmfulness of EMFs, a few studies have demonstrated links to cancer, particularly leukemia in children, and some research has shown that even low levels of electromagnetic radiation may trigger allergies in sensitive individuals, and may affect the metabolism, immune system, and ability to cope with stress. Measurements taken in the Solar Living Center register insignificant readings, except in very close proximity to the computers.

The biggest factor of the building's energy consumption is implicit in its design. We chose a straw bale building because its high insulating value eliminates much of the need for mechanical heating or cooling systems. Most heating and cooling needs can be met passively with solar energy (see "Designing the Climate Response Systems" later in this chapter). Our building does not have a centralized HVAC system!

To meet our cooling needs, we installed five small, solar-powered evaporative coolers (units typically used in recreational vehicles or small cabins). Even though midday temperatures can reach well over 110 degrees in Hopland, we have not yet turned on the water to these coolers. At the end of our first year of operation, we began to remove the evaporative coolers to be used elsewhere, and replaced them with fans only. The fan loads are minimal, using under 200 watts when all five fans are running. On the most still of evenings during the very hottest days in the summer, we turn on the fans to force air evacuation of the building overnight. This nighttime flushing cools the mass of the building itself, so that the mass can absorb the next day's heat.

The hardware

Our selection of hardware components for the power system was based on performance criteria exclusively, not on preference for certain Real Goods vendors, many of whom were anxious for their products to be displayed in this setting. We designed a power system that demonstrated principles of wise design consistent with the project mission. As a result, the Solar Living Center showcases the best technologies available.

We resisted installing hardware just for technological dazzle. At one point, we toyed with installing a solar parabolic dish Stirling generator made by Cummings. Even though we were tempted by the sexiness of such a unit, we concluded that it was overkill for our needs. It would have added interest for the hardware junkie, but it was simply not the best technology for the intended use. (A good decision, it turned out, as Cummings has since abandoned this product.)

Siemens Solar generously donated 10 kilowatts (10,000 watts) of photovoltaics (mostly PC-4 solar modules). One tracker was mounted exclusively with M-55 (55 watt) modules with a new anti-reflective coating system that has since become a standard feature on all their modules. These comprise the entire photovoltaic system.

Although we are energy independent at the Solar Living Center, we are by design not literally off-the-grid. We decided to establish an intertie with our local utility, Pacific Gas & Electric, for several reasons. This intertie allows us to route excess power into the utility, and to withdraw power if there is a shortfall.We think this is the future for solar energy. If solar is ever to expand beyond the remote homesite into the mainstream, it will have to be in cooperation, not competition, with the established power-generating companies.

The Sponsor Story

Stephen Morris

The Solar Living Center made the transition from concept to reality when the memory of the 1992 Olympics was still fresh in everyone's minds. When the idea first surfaced to have participating sponsors for the project, the initial reaction was "Who would want to help Real Goods build a solar living center?" But the answer came very quickly, "Anyone wanting high visibility exposure to an audience interested in cutting edge, environmental products," that is, the Real Goods customer.

The initial expectations were quite grand, but the program gained momentum only when a tight ethical boundary was drawn. Sponsorships would be solicited for materials only, not money, and no compromises to the design or building process would be made to accommodate the needs of a sponsor.

The renewable energy companies were the first to recognize a win-win situation. Siemens Solar contributed the solar panels, and without too many calls, sponsors were lined up for the inverters (Trace), power center and controllers (Ananda Power Technologies), and trackers (Small Power Systems).

At the Eco-Expo in Los Angeles, many manufacturers of building products donated items to be used in a dream environmental house, and they were approached about having their products featured in something with a lifespan to be measured in centuries (we hope), not hours. Some companies understood what we were trying to accomplish and agreed quite readily to donate materials (James Hardie Building Products, Waterless Company, Pittsburgh Corning, Leviton Manufacturing, and Insteel Construction Systems). Others declined to participate, never quite understanding the concept of "solar living" or who might be interested in it.

Contributors were sought for the landscape component, too. New World Manufacturing gave us a tank liner; Skylark Inc. donated graceful flow forms; AGWA contributed the graywater system; and the recycled benches for the courtyard came from Northward Industries.

We knew that our sponsorship program had fully bloomed, however, when the California Rice Industry Association agreed to provide the straw bales for the main showroom. To our knowledge, this is the largest straw bale retail store in the world, and more than one rice farmer has stopped by to express pride in participating.

The legacy of the sponsorship program is that it allowed other companies to participate in one small company's dream. Their contributions enable the dream to grow larger. The dividends will be paid for many years.

Real Goods sized its solar and wind energy systems to match power production and consumption as closely as possible. Conservation steps included the use of energy-efficient computers in the store, compact fluorescent bulbs in all indoor and outdoor fixtures, and of course, design of the building for daylighting and passive heating and cooling. The photovoltaics can more than keep up with daytime power demands; at night the wind can usually generate enough energy for the security lighting. In the event of a power outage, the store could operate normally for six to eight hours from electricity stored in its battery bank, and even longer by implementing additional conservation strategies.

PG&E does not yet have many grid-photovoltaic intertie systems. The Solar Living Center, the first known commercial installation, provides a good case study (or as we sometimes call it, a "place" study) that demonstrates how an intertie can be a winning proposition for both utility and small business. Energy storage in batteries is not as economical as storage in the grid, even at the commercial buyback rates that we get from PG&E. Typically, we receive 2¢ per kilowatt-hour for what we produce; the amount fluctuates from month to month depending on PG&E's "avoided costs," meaning the amount they save by not producing power to meet our needs in that month. We purchase power at 12 to 14¢ per kilowatt-hour. Obviously, PG&E understands the theory of "buy low, sell high." Yet, even at this exorbitant exchange rate, it is still cheaper for Real Goods to "store" excess power with PG&E than with conventional lead-acid batteries. Lead-acid battery storage systems cost between 15 and 25¢ per kilowatt-hour, for a differential of 5 to 15¢ per kilowatt-hour. Also, the utility is a long-lasting "battery" and is infinite in its storage capacity. We can literally pack watts away in either the summer or winter to be used at another time of year.

JEFF OLDHAM

All of the wind and solar inputs are routed into the electrical room, a straw bale building that maintains temperatures appropriate for the equipment. The generating capacity is about 72 kilowatt-hours per day from the photovoltaics and 3 kilowatt-hours from the wind generator. Here, staff member Gary Quast explains the system to visitors. All of this equipment is displayed as part of the Solar Living Center education experience.

Coordinating with PG&E was painless; they were cooperative and friendly. Gary Quast from their Santa Rosa office was quite amenable to our project and did not make us jump over unnecessary bureaucratic hurdles. On the fateful day of going "live," I checked and double-checked every connection. Then I programmed the inverters to "sell."

Every electrician knows the feeling: You are about to throw "the switch." You turn your head away, close the only two eyes you own, grit your teeth, and commit the circuit! More often than we like to admit, all hell breaks loose. I initiated this tie-in with the push of a button. There was a deafening silence, beautiful and wonderful in a way that only an electrician could understand. Nothing blew up or even groaned or sparked. The utility meter just began to slow and then to spin backwards. Solar poetry in motion.

JEFF OLDHAM

We sized our system to provide the precise amount of energy we wanted to sell. Did we want to buy a little, or did we want to get a check back from PG&E each month? Our first reaction was that we wanted money back. John Schaeffer thought it would be great to post the checks received from the utility on a bulletin board. But while this would have been gratifying from a consumer's perspective, the economics of utility buyback rates did not encourage surplus generation. Over the life of the PV system, it costs us about 8¢ per kilowatt-hour for photovoltaic power; while this is cheaper than the utility price of 12¢ per kilowatt-hour, it is four times the 2¢-per-kilowatt-hour buyback rate. It would have been bad economics, therefore, to have oversized the system to routinely generate electricity we did not need on-site.

Final design criteria called for the generation of slightly less power than we would need in a day. Since we are paid only 2¢ per kilowatt-hour, it makes economic sense to use, not sell, every watt we produce. The ideal is to match production and consumption as closely as possible. (Don't forget, there is a capital cost to creating a power system that is directly related to capacity.) My original expectation was that we would make surplus electricity in the summer and purchase power in the winter, but I had not anticipated that we would eliminate the big seasonal load of the irrigation pump in winter. Ironically, this means that we are even closer to the ideal than we anticipated.

For the solar gearheads, here are the system specs. For a full translation, consult the Real Goods *Solar Living Sourcebook,* call a Real Goods technician, or come to one of the classes we conduct at the Solar Living Institute. Normal folk can just skip to the next page!

- The main energy components are 10,000 watts (more or less) of photovoltaic cells, on seven active azimuth trackers. Five trackers made by Wattsun, each with an array of sixteen PC-4 modules, generate 1,200 watts of power. One Small Power Systems tracker with eighteen PC-4s generates 1,350 watts, and another Small Power Systems tracker with twenty M-55 modules yields 1,100 watts. On the south face of the storage building, we have integrated a seasonally adjustable array of twenty-four PC-4s for 1,800 watts of power, which also provides southern shading for that building.
    - A 3,000-watt Whisper wind generator complements the solar-electric components. The Whisper is a very simple wind machine made in the U.S. Its two-blade design starts up in a 7-mile-per-hour wind, but it is built to withstand 120-mile-per-hour hurricane-force winds. The tilt-up tower makes infrequent servicing safe and easy. The Whisper represents one of the best values on the renewable-energy market today.
        - All of the inputs, wind and solar, are routed back to the electrical room. This is also a straw bale building that maintains appropriate temperatures for the equipment and battery bank. The wind genera-

tor and photovoltaics are regulated and protected by an Ananda Power Center that contains three 60-amp photovoltaic charge controllers, with three 1,500-watt TDR load diverters for the wind generator. Four Trace Engineering SW5548 sine wave inverters provide the line-tying back to the grid through a 400-amp, two-pole disconnect ahead of the main service, which is a 400-amp, 220/120-volt single-phase service.

- The four Trace inverters are split into two pairs of two. Each pair is tied together for an output of 220/120 volts, and each pair is then dedicated to a panel in the store: the lighting panel and the plugload panel. We also have a modest battery bank of 440 amp-hours at 54 volts nominal. All of the equipment is 48 volts, but in order to sell power at closer to the peak power point of the photovoltaics, I threw in another 6-volt battery. The batteries are typical golf cart batteries, the 220-amp-hour 6-volt Interstate 2200. The nominal 54-volt system is floated at 60 volts (our sell point), which puts it within just a volt or so of the peak power point of the modules when four are wired in series. It also gives a little bit of headroom, so we can perform an equalization with the photovoltaics as well. This avoided the expense of a peak power point tracker and was well within the operating limits of the Trace inverters.
    - The particular Trace inverters that we chose require a minimum of 220 amp-hours of battery storage to operate properly. The Traces also provide the function of a standby system. In the event of a power failure, the inverters automatically transfer to start drawing the power from the battery bank, without disruption to the store power or our main server in the storage building, where a dedicated circuit was pulled over from the power panel in the store.

Under normal conditions, without implementing any conservation, the store can operate for six to eight hours from the battery bank. If we implement conservation practices, we can stretch it to a good ten to twelve hours, the equivalent of a full day of operation. This assumes that there is no sunshine or wind. If the sun is out during a power failure, the photovoltaics can more than keep up with the demands of the store. If the wind blows during the night, it is likely that we can keep up with the demands of the security lighting. Thus, the battery bank is only tapped in the event that there is no utility, sunshine, or wind. If all those things happen, then we are on battery power and will have to live within the limits of that finite amount of storage. It should be noted that there has never been a PG&E power outage in Hopland longer than six hours.

We need the Ananda TDR load diverters for the wind generator in the event that we lose the utility tie to the building during high winds in the middle of the night. I imagined a

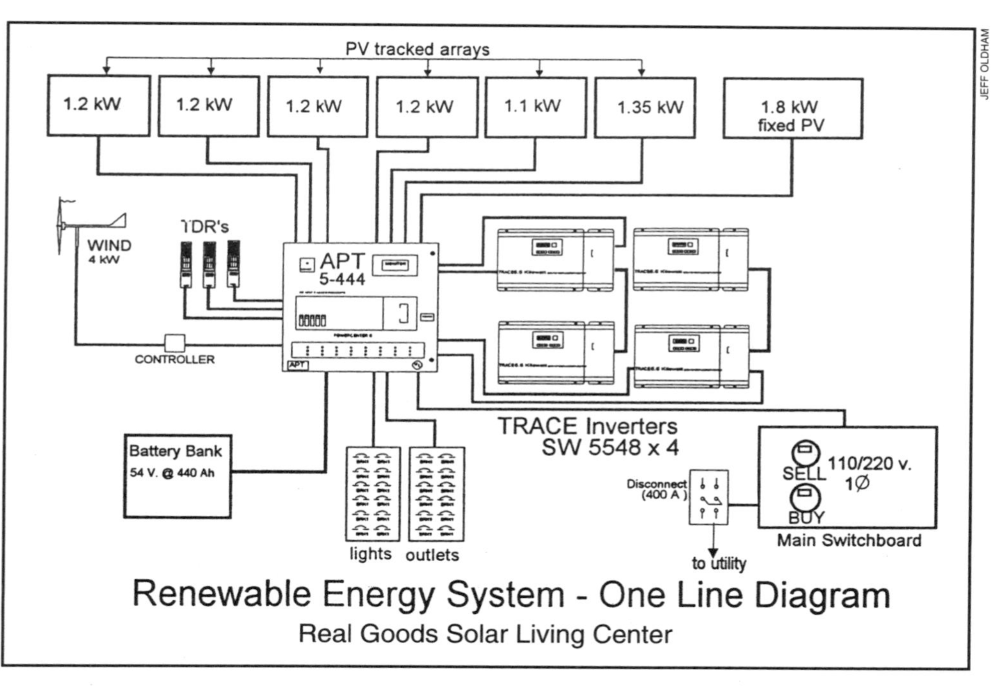

JEFF OLDHAM

Real Goods established the first intertie between a public utility and a commercial enterprise producing its own renewable energy. The intertie with Pacific Gas & Electric allows the sale of excess power to the utility and the withdrawal of power in case of a shortfall. The Solar Living Center demonstrates that such cooperation can benefit both the utility and the business.

scenario in which the wind generator produced too much energy for the battery bank, becoming elevated in voltage to a point of overcharging the batteries and perhaps boiling them off, or swelling the plates and shorting them internally. Under that rare circumstance, the TDRs will kick in and waste the energy as surplus heat into the room itself.

We have been quite pleased with the performance of the system. I would like to make about 10 percent more power, and I certainly wish the buy/sell exchange ratio between us and the utility were more favorable, but these are minor complaints.

As we grow, we will consume more power and will add more photovoltaics or perhaps more wind generators, dedicating them to their own inverters and line-tying back into the main switchboard. The generation capacity of the system is about 72 kilowatt-hours per day from the photovoltaics and 3 kilowatt-hours per day from the wind generator. There are many times during the day when we are producing surplus power beyond our consumption for the entire site, and other times when we fall short. On average, we buy 20 kilowatt-hours per day from PG&E and sell back 6 kilowatt-hours per day. The surplus is fed back into the grid.

Subsystems

At the front entrance, we wanted to feature a beautiful waterfall. To operate this, we have eight PC-4 75-watt modules wired into a 24-volt system, a 24-volt Air 303 marine generator, and four 6-volt, 350-amp-hour, L-16 batteries wired at 24-volts, for a total capacity of 350 amp-hours. A centrifugal circulation pump supplies the waterfall; it runs at about 8 amps at 24 volts. The waterfall feature runs during the daylight hours, operated by a photo cell and a low-voltage disconnect system that turns it on at dawn and off at dusk. At dusk, a lighting controller turns on the two 24-volt, 13-watt compact fluorescent floodlights that illuminate the Real Goods logo sign at the front entry gate, runs on a timer for about three hours, the exact duration depending on the time of year, and then shuts down. The panels are fixed-mounted for a winter sun angle at the top of the gate structure itself.

JEFF OLDHAM

One of the more visible, and delightful, parts of the energy design is how solar energy enables us to enliven the Solar Living Center with water. There is hardly a place on the site where the gurgle and babble of water does not bring life to what was formerly a sun-baked, arid plain. It has been proven that the sound of running water is the most soothing sound to human beings, and we wanted to maximize those effects.

A photovoltaic-direct water-pumping system operates both our irrigation water and other water features. This is an elegant use of water. We have another PV-direct system for demonstration on the site, a 1½ horsepower, 120-volt direct-current submersible pump, manufactured by Solarjack and powered by one of the Wattsun trackers. This array is a sixteen-panel 1,200-watt system wired for 120 volts DC nominal. We have been impressed with the performance of this pump. The well is 80 feet deep, and the pump sits at about 60 feet. The water level fluctuates from 2 feet below the surface in the winter to about 20 feet in the summer, when

The Solar Living Center is sited over a copious gravel-based aquifer. Water is pumped from a well by a PV-direct system into a 3,000-gallon, reused redwood tank, then overflows into a series of flowforms, channels, fountains, and pools. It is drawn out of the bottom pool by another solar pump to recirculate through the system. Along the way, the water provides irrigation for the gardens and trees, evaporative cooling in the Courtyard, educational and fun features for children and adults, and a symbolic message in the Solar Calendar. Because the pumping system is powered by the Sun, more water flows during the longer, hotter days of mid-summer, when the demand for irrigation and cooling is greatest.

we do most of our watering. The pump delivers about 45 to 47 gallons per minute. It pumps whenever the sun is out, with an output linear to the amount of sunshine. On cloudier days it pumps less, on sunnier days more.

Solar-direct is an appropriate way to irrigate, because the longer and hotter the days, the greater the demand for water and the more that is pumped. At the height of the summer, around the Summer Solstice, the yield is at peak. Conversely, the yield is lowest in the dead of winter, when we are in the midst of our rainy season anyway. Nature has a way of balancing resource and demand that you fully appreciate when you are creating your energy by harvesting the resource.

The water is pumped out of the well into a 3,000-gallon, reused redwood water tank (see chapter 3). At the opposite end of the series of flowforms and ponds, we draw the water out with a 1½ horsepower, 220-volt irrigation pump. This way, we get full water circulation through both ponds. The water that is not transpired by the trees goes back into the ground, ready for our next pumping. We get a multitude of uses out of this water. We get evaporative cooling in the Courtyard area, our first solace from the triple-digit temperatures in the summertime. We can divert some into the children's area, where it is used for education, cooling, and fun. A little more is diverted into the fountain, where it circulates and overflows back into the main rill and accentuates the message of the solar calendar. This constant flow through the fountain maintains water clarity without any chemicals. We move about 24,000 to 25,000 gallons per day through the system. The ponds hold about a million gallons of water, which is exchanged approximately once a month. This keeps the ponds very clear, our water fresh, and our aquatic plants and fish very happy.

In the children's area, children can play with a conventional, marine-style hand bilge pump, which can produce about 10 gallons per minute if they are vigorous. We saved our scrap PVC conduit, ripped it down the centers, cut it in 1- to 3-foot lengths, and rounded off the corners. Children can place these on the sand, overlapping one end on another, to create an aqueduct to divert water through the sand pit. It is hard to have a better frolicking combination for kids than sand and water! Another submersible pump sits down in a shallow well that is supplied by the main rill. This is also a solar-direct pumping application. The solar module is a 22-watt, unbreakable panel from United Solar (model UPM 880). It is certainly the best choice in the children's area, able to withstand any abuse. It is mounted on a manual tracker, down at kid level, so that they can spin the module around to learn the impact of tracking on the production of the submersible pump. The pump discharges into a small showerhead fountain in the rill of the children's play area. The young explorers quickly

BAILE OAKES

The delight of creative play with water, sun, and sand engages children in understanding the dynamics of renewable energy. A submersible pump connected to an unbreakable solar module discharges water from the main rill into a fountain in the play area. Children learn that manipulating the module to face toward or away from the Sun changes the flow of water through the channels they can construct of sand and scrap PVC. A hand pump allows them to add more water to the system. The excess runs through an aqueduct back to the main rill or through the sand into a drain that directs it to irrigation needs lower on the site.

discover that rotating the module to directly face the Sun maximizes the height of the fountain. If they block it from the Sun, the level of the water drops or the fountain stops altogether. Cover half the module, get half the water. It is exciting to watch the process of discovery. Some clever kids have even contrived to use a short piece of scrap PVC to prop the panel up to face the Sun, freeing one of their buddies to join in the sand and water mayhem.

For the edification of adults, Baile Oakes designed a global warming display. Baile explains, "my goal with the global warming display was to physically involve visitors in the process of understanding the impact of carbon dioxide on the atmosphere, and to emphasize Real Goods' goal of preventing the production of one billion pounds of carbon dioxide in 1990s." A three-dimensional map of the San Francisco Bay and the Sacramento and San Joaquin deltas enclosed in a tank of water shows two distinct tide lines: current levels and with the 3-foot rise in sea level that global warming is predicted to cause during the next fifty years.We rigged up a photovoltaic panel and a Sears recumbent exercise bicycle converted into an electric generator. Underneath the front flywheel, a pulley belt spins a DC electric generator as the visitor peddles the bike. The visitor may produce renewable energy by riding the bike or choose the renewable energy from the photovoltaic panel to run the pump and drain the Bay. It takes a lot of pedaling to produce the same amount of energy as the Sun! It is sobering for Bay Area dwellers to realize that global warming could put their homes underwater within their childrens' lifetimes!

While sitting at the bike controls, the visitor views displays created by artist M. Wuerker to explain the effects of fossil fuels. For example, he or she would need to pedal the bike fast enough to produce 240 watts 24 hours per day, 365 days per year to offset the average amount of carbon dioxide that each of us adds to the atmosphere from our usual residential use of energy. This does not take into account the per capita carbon dioxide produced by transportation, industrial, or commercial use of fossil fuels, nor the 55 percent of this carbon dioxide that is absorbed by the ocean each year. With those considerations, one would need to pedal ten times as much to offset the per capita carbon dioxide emissions.

To illustrate the point that we can all help to offset this buildup of global warming gases, the visitor is also given the choice to use pedal energy or the Sun's energy to drain the sea level in the tank and prevent flooding, or to operate two electric fans that cool the pedaller. We all have choices to make, and comfort seems to be winning in most arenas.

Throughout the project, we have made every effort to make technologies accessible, simple to understand, educational, and fun. When people can experience a phenomenon by touching, operating, and witnessing, they become believers. Solar and other forms of renewable energy are the answer. The question is, when will the federal government figure

JEFF OLDHAM

Predictions suggest that global climate change caused by fossil fuel consumption could raise sea level up to three feet during our children's lifetimes. One of the most severely impacted areas would be the San Francisco Bay, an hour and a half south of the Solar Living Center. With the global warming display, visitors can pedal a recumbent bicycle that generates electricity to pump water from a tank enclosing a three-dimensional map of the Bay area, preventing flooding. Or they may choose to use their pedal energy to operate fans to keep them cool as they ride. A photovoltaic alternative illustrates how much pedalling is needed to equal the power of the Sun.

this out? The Solar Living Center has confirmed what all of the surveys have been telling us: Americans love and want renewable energy! These are technologies that are available and cost-effective now.

Designing the Climate Response Systems

We wanted the Solar Living Center's power supply systems to provide thermal and visual comfort to the building's occupants while using a minimum of fossil fuels. Our objective was definitely not to freeze in the dark. Rather, we chose to work with the local climate and harness the naturally available forces to create a comfortable, enriching, and environmentally connected interior environment. We employed a number of passive "macro" strategies:

- maximize solar gain for heating during the cool season;
- minimize solar gain for cooling during the hot season;
- maximize daylighting for visual comfort and occupant well-being;
- utilize winds for ventilation when desirable;
- protect the building from winds when undesirable;
- establish a competent thermal envelope to protect the building interior from undesired thermal transfer in both summer and winter.

Climate and site analysis

To understand the climatic context for the Solar Living Center, we examined the site carefully and analyzed local and regional weather data. The 12-acre project site lies in a wide valley just south of the Hopland town center. The surrounding area is flat and open, and devoid of prominent topographic features in the near vicinity, with the exception of Duncan Peak to the southwest. To the north and west, a relatively small ridge of hills parallels the site southward at a distance of roughly one and one-half miles. The valley is surrounded by rolling hills typical of this part of Northern California, with elevation changes not exceeding 1,500 feet. The site sits at an elevation of 490 feet above sea level, a latitude of 38.58 degrees north, and a longitude of 123.70 degrees west. There are no significant solar obstructions anywhere near the site. The amount of solar energy that falls upon a particular spot is called "insolation," and is usually expressed in terms of kilowatt-hours per square meter per day. The annual average insolation in Hopland is 5.5 kilowatt-hours per square meter per day.

The most suitable source for data about the local climate seemed to be the Ukiah airport, located roughly 15 miles north in a geographically similar valley. Weather data

Climate analyses of the site provided the information needed to maximize thermal and visual comfort in the building while minimizing energy use. Passive strategies, such as shading, daylighting, insulation, night-flushing, thermal mass cooling, and natural ventilation, were coordinated in the building's design so that the active power systems could be efficient and appropriate. This rooftop heliodon aids in the study of daylighting.

ADAM JACKAWAY

recorded there is relatively extensive and, most importantly, has been collected continuously for over fifty years (however, as noted earlier in this chapter, we discovered that this data had limitations in relation to our particular wind-power prospects). Upon completion of the data collection, the information was entered into a spreadsheet, from which charts and graphs were produced for easy visualization and summation of the local climatic forces.

Overall, the climate can be classified as relatively mild in every season except summer. Spring and fall are characterized by warm days and cool nights and are surely the premier seasons. Winter temperatures rarely dip below freezing, and daytime highs are often pleasant. Fog and precipitation are most prevalent during the winter, but afternoon clearing is common. Winds are also most common in winter, generally blowing from the north-northwest, while storm systems can arrive from either the northwest or the south. Summer temperatures swing significantly over the course of the day, with uncomfortable daytime highs typically associated with oppressive and unobstructed sunshine. Clear skies and low humidities predominate for much of the year.

To establish a design framework combining climate data with our design goals, we designated three basic categories: heating, cooling, and lighting. For each category, we prepared a brief climatic summary, along with initial design implications.

Responding to the Sun: Heat and light

The climate analysis indicated that our main challenge was to deal with the summer sun. This suggested a carefully considered shading strategy. Literally from the first week of design, we began making models to investigate the performance of our design ideas. We used these models simultaneously to examine shading competency, daylighting potential, and glare mitigation. Investigations varied in complexity, sometimes consisting of a quick hold-the-model-up-to-the-Sun test, and at other times of more lengthy and systematic sessions with the Heliodon at the Pacific Energy Center in San Francisco.

Not surprisingly, the final building form opens toward the south in both plan and section. Summer shading is enhanced by the effectiveness of south-facing overhangs, supplemented by the limited use of eastern and western glazing where shading proved difficult due to low angles of incidence. Conversely, winter solar gains are most easily admitted from this orientation, while limited northern glazing reduces heat losses.

Daylighting from a southern glazing wall can be tricky, but if proper shading is maintained, this orientation offers the potential for direct beam accents. Diffuse daylighting is encouraged through the use of floor-to-ceiling glazing and through the long, curving, east-facing clerestory windows.

Strategies for solar shading and solar gain. To understand the solar shading and collection strategies, it helps to conceptualize the southern facade as three horizontal bands. The bottom third of the glazing is shaded year-round with vines growing on a trellis that runs the length of the facade. This prevents overheating in the summer and minimizes direct beam glare and photodegradation at the front of the showroom—problems that can exist year-round. In addition, the elimination of direct sun upon surfaces directly outside of the building reduces visual contrast between inside and out, easing transition glare as you enter and depart. The upper third of the glazing, situated above the roll-down canopies, is shaded from February through October by the fixed roof overhangs, eliminating solar gain through this portion of the windows for all but the coldest period of the year. The

The southern facade of the building accomplishes more than one function simultaneously: daylighting, shading, and solar gain. The bottom third of the floor-to-ceiling glazing is shaded by a grape trellis, preventing overheating and reducing glare. The upper third is shaded by fixed roof overhangs during all but the coldest period of the year. The middle third of the glazing is fitted with shading devices that are operated manually from within the showroom, allowing store staff to admit or shield solar gain to the interior.

middle third of the glazing plays the most dynamic role. Fitted with operable shading devices, this band of glazing admits or shields the space from solar gain, as conditions in the internal environment dictate.

ADAM JACKAWAY

Shading devices. Although we explored many shading devices for the middle third of the main facade, we eventually settled on roll-out hemp awnings. These simple yet effective devices have many benefits Inexpensive and relatively low maintenance, awnings have been used for centuries on storefronts throughout the world. We selected hemp for its durability, beauty, and reputation as a link to sustainable agriculture. From a lighting standpoint, the translucent quality of the awnings promotes daylight penetration. Architecturally, we felt the canopy shape echoed the forms of the roof and was consistent with the overall aesthetics. For the two most easterly bays, a rotatable vertical-fin shading system is proposed (yet to be installed), which should respond more appropriately to the southwesterly orientation.

The most difficult shading conditions occurred, not surprisingly, along the southwest facade. This orientation is problematic because it lies in direct view of the Sun exactly when gains are least desirable: in the mid to late afternoon. By this time of day, the air has reached its hottest temperature and the building has had most of the day to absorb energy from both the air and the Sun (radiantly). Initial investigations for this facade determined that openings would have to be very small, or else heavily shaded, even in winter, when solar thermal gains are desirable. Windows at eye level would pose significant glare problems for building occupants.To solve these problems, we employed a sawtooth plan for this wall, resulting in a series of glazing facets reoriented toward the south. These windows are now easily shaded by a simple series of horizontal overhangs that provide shade when needed.

A rooftop heliodon table was used to study the daylighting in the showroom. The model is placed at the proper altitude and azimuth for different times of day and year; the sky itself accurately models the daylight conditions.

Daylighting: Overall strategies

Daylighting was of paramount importance in the design of this building, in order to foster occupant well-being, reduce energy consumption, and save money. Accordingly, the structure's sweeping curves are intended to capture natural light. The benefits of this shape are twofold: First, the curve establishes an expanded floor-to-ceiling height at the glazing wall, enabling light to enter the building partially from above and reducing sidelighting glare. This allows the lower third of the glazing to be fully shaded (as described above) without incurring a significant daylighting penalty. Second, the ceiling's curve enables its rear portion to have an increasingly perpendicular view to the light source (the Sun). Accordingly, the roof is finished in white to reflect this light downward to the showroom floor, helping to illuminate the northernmost areas. The building is shallow, providing a good sectional ratio of window height to room depth. Interior surfaces are light colored to promote further light distribution through enhanced reflectance.

Clerestories. In order to provide greater visual interest and add some drama to the daylit environment, we broke the roof into facets at the division of each bay to form the overlapping leaves or "seashells" (as Bruce King describes them). By stepping the roof facets up toward the west, we opened a series of curved, east-facing clerestories that let in additional light and sparkle. Due to their orientation and the overlapping of the roofs, they do not carry

6:00 AM, Sept. 21

7:30 AM, Sept. 21

9:00 AM, Sept. 21

DAVID ARKIN

10:30 AM, Sept. 21

12:00 PM, Sept. 21

1:30 PM, Sept. 21

3:00 PM, Sept. 21

4:30 PM, Sept. 21

6:00 PM, Sept. 21

This sequence of stills from a videotape of solar gain analysis on PG&E's heliodon reveals the impact of direct sunlight at one and one-half hour intervals on the Equinox. Note that no direct sun enters the building after 10:00 a.m. A tiny fiber optic lens—the same used by David Letterman's "Monkey Cam"—gives the model a life-like, time-lapse quality. The heliodon and other tools (including energy strategy advice) at PG&E's Energy Center are free to the public; several visits were made while tuning the showroom design.

a significant summer thermal penalty. Additionally, due to their height above the occupants, their contribution of glare is minimized.

We subsequently extended the clerestories into vertical glazing at the rear, affording further daylighting and providing view windows to the north. In the early morning on a clear day, the direct sun through these apertures is marvelous (although most of us have only seen this effect in the model and photographs! Someday we will convene a sleep-over for the full effect.)

Light shelves. To further redistribute light, we installed light shelves along the interior perimeter of the southern facade. The shelves are diffusely reflective and bounce both direct sun and diffuse skylight back toward the rear ceiling. This evens out daylight. To avoid dark areas below the shelves, we constructed them with a translucent plastic. Direct solar gain, desirable for wintertime heating but a potential cause of glare and photodegradation, is intercepted by the shelves and absorbed and/or redirected toward the rear.

As we considered the depth for this light shelf, we stumbled across a serendipitous secondary use. Reasoning that the light shelves should grow deeper as each window bay grew taller, it became apparent that this geometrical match provided an opportunity for the shelves to become operable and to rotate upward at night to provide added thermal insulation along the southern facade when daylight is no longer available and thermal transfer is undesirable.

Responding to the winds: Protection and ventilation

The building's curved geometry provides protection from winter winds, which typically blow from the north-northwest. The low profile of the northern facade, largely devoid of windows, serves as a buffer to winds, and the curve smoothly redirects air flow over the building.

Additionally, the R-65 staw bale and PISE™ (pneumatically impacted stabilized earth) construction along the northern perimeter minimizes thermal transfer losses.

During the cooling season, winds aid in natural ventilation. As winds blow across the roof, the steps create negative pressure zones on the outside of the operable clerestories, drawing air out of the building at the ceiling level where hot air collects. (Wind tunnel analysis of this concept during schematic design indicated a high likelihood of success, which has now been validated by the building's performance.) The clerestories also promote stack ventilation by providing an effective vertical height between inlets and outlets.

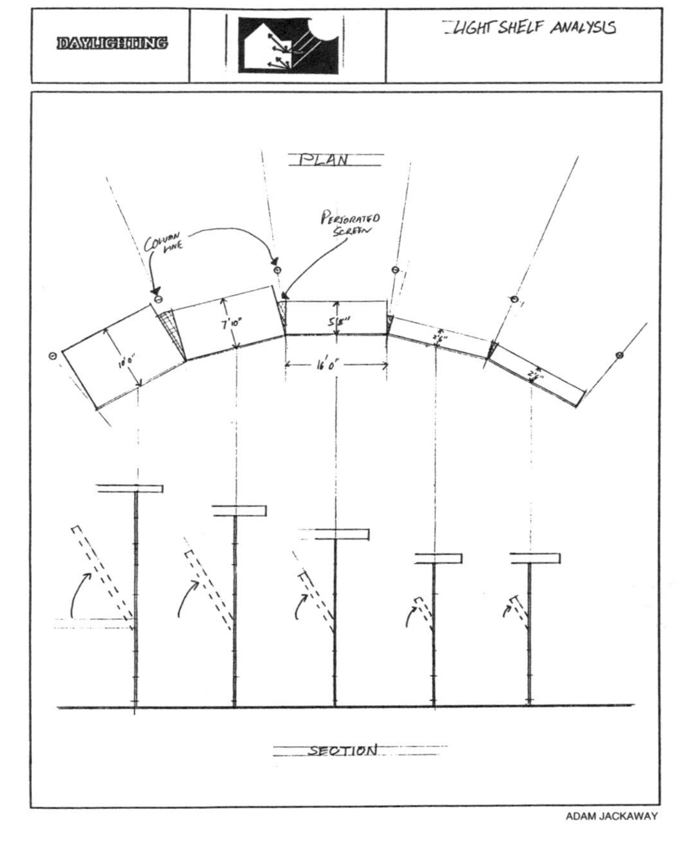

ADAM JACKAWAY

DAVID ARKIN

Light shelves constructed from translucent plastic installed along the interior of the southern facade reflect direct sunlight and diffuse skylight toward the rear ceiling to even out the lighting, reduce glare and photodegradation, and daylight the rear of the store. These shelves are manually rotated upward at night to provide thermal insulation during winter months.

From the outset, we felt the most promising ventilation strategy would be night-flushing. Due to the dryness of the climate, diurnal temperature swings are significant, and the cool nights provide an opportunity for free cooling of the building's thermal mass. With this principle in mind, the clerestories are opened overnight to allow heat built up through the day to escape. The slab floor is recharged with "coolth," enabling the building to coast through the following day without need for additional cooling. The beauty is in the simplicity.

The thermal envelope. Thermal transfer through the building envelope is kept to a minimum through the use of thermally resistant building materials. The roof is insulated to R-58 with 12 inches of loose cellulose fill (100 percent recycled newspaper), a radiant

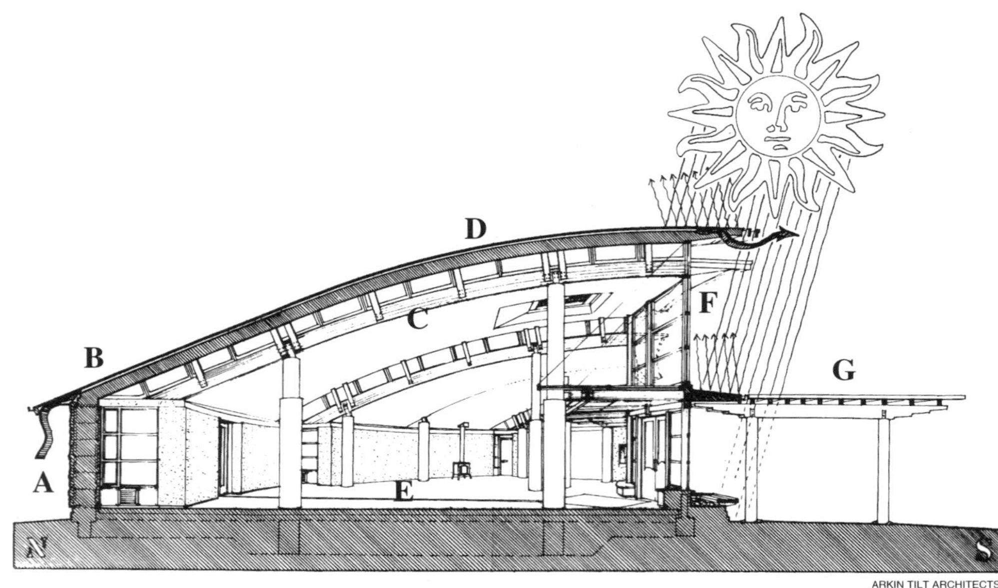

ARKIN TILT ARCHITECTS

Hot Day Cooling Mode

A The thermal mass and high insulation value of the straw-bale and PISE™ (sprayed soil-cement) wall protects against the thermal transfer of 100°F+ outdoor summer temperatures.

B Air space in roof ventilates heat from radiant barrier over 12" of cellulose insulation (R-60).

C Clerestory windows are closed when outside temperature exceeds interior temperature.

D White Hypalon™ (synthetic rubber) roof membrane reflects gain from solar radiation.

E Thermal mass of concrete floor and columns absorbs heat from people and equipment; stores "coolth" from previous night flush.

F Overhang and awnings shade windows, controlling solar gain. Light shelves and curved white ceiling distribute daylight evenly, reducing need for heat-producing lighting fixtures.

G Trellis shades walls, windows, and walkway in summer; allows gain in winter; and controls glare.

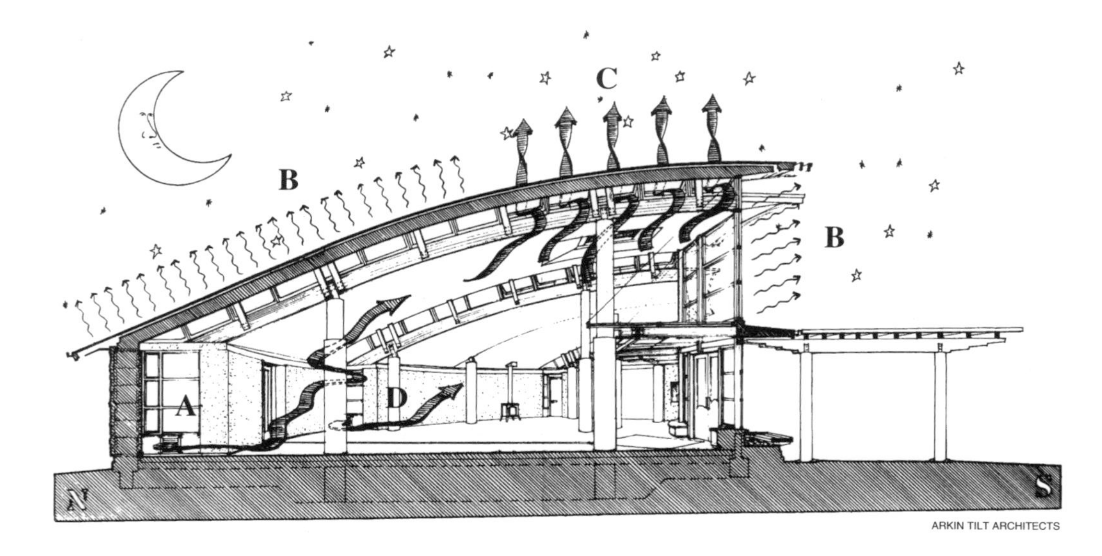

Night Cooling Mode

A Fans in the evaporative coolers run after hot (100° F+) days for additional air changes.

B Roof and high windows radiate heat to the night sky.

C A "stack effect" draws out warm air through clerestory windows and draws in cooler air through openings near the floor.

D Night sky radiation and cool night temperatures are used to "charge" the thermal mass of the building with "coolth" for the next day.

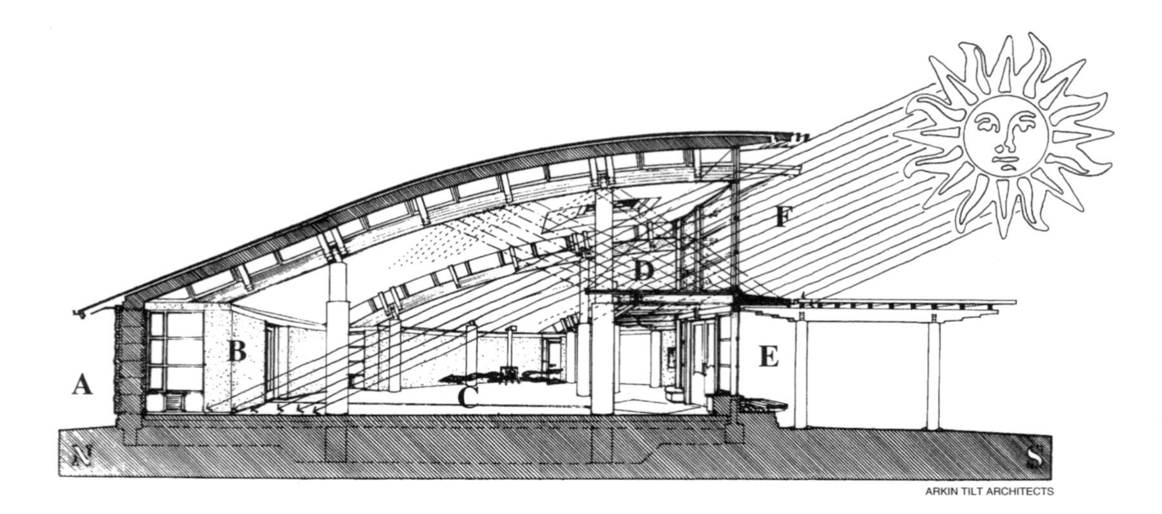

Cold Day Heating Mode

A The mass of the highly insulated straw-bale and PISE™ walls produce a thermal "flywheel" effect, storing and releasing heat.

B Stored heat in the thermal mass in the concrete floor and columns is also released to maintain comfort.

C Efficient wood-burning stoves (working display models) are the only source of supplemental heat.

D Lightshelves control glare and direct gain, reflecting light onto the curved ceiling.

E Doors and windows can be opened to provide immediate cooling if the temperature indoors is too warm.

F The low winter sun penetrates the building through substantial south-facing glazing.

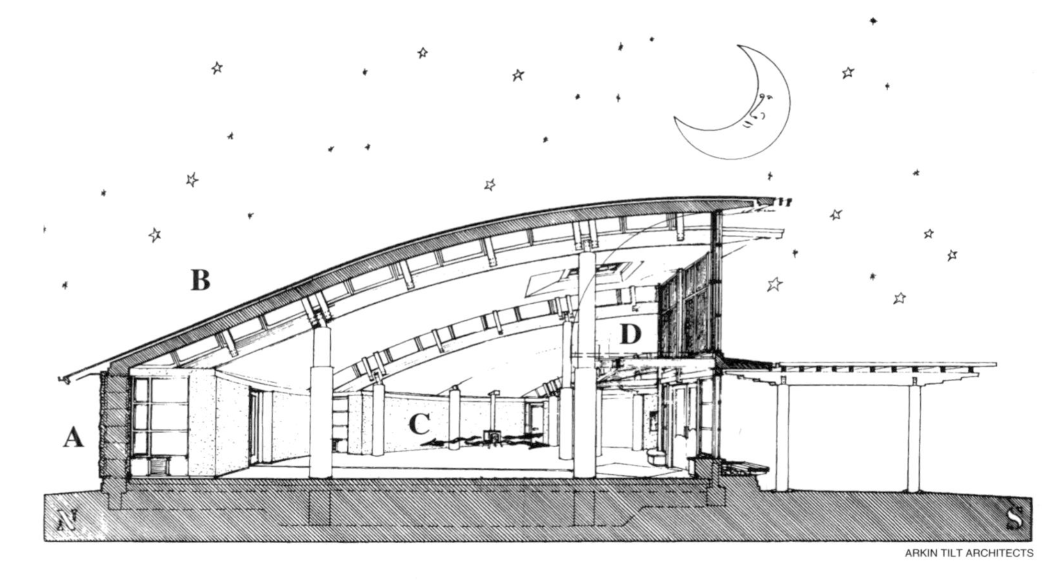

ARKIN TILT ARCHITECTS

Night Heating Mode

A The insulation in the straw-bale and roof helps to retain the day's heat inside the building mass.

B The 12" cellulose (recycled newspaper) insulation in the roof provides an R-value greater than 60.

C The wood-burning stoves can be left on a slow burn on the coldest nights, balancing heat loss.

D Lightshelves are hinged and can be folded against the high glazing to reduce heat loss to the night sky.

barrier, and a 1½-inch air space. The white Hypalon™ roofing is also a radiant barrier that reflects 85 percent of the light (not included in the calculation for the R-58 rating, but something that improves upon it). The aluminum radiant barrier is R-14.

The opaque side walls are comprised of straw bales with an R-value approaching 65 (on their sides, the 21-inch bales are about R-57, with an additional "guesstimate" of R-8 for the PISE™ finish). Finally, the glazed southern facade is all double-paned, low-emissivity (low-E) glass, coated to allow light to enter, but regulating heat flow and ultraviolet penetration, for an R-value of about 2.8 compared to about R-2 or less for conventional double glass.

A low-consumption conditioning system. Throughout the schematic design phase, we debated ideas for heating and cooling the showroom. Ultimately, the building relies upon passive strategies for most of its heating and cooling needs. Supplemental conditioning is provided by evaporative coolers and wood stoves, respectively. I wistfully recall, however, one of our rejected conditioning strategies.

In this approach, the Sun's heat would be collected during the winter in a bank of solar hot water collectors installed outside the building. The heated water from these panels would pass through a storage tank containing a heat exchanger, where it would release its energy to a liquid-based radiant system running through the showroom floor. Pumps for this system would be powered by energy collected by on-site photovoltaic panels. We speculated that the radiant floor system might even be run in reverse in the summer, with the collectors used at night to radiantly cool the water stored in the tank, then released during the day to maintain a cool internal slab. The radiant floor system is appealing because it operates independently of interior air temperatures, thereby "conditioning" the building occupants directly, so that comfort would be less a function of air temperatures. This is advantageous in a retail building, where the air changes per hour are high due to the frequent opening and closing of the entrance doors.

Alas, the system was deemed too complex and expensive by our progressive yet pound-wise client. Moreover, this type of system is not without disadvantages. Radiant floor systems have a long start-up time, and can be difficult to operate effectively during swing seasons when heating and cooling are required on consecutive days. Additionally, the notion of using the floor to cool is untested and might result in condensation. Perhaps this is what gave Real Goods "cold feet." In the end, we chose simplicity over high-tech, and developed a reliable, elegant system.

Although we succeeded in producing a low-energy building, there is always room for improvement. It is imperative that we study the building carefully to learn how it is saving energy and where savings might be improved through better operation or a better design. Monitoring of various levels of detail has occurred, but it will take a rigorous, yearlong monitoring project by Real Goods and the design community to fully understand the true processes at work. With Real Goods' commitment to the development of knowledge, I have no doubt that we will understand the building much better in five years than we do now.

Collaboration is the key to integral, ecological design. David Arkin and Bruce King (pictured her) along with Adam Jackaway and Jeff Oldham (pictured in chapter 5) share not only the success of the showroom building, but close friendships as well. It's no secret that designing and building this project was a great deal of fun.

David Arkin, AIA, was the Project Architect of the Solar Living Center. He and his wife Anni Tilt have since established their own practice, Arkin Tilt Architects, specializing in ecological planning and design. He is a board member of Architects Designers Planners for Social Responsibility (ADPSR) and a founding member of the California Straw Building Association (CASBA).

A structural engineer who was initially skeptical of the plans for a large commercial building constructed from straw bales, **Bruce King** is now a widely recognized specialist in environmental building techniques. His book *Buildings of Earth and Straw* (published by Ecological Design Press and distributed by Chelsea Green) is an essential reference for any architectural project utilizing natural building materials.

We met **Adam Jackaway** and **Jeff Oldham** in chapter 5.

CHAPTER 6

A New Way of Working

David Arkin, Adam Jackaway, Bruce King, Jeff Oldham

I've always thought of architecture as a kind of philosophical carpentry. It's very much the Zen idea—you don't find truth through precepts or concepts, you find it through doing. And from that you can learn something larger. —*Richard Fernau*

David: One of the greatest lessons that we learned by designing and building the Solar Living Center was the importance of *collaboration* in the creation of integrated, ecological design. As project architect, I experienced this collaboration from the first visit to the site I made with Sim Van der Ryn, to the design of the sculpture at the center of the oasis fountain with Baile Oakes, Stephanie Kotin, and Chris Tebbutt. The level of integration we achieved was made possible only by eroding the traditional boundaries of duties in both design and construction. Of course, it was also a great deal more fun.

This chapter was written collaboratively by four members of the design and building team. It was our temptation to present the design of the building as a series of chronological events, but in fact the process was very cyclical, with the climate analysis informing material selection, materials informing structure, structure informing form, form informing climate control, and so on. In this way, the design process models natural systems, which are constantly feeding back information and tuning themselves accordingly. As a branch grows in search of sunlight, so too did our design evolve as a natural fit to its climate and setting.

A Natural Process

Therefore, we elected to discuss our different ways of meeting some of the criteria established for the project. Below are five of the many goals of the Solar Living Center, paralleling the five principles of ecological design outlined by Sim Van der Ryn in chapter 4:

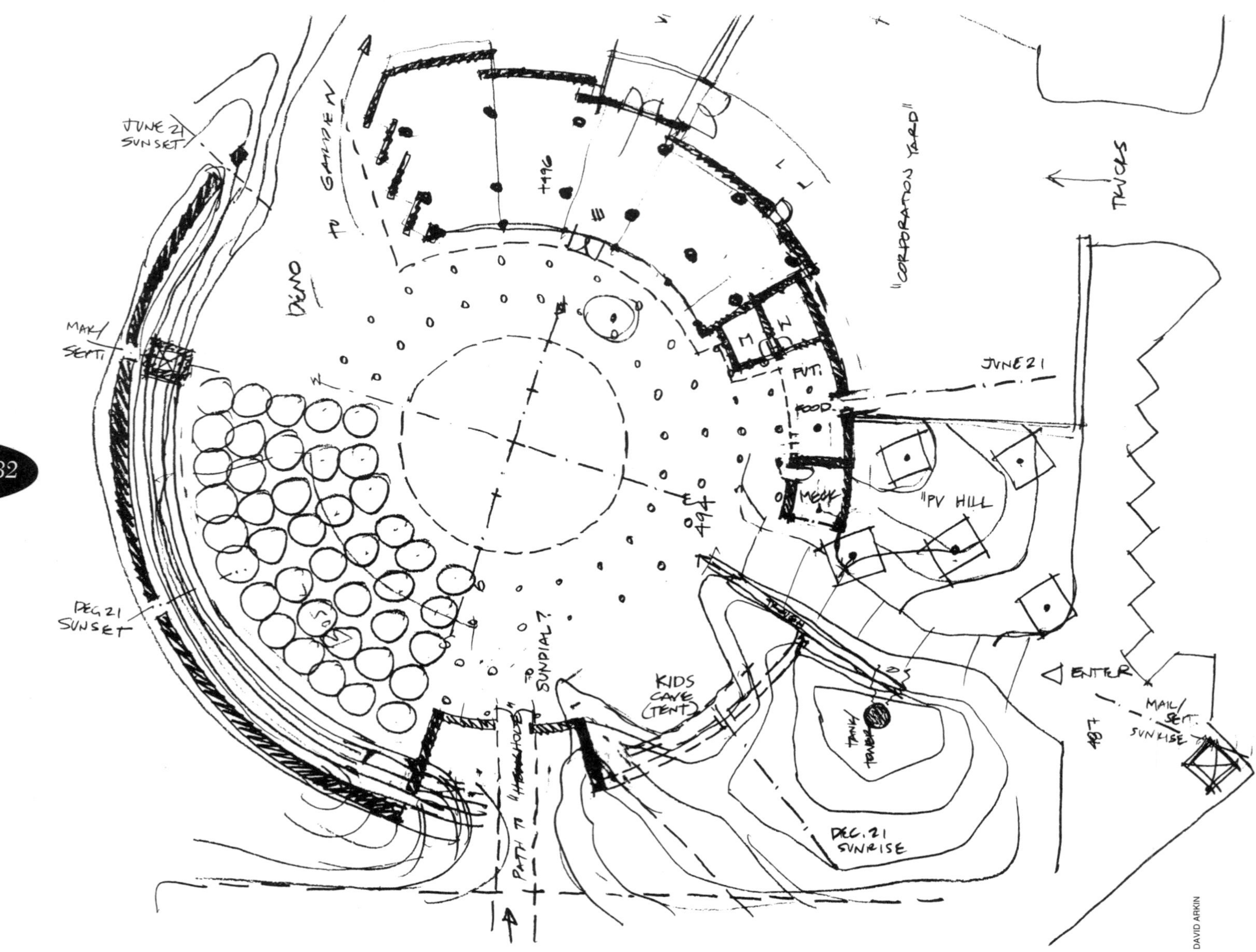
JUNE 21
SUNSET
MAY/
SEPT.
DEC 21
SUNSET
TO GARDEN
DEMO
"CORPORATION YARD"
TRUCKS
JUNE 21
FUT.
FOOD
MECH
"PV HILL
ENTER
MAIL/
SEPT.
SUNRISE
KIDS
CAVE
(TENT)
SUNDIAL?
DEC. 21
SUNRISE
496
494
497
M
W

DAVID ARKIN

Goal 1. Create a Climate-Responsive Building (Solutions Grow from Place)
Goal 2. Create an Educative Environment (Make Nature Visible)
Goal 3. Design for Low-Impact Construction (Ecological Accounting Informs Design)
Goal 4. Involve Everyone and Have Fun (Everyone Is a Designer)
Goal 5. Feedback: Measure Successes and Failures (Design with Nature)

"The design process mimics natural systems, which are constantly feeding back information and modifying themselves accordingly. As a branch grows in search of sunlight, so too did our design evolve as a natural fit to its climate and setting." Along the way, many options were explored and discarded or incorporated into the final plan.

While the process was integrated and cyclical, a basic methodology and sequence is typical (or, we submit, ought to be typical) to the design of most buildings. The design process begins with a careful site analysis and collection of climate data. Our initial site visits included mapping the relationship of the site to the greater landscape as well as the path of the Sun. We also reviewed the program established by Real Goods in relation to the impacts it would have on climate control. For example, the primarily daytime occupancy afforded us the opportunity to utilize night-flushing for summer cooling. From this data analysis, we reached some general conclusions that in turn shaped design studies.

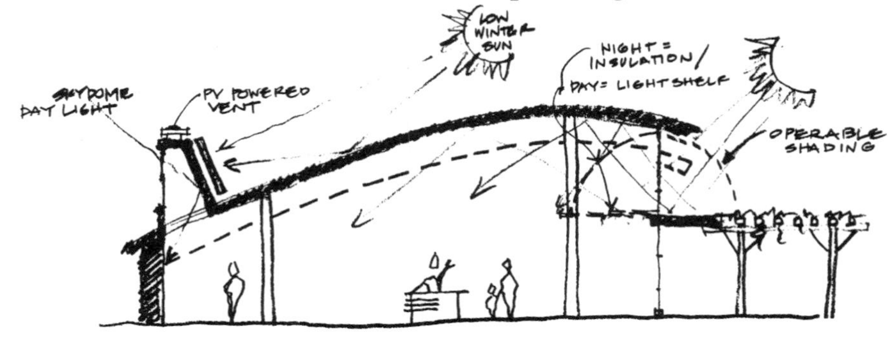

The initial gesture of a design of the showroom was a bermed structure Sim and I had presented in the design competition as part of the architect selection process. This building was curved in plan to embrace a circular oasis, but featured a sod roof built against a bermed/levee wall to hold back one-hundred-year floods. We called this scheme the "bunker." As the building rose out of the flood plain, having the wall support 18 inches of wet earth in the event of an earthquake made less and less sense, for insurance and other reasons. We explored two less interesting options, the "box" and the "basilica," before concluding that the curved "bowstring" was both the most elegant and the most facile at distributing daylight. Adam Jackaway and intern Norm Bourassa built 1/4-inch scale models of the "bowstring" and "box" to be tested and videotaped on the Heliodon table at PG&E's Pacific Energy Center in San Francisco. A Heliodon uses a stationary light source and a table that adjusts and rotates to simulate the path of the Sun through the course of a day at various times of the year.

With consensus among both the design team and Real Goods that the curved roof was the most dynamic and appropriate form, we performed thorough daylighting and thermal analysis. Adam built and tested a 3/4-inch scale section of one bay of the design for even daylight distribution. Thermal analysis testing included several trips to PG&E's Heliodon, a run in the Boundary Layer Wind Tunnel at UC-Berkeley, design modifications, and a double-check of our cooling loads by Sol˚Data energy analysts of Santa Rosa. Simultaneous with this work, we engaged in long-distance site design collaboration with Chris Tebbutt and Stephanie Kotin. Civil engineers Terry McGillivray of Mendocino Engineering and Bob Pedroncelli, who coordinated with CalTrans, helped transform the site design into a built landscape. Leslie Lorimer of our office directed construction of a 1/16-inch scale model of the site that illustrated the Solar Living Center at full build-out with mature vegetation. This

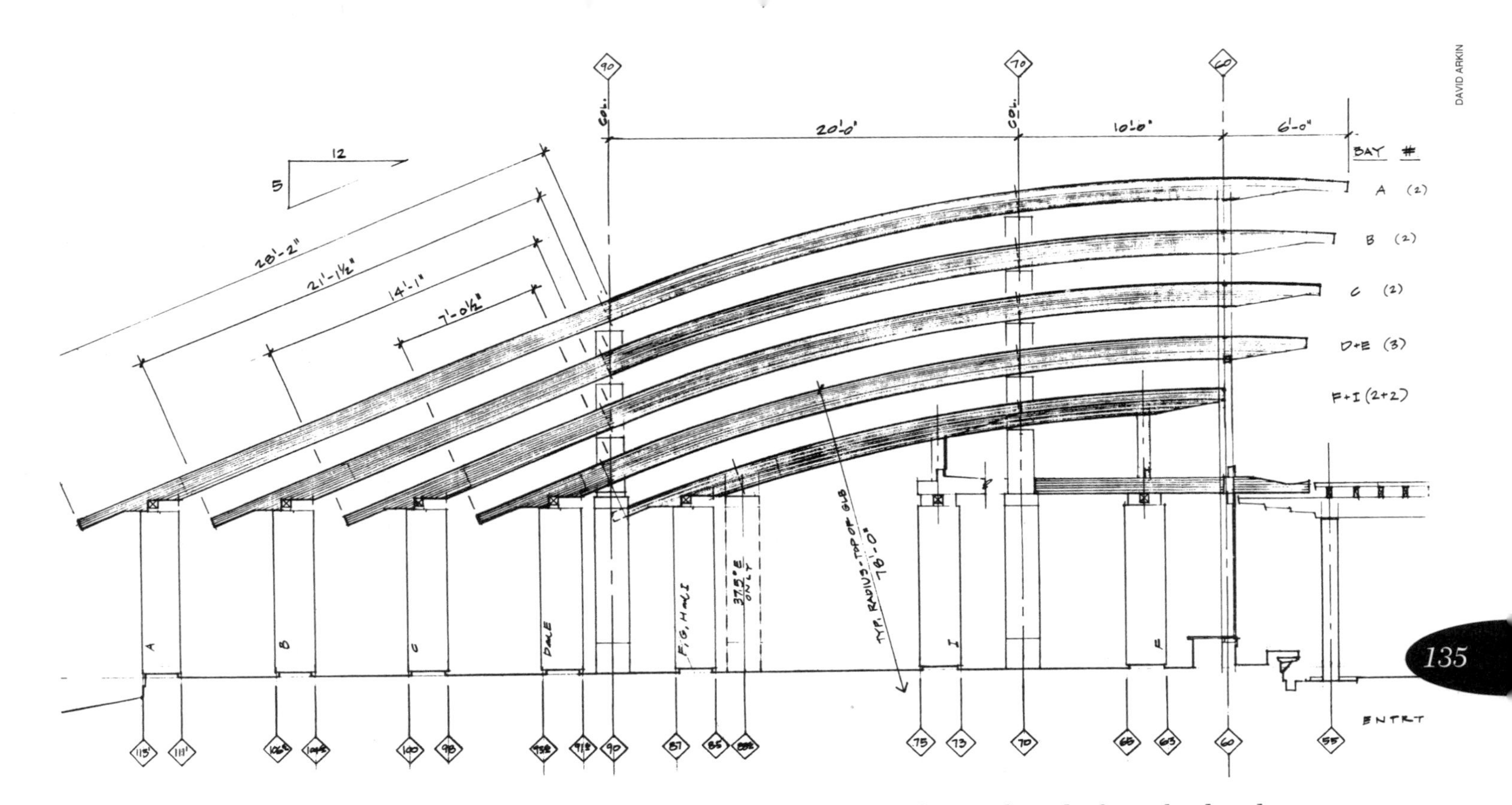

DAVID ARKIN

Every stick of wood used in construction was either recycled or certified sustainably harvested. To create the curved roof trusses, glu-laminated beams ("glu-lams") were made of Douglas fir grown, milled, and manufactured within 40 miles of the Solar Living Center. Utilizing local materials, which reduces the energy (and dollar) costs of transportation, was just one of the sustainability factors calculated and considered by the construction team.

model was on display in the temporary showroom at the north end of Hopland and was a valuable tool in presenting the design to the local community.

Development of the design incorporated many of our early material choices, most notably straw bale, with further research and other product choices to meet our performance needs. Bruce King and I worked closely in developing a structural system that met our goal of reduced environmental impact while maintaining life safety and health standards. He went out of his way to research concrete and suggested several alternatives, such as fly-ash additives to reduce the Portland cement content. Our earliest sketches of the building featured trusses of Douglas fir reclaimed from demolished buildings. The costs of the curves in both plan and section dictated moving to glu-laminated beams instead. We soon concluded that milling beautiful old timbers of vertical-grain fir into small 2 x 6 members to laminate made little sense. Rather than endorse the clearcutting of forests one hundred years ago, we decided to support the best forestry practices of today. We used certified sustainably har-

vested Douglas fir that was grown, milled, and manufactured into glu-lams all within 40 miles of our building. This greatly reduced the embodied energy and dollar costs in transportation, which often account for most of wood's impact. Tim Kennedy, Real Goods' assistant project manager, researched the embodied energy, toxicity, cost, availability, recycled content, and recyclability of hundreds of materials. A great number of the material choices were made through a less-than-scientific but nonetheless rigorous review by Jeff, Tim, and me. One of us would propose a material and the others would critique it. Egos were left behind in favor of making the best choices.

We also had early meetings with local builders David Raitt, Pierre Horn, and Howie Hawkes of Mendocino Housewrights, and Steve Gresham. As they would be considered for building the project, their input served the dual role of getting them familiar with the project early as well as getting valuable feedback on improving the design and details. After waiting a season to begin construction, we ultimately held competitive bidding and selected TDM Construction of Ukiah. Tom Myers brought an "open book" attitude into the project, and while he was working under a fixed price, he immediately became a member of the team and we worked closely to modify elements of the project to meet our budgets. This collaboration was atypical to the frequently adversarial contractor/architect/owner relationship. Tom moved his office, literally, to the site, and shared the space with Jeff and Tim. The communication this engendered, and Jeff's facilitation of it, cannot be overstated.

Simultaneous to contractor bidding, the project was submitted to the Mendocino County Department of Planning and Building Services. The county sent the final documents to a contract structural-plan-checker, with whom we had not had any previous communication. A remarkable laundry list of comments came back. Jeff and I were able to hold a meeting with the county's plan checker, John Anastasio, and this face-to-face meeting was helpful in resolving many issues, though we can't quite say he became a member of the team. We were patient and eventually got our permit to build.

Waiting a year to begin construction was beneficial for many reasons, not the least of which was averting the floods of 1995. The site had been graded and planted that summer, and a storage building was erected in the fall. The northern edge of the site is Feliz Creek, a tributary to the notorious Russian River, which it joins a quarter mile from the site. Two-thirds of the site is a floodway, and in the rains of January and again in March the site became just that. Of course, we were prepared and had designed the site to handle these events, never imagining that it might be put to the test so soon. The newly graded site, including infant vegetation, survived excellently.

Early meetings had included Real Goods' store manager Nancy Hensley, and I had toured the existing store on Mazzoni Street, soliciting input and needs from the store staff, but formal review and interaction with the full-time users of the project had been limited. As we were about to begin construction, we also held a series of presentations with the staff to introduce them to their new environment. Admittedly, these meetings happened late in the process, and we were fortunate that all loved the design and were subsequently very happy with the completed showroom.

After prolonged permitting and financing processes, construction began in July of 1995. Tim monitored the material and subcontractor mileage recording and the job-site recycling programs. Jeff and Tom and I began our daily rituals of phone and fax communication. The 1/4-inch scale model we had used for daylight testing was at the site and became a valuable tool for communicating to subcontractors ("subs") and each other. North Coast Structures of Windsor, TDM's framing sub, became an important member of the team. Ed Winkelmann, Scott Haviland, and Michael Douglas went out of their way to meet our goals and facilitate use of certified sustainably harvested lumber, as well as to maintain the highest quality in their work through to the end. As project architect, I worked closely with all the subs and, together with Jeff, nurtured the team spirit required to pull off the project. Billy Timmons and Len Thomas of North Coast Structures commented to me one day, as things were finally taking shape, that they had really had doubts early on, but they were quite proud to be part of the construction of the SLC. Steve Gresham, who installs many of Real Goods' photovoltaic systems around the county and around the world, was hired by TDM to supervise construction and deserves recognition for his temperament and leadership.

Changes were made throughout construction, but change orders were processed in the spirit of collaboration and were talked through before the prices were issued. In some cases, Tom had bid low, such as for the translucent light shelves for which he had budgeted $5,000, but whose materials alone cost $12,000. Rather than force him to take a loss, we worked to develop an alternative that met our performance needs at a lower cost. Real Goods asked recognized high-efficiency lighting designers Robert Sardinsky and James Benya to assist with artificial lighting. Throughout construction, Tom and Jeff and I collaborated closely with Chris Tebbutt and Stephanie Kotin, and later with artists Baile Oakes and Peter Erskine, who were introduced late in the construction but integrated into the team. I especially enjoyed working with Tom's key carpenter, Manuel Paz, who was patient, meticulous, and insightful as we adjusted the door head and jamb details in the field.

Discussions of durability and maintenance led to the conclusion that no finish at all would be necessary if the appropriate materials were selected. For example, unpainted galvanized sheet metal gutters and flashing are resistant to deterioration; painting once just means repainting later. Real Goods insisted that details such as the floor and ceiling finishes by the Otto Design Group incorporate materials of no or low toxicity.

The OTTO Design Group was hired to design and build the store displays and several other features. Phil Otto, Scott Stewart, and John Fitzgerald brought to the task considerable experience in incorporating recycled and reused materials due to their work on the many Urban Outfitters and other interiors they've designed and built. Beyond the fixtures themselves, they are responsible for the floor and ceiling finishes, the concept of the entry gate, the sculptural trellis along the entry drive, and the remarkable drinking fountains of scrap metal. Despite persistent rains, the entire team worked overtime and then some to complete the project for a May 1996 opening of the retail showroom. Jeff contracted mononucleosis, undoubtedly related to the long hours he'd been logging after Tim Kennedy's departure, but Vicki Oldham, Jeff's wife, moved in deftly to complete the job. Solar Living Center director Mark Winkler also joined the team, and quickly found a shovel in his hands. We were putting finishing touches in place right up to the grand opening on the Summer Solstice, but none of the twelve thousand visitors that weekend noticed, and the building and site were deemed a smashing success.

While the building was essentially complete, the design process was not. User education and interaction and postoccupancy performance analysis are ongoing as this is being written. Jeff and I conducted tours of the building with the store staff, both to instruct them in the operation of the building's passive features and to answer questions relative to the tours they were hosting. In the fall of 1996, a class of UC-Berkeley's College of Environmental Design Architecture School studied the building's passive design performance. Two students (Susanne Richardson and Lara Teixeira) authored an operator's manual to orient new store staff, while others recorded temperature and humidity data. Real Goods is monitoring energy consumption and soliciting staff and visitor feedback. There is every indication that the project is meeting or exceeding most of our goals. Again, we feel this analysis is still part of the design process, and we are still "tuning" the building accordingly, trying to optimize performance. In the following sections, we discuss in our own voices how we collaborated to meet the goals established early in the process.

Goal 1. Create a Climate-Responsive Building

Adam: In the last hundred years, technological advances in the areas of lighting, heating, air conditioning, and glazing have opened up a world of new design possibilities. Buildings may now exist in virtually any climate without utilizing local natural forces to aid in thermal or visual space conditioning, relying instead upon a myriad of mechanical systems to create habitable interiors. Within a relatively short time, architects have begun to depend upon these technologies to an alarming degree.

Prior to this dependence, understanding the weather, the regional climate, and the role of the Sun as a source of both light and heat was a prerequisite in the design of a building. Inherently, the outdoor environment had a big role to play in the shaping of the indoor environment. But as the ability to mechanically condition artificially any type of indoor environment became a reality, knowledge of natural forces was unfortunately rendered unessential. It is now possible to keep a building warm in the winter, regardless of its shape or orientation. Electric lighting enables buildings to be constructed without regard to daylight, and air conditioning keeps them from overheating in the summer. As a result, designers are losing touch with the environments in which their buildings are sited.

As this transition first became a reality, it was seen as a tremendously freeing breakthrough. Designers could focus more upon other issues, and often employed this new freedom to experiment with new shapes and styles. Yet although these technological advances have no doubt brought about many beneficial changes to both the architectural aesthetics and usage of our buildings, they have not been without their drawbacks.

I believe that buildings that are climate-blind (ignore their climate) shortchange our built environment in three essential ways. First, such design is typically far more energy consumptive than climate-sensitive design, hastening fossil fuel depletion and furthering environmental degradation. Second, by ignoring the climatic context of our building sites, we miss opportunities to develop an architecture of place rich with regionalism and diversity. And finally, but perhaps most importantly, by divorcing our interior environments from exterior environments, we deprive building occupants of the joys and benefits associated with connection to our natural world. I believe that occupants will always favor dynamic, responsive interiors over stable, sterile ones. I also believe that we have a responsibility to understand and work with the beneficial and challenging forces in our climatic contexts as we add to the built environment.

David: Creating a climate-responsive building meant coordinating all aspects of the design, from landscape to details, toward this goal. Chris and Stephanie understood our need for shade in the oasis and responded with their elegant drip-ring structure and gray poplars which, with their huge leaves, provide nature's form of seasonally operable shading. Similarly, we selected a Japanese grape for the trellises. This grape leafs out late in spring and holds its foliage late into fall, and thus compensates for our relatively cool spring and hot fall seasons. The trellis was modeled and tested on the Heliodon table, as were the light scoops intended to reflect direct sunlight to the rear of the showroom (these have yet to be installed, and most days the lights in the back of the store are on). The Pacific Energy Center ran a time-lapse test of the model under natural sky conditions to test its performance.

Japanese grape was chosen as an appropriate climber for the shade requirements of the southern facade trellises, because it leafs out late in spring and holds its foliage late into the fall, corresponding to Hopland's cool spring and hot fall seasons.

Wall and roof systems were

The walls of the building are constructed of 23-inch thick rice straw bales coated with concrete gunite and finished with soil-cement, for a combined R-value of about 65. Introduced widely to the American public by the publication of The Straw Bale House *(Chelsea Green Publishing, 1994), straw bale construction is one of the most environmentally attractive methods available.*

selected specifically for their climate-appropriate performance. The straw bale walls with 3 to 4 inches of concrete gunite and soil-cement finish achieve an insulative value of R-65 (a typical 2-by-6 wood stud wall with fiberglass insulation is R-19). The roof features 12 inches of cellulose insulation below a radiant barrier, which by itself is R-10. A 1½-inch air space above the barrier ventilates the roof for any solar gain that gets beyond the white Hypalon™ membrane roof, which reflects 70 to 75 percent of the solar radiation it receives. This venting is optimized by the shape of the building, which draws cool outside air in low and vents warm air high through the chimney effect. Warm air is also drawn out by the low

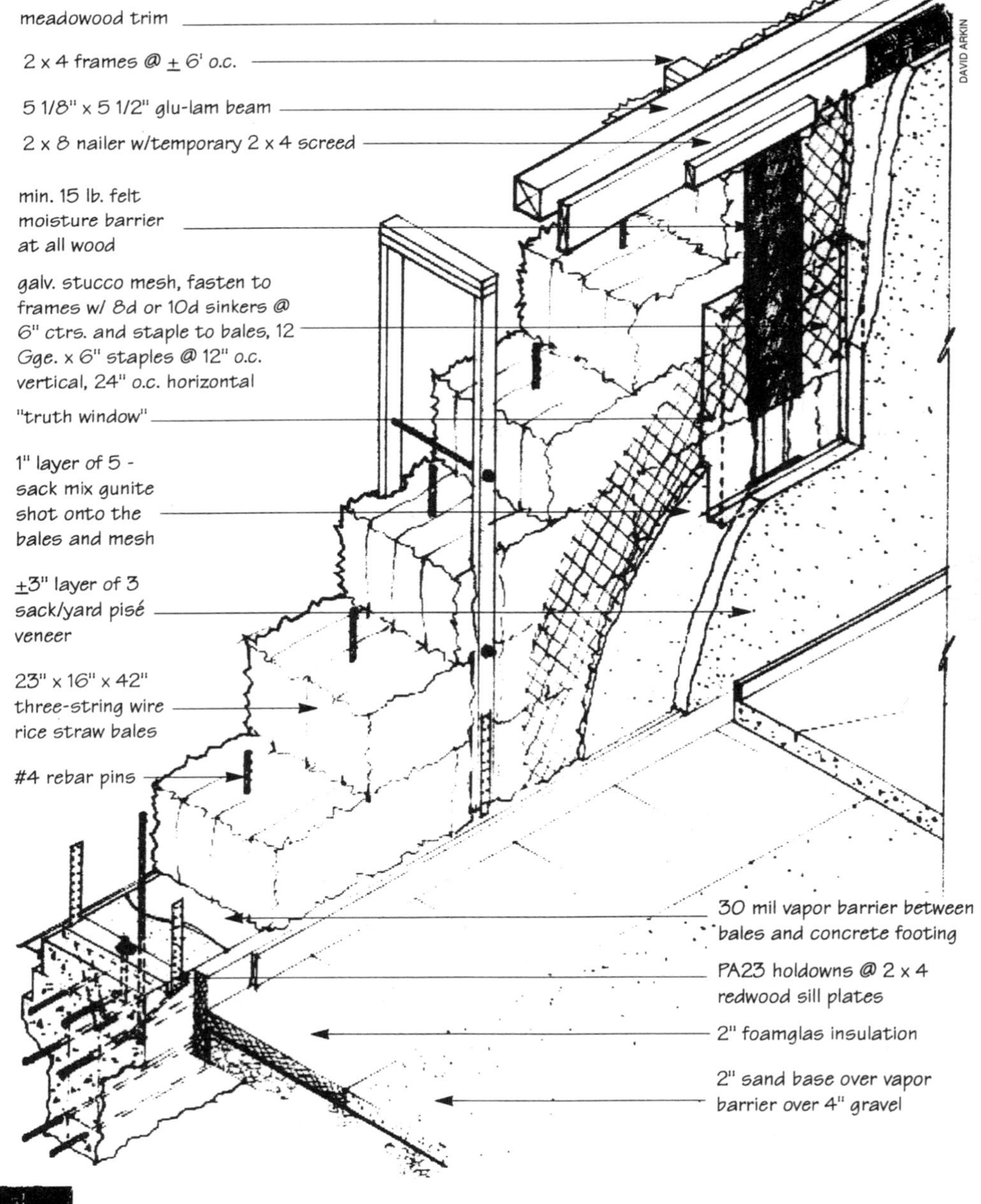

illustration by David Arkin, AIA, Project Architect

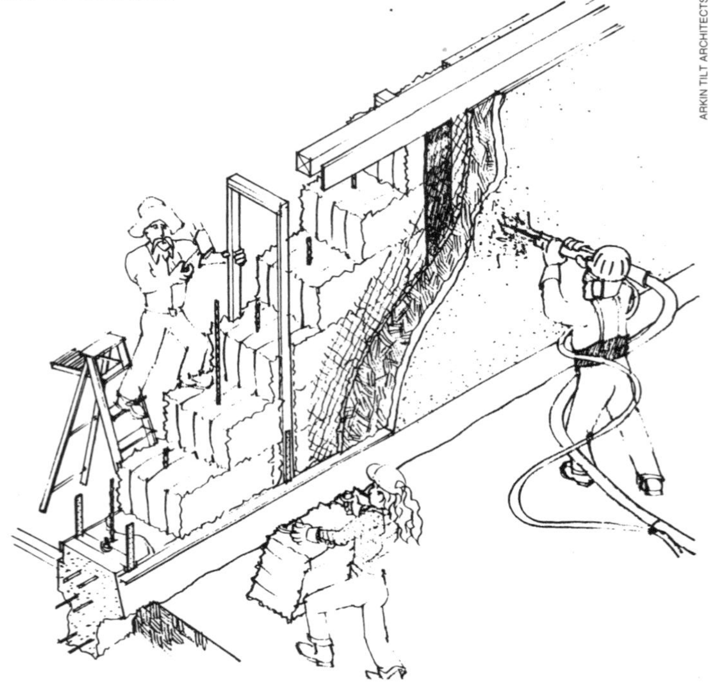
ARKIN TILT ARCHITECTS

Several stages that occur sequentially in the actual construction of straw bale walls are shown simultaneously in this cut-away illustration from Bruce King's book Building with Earth and Straw.

pressure created by the northwest breezes over the building. Similarly, we made the clerestory windows along the stepped roofs operable to take advantage of these same principles and aid in night flushing.

The straw bale walls are only 8 feet high. All walls above this level are R-Control sandwich panels (Stress-Skin) with a smooth Hardi-board fiber-cement finish. The tall southwest wall takes the brunt of afternoon sun and features a ventilated cavity behind the Hardi-panels to further reduce unwanted gain. Because of the extensive shading study, we did not need high-performance glazing, and have more economical 1-inch dual-glazed low-E glass throughout the building. The un-thermally-broken aluminum frames became a cost compromise, but the substantial thermal mass in the floor, walls, and columns compensate for losses. The insulating light shelves, when closed on winter nights, greatly reduce thermal transfer on the large area of south-facing glazing.

Through the careful study of climate and shaping of a passive building, one can often reduce the dependence on heating and cooling equipment and thus realize great savings in the building's operating costs. In the SLC, we were able to almost eliminate these systems altogether. We use two products that Real Goods sells. Evaporative coolers (also known as "swamp coolers") aid summer cooling. Ours are 12-volt direct-current, placed in the stepping bays at the rear of the building to utilize cooler shaded air close to the ground. We anticipated relying on them to get through extremely hot periods. While the fans are used to boost night flushing, the water to the evaporative coolers has never been turned on. Likewise, wood stoves are on display and installed in the showroom. These have been used on the coldest of winter mornings, but are more often only burning for ambiance. Again, the substantial mass inside the insulating envelope is able to handle the stove's output without overheating the space, and natural ventilation is feasible even in the middle of winter. On

Highly insulating, soundproof, and nontoxic, the basic material is an agricultural byproduct, and is thus inexpensive and renewable. The straw bale construction process itself is relatively simple, quick, and even fun. Here, a worker pins straw bales with rebar.

temperate days throughout the year, the windows and doors can be held wide open, which is refreshing in a number of ways.

Bruce: The basic building shape is a series of "seashells" open to the south, with low, highly insulated straw bale walls on the north, and high, glazed walls facing south to "scoop up" the solar light and warmth. They unfortunately also scoop up the powerful southern winds that accompany winter storms, so that despite the building's location in an area of highest seismic risk, wind loads governed the structural design.

DAVID ARKIN

If we ever had any doubts about the ability of the concrete "tree columns" to resist big winds, those doubts were completely erased when a record wind storm hit the area in December of 1995, causing extensive damage all along the California coast. The building was at its most vulnerable at that exact time, because though the straw bale walls and roof were in place, no glazing had been installed on the huge south walls. The building was literally a huge scoop facing directly into the storm. But there were no problems—other than that this engineer didn't sleep much that night.

This was particularly gratifying because, as the structural engineer, I had successfully argued for somewhat more relaxed wind design standards than county building officials originally suggested. My suspicion was that code enforcement has become excessively conservative, forcing much higher costs (both as money from owners and resources and energy from the environment) than was warranted for basic life safety. I would hope that the lesson imparted might free other building designers to let actual site climatic conditions (as opposed to bureaucratic overkill or fear of litigation) drive design. We can relax a bit, here.

Jeff: My on-site experiences have been quite memorable. Although it was exciting to help design this innovative building, the positively elating experience was to realize that in practice our design exceeded our

REAL GOODS

At the most vulnerable moment during construction, with straw bale walls and roof in place, but no glazing on the southern facade, the record wind storm of December 1995 hit the coast of California. The open, curved building was like a huge scoop facing directly into the wind. Bruce King, the structural engineer, based his design standards for the concrete "tree columns" on actual site climatic conditions. The columns successfully resisted the big winds.

expectations. Translating design into constructed reality can be frustrating and disappointing. This is one of the rare cases where the building actually performs better than anticipated and the process was gratifying and impressive.

Early in the building process, it became clear that this building would be extraordinarily soundproof. My assistant, Tim Kennedy, and I tried to communicate through an unfinished 8-foot-high straw wall, to push a straw needle back and forth. Hollering at the top of our lungs, we were unable to hear each other at all. This hysterically futile experience told us that we were on the right track. Once the roof, PISE™, and windows sealed the building, it became obvious that we had a winning plan.

Impervious to outside temperatures, the building is a testament to mass and passive building principles in all their glory. We have no need for the evaporative coolers, and the wood stoves are used more for atmosphere than necessity. My favorite anecdote took place shortly after the grand opening on a 100-degree July day. A woman entered the store and reprimanded our staff for wasting energy by having the air-conditioning system turned down too low. She was impressed to learn that we have no air conditioner and that she was experiencing the triumph of mass and passive design over the elements. The biggest performance test occurred during the Summer Solstice grand opening celebration. The outdoor temperatures ranged between 102 and 103 degrees Fahrenheit, with ten to thirteen thousand people pouring through the open doors for three days. Thousands of bodies squeezed through the store, radiating 500 or so BTUs apiece and doing their best to counteract the mass of the building with a mass of flesh. During this time the building temperature didn't exceed 86 degrees Fahrenheit, passing a true performance acid test. Summer days in Hopland are typically in the triple digits, yet the indoor temperature remains in the seventies, rarely even reaching the upper seventies. I think we have a real success.

Goal 2. Create an Educative Environment

David: Our intention at the outset was to create a place that could teach you something at every turn—even at a passing glance while driving by. From the entry drive past constructed wetlands and restored riparian areas to a parking lot with electric vehicle charging stations; from approaching the oasis through a hillside of tracking photovoltaic panels to the PV Equipment Room, which displays the storage and inversion of electrical energy; from the cool, green "parallel universe" of the oasis to the calm, light showroom; and from the global-warming exhibit to the myriad of reused and recycled materials in the restrooms, this place is relentless in its education.

This was very much by design. And it was furthered by frequent rereading of the vision statement John Schaeffer had prepared before any of us had been given the task. Perhaps the greatest lesson here is the value of clearly stating one's goals at the inception.

Another expression of education was a decision we made to be honest about our use of materials—sometimes brutally honest. Jeff and I were discussing finishes and, after going around with nontoxic versus low-toxic and such, concluded that the best finish may well be none at all. In other words, select materials that by their nature are suited to the task at hand. This thinking guided our process.

Some examples include the PISE™ finish on the straw bale walls. This material was quarried at the Fetzer Winery site about two miles up the road. Fetzer was constructing a building with 18-inch-thick PISE™ walls and had some extra material on hand. The soils at Fetzer are a natural red-brown tone, quite beautiful, and are the color you see on the showroom. David Easton and East Bay Gunite applied PISE™ with a gunite machine, which wet the dry material as it sprayed through the nozzle, creating a very strong finish in one coat. A sample shoot on some bales gave us some finishes to choose from, and we

DAVID ARKIN

The material for the PISE™ (pronounced pee-ZAY) finish on the straw bale walls was quarry surplus from a construction project at Fetzer Winery, a couple miles away. The soil was sprayed directly with a gunite machine, creating a beautiful, strong finish that needs no further preparation or maintenance.

selected the screeded "cottage cheese" effect for the interior, but liked the as-blown "Flintstone finish" on the outside. Here again, the application of the material—spraying in place with a gunite rig—is revealed in the appearance of the material today.

Another example is the use of unpainted galvanized sheet metal for the flashing and gutters. While these are usually painted, the galvanized surface is resistant to deterioration. Painting them now would have meant repainting down the road. Against the redwood trim, also left natural (but given a penetrating sealer), the galvanized metal is quite at home. Downspouts are chains and scuppers that celebrate rather than hide the natural process of rainwater reaching the ground.

Finally, an obligatory "truth window" was left on the interior of the showroom to reveal the straw bale construction of its walls. Doubtful visitors can see and feel what the building is made of and how it was built. While the bale walls were being erected, a dozen or so carloads of folks each day pulled off the highway to talk about straw bale construction. Jeff and Tim began to schedule tours of the uncompleted building every other Friday. And I suppose this book is yet another example of the educative experience this project embodies.

Adam: One of the aspects of this project that brought me the most joy was the fact that in addition to having the wonderful task of designing a truly climate-responsive building, it was explicitly stated in our project goals that we were to make these elements stand out in order to educate the building's visitors. Accordingly, throughout the design process, we continually factored the readability of our strategies into our evaluation processes. Not surprisingly, the project is dominated by clear forms, simple (although not straight!) geometries, and clearly delineated processes.

Many of the strategies we explored during design development had great potential for education but were often excessively complex in their operation, overly expensive, or just plain overkill. As it turns out, I think the final product has been successful as an educative building, in that its sheer simplicity and logic makes it readily understandable. Yes, one

The intention of the Solar Living Center is to teach at every turn. The construction team learned during their process, and the building itself serves as a model of what it is possible to achieve with sustainable design and renewable energy. A "truth window" in the interior of the showroom allows visitors to see into the straw bale wall and better understand how it was built.

Visitors can observe Bill Simmons and other Real Goods staff members operating the shading and ventilating devices to maintain comfortable lighting, temperatures, and air quality in the showroom. Not only do staff members feel good about the quality of their working environment (because it is healthier), they feel connected to the natural environment (because they respond to its daily and seasonal cycles). And they communicate their excitement about the place to people who come to learn and shop at the Solar Living Center.

certainly can have various levels of understanding of this place, but visitors generally are able to grasp the main impetus for the shapes, mechanisms, and forms without lengthy explanations. Additionally, visitors are given many insights into the inner workings of the place, such as the truth window and the power-monitoring building, which add significant depth to the experience.

There was one educational feature, however, that I wish had made it to the final design. David and I had discussed creating an overlook to the building (possibly from the other side of the courtyard), or a deck or balcony along the southern facade overlooking the courtyard. Along the railing of this balcony, we proposed installing an illustration of the building and courtyard with arrows pointing to and describing all of the interesting features at the site. I envisioned this feature to be much like the overlooks at national parks where each of the prominent features in your view are identified and described. I still think there is great power in this approach. Perhaps something along these lines can be added at a later date.

JEFF OLDHAM

Education also occurs at the SLC through what might be termed operation activities, where visitors learn by observing the Real Goods staff operating the building. As I recollect, this was not initially an explicitly intended methodology, yet it may turn out to be one of the most inspiring. Looking back, I think its origins can be traced to some early correspondence between Jeff Oldham and me about the potential for using movable shading devices.

Early in the design process, while working on some overly complex movable shading strategy, I suddenly developed a fear that although this crazy strategy might work, the client might never understand or operate it and the building would overheat. Willing, able, and knowledgeable operators would be absolutely essential to successful implementation of movable devices. I faxed Jeff at Real Goods to inquire about the staff's desire to be involved with the operation of their building. Much to my delight, a return fax assured me that our client was not only willing to be able and become knowledgeable, but they *demanded* to be involved with the operation of their building. A finer client you cannot ask for.

Bruce: For me, personally, this project was far more than educational; it was a welcome clarion call to discover and explore the green building movement from a structural engineer's perspective. At the time, I had so little data or literature to guide me (though I eventually found a fair amount) that I resolved to make life easier for other engineers who might be called on to work with earth or straw as structural materials.

So I gathered all the anecdotal and testing information I could, and wrote a book: *Buildings of Earth and Straw: Structural Design for Rammed Earth and Straw-Bale Architecture* (Ecological Design Press, 1996; distributed by Chelsea Green). And now, three years later, it is hugely gratifying to see both earth and straw construction burgeoning in popularity. This simple little book, spawned directly out of the SLC project, may help to ease the acceptance of natural building materials into mainstream construction everywhere. The SLC is a wonderful example of "alternative" construction for all to see and touch, or at least read about.

Jeff: We have always said that education is Real Goods' most important product, so of course we incorporated this philosophy within our design. The building provides active and passive educational opportunities. It is a working display of sustainable development, passive building design, and renewable energy integrated into a practical, beautiful building. The truth window allows a view into a cross-section of the building. The children's playground/education area provides hands-on experiences for children of all ages, with working displays showcasing the power and potential of the Sun. Workshops and tours are provided for both the professional and layperson.

Since the beginning, the site has been a magnet enticing the curious through our gates. A construction site is a hazardous venue for touring, and not wanting to impede progress, we kept site tours to a minimum. Many people, particularly professionals, press, and shareholders, were anxious to get an early peek at the site. Even in the earliest phases of the project, these visitors could see the vision being born from the earth. Their excitement, delight, and encouragement reassured us that we were on the right track. There were many stresses in the construction project, but the positive input of these visitors kept us inspired and fueled the energy it took to persevere through the process.

Experience is the best educator. Workshops and site tours give professionals and laypeople the opportunity to explore sustainable principles and techniques to use in their businesses and homes. Hands-on activities for children of all ages combine fun with learning. What better way to learn about solar energy than to power your own mini-aqueduct project with a movable module? (For more information about the educational displays, see "Subsystems" in chapter 5.)

BAILE OAKES

After the building was complete and visitors began to pour in, we were showered with praise and thanks for the amazement, hope, and inspiration the site evokes. My most satisfying experience throughout the entire process occurred during the grand opening. The children's play area was inundated with little squealing children, my daughter among them. They were running around covered from head to toe with wet sand, laughing, creating waterfalls, dams, and aqueducts, with water and sand flying in all directions. It delighted me to see the joy on their faces and to know that I had played a part in providing such a playground for these kids and all those yet to come. It really made the whole process worthwhile.

Many architectural classes from universities have visited the site. It is an inspiration for these students to see this ecological development in practice, to know that dreams can be incorporated into their future careers. Construction can go beyond cookie-cutter techniques, and the mistakes of previous generations are not fated to be endlessly repeated. There are new, alternative, and better ways to design and build, and in actuality there are clients willing to invest in these sustainable principles and techniques.

Goal 3. Design for Low-Impact Construction

***David**:* In addition to trying to minimize the energy and resources the showroom would be using on an ongoing basis, we sought to minimize the impacts of its construction as well. We acknowledged that any building activity was going to have some impacts, but through consciously studying and monitoring these impacts we might reduce them to some degree. As mentioned earlier, we started by selecting materials that by their nature accomplished the job at hand.

Beyond its thermal and user-friendly properties, straw bale construction is attractive in its creative use of what is currently considered an agricultural waste byproduct. Over one million tons of carbon dioxide and particulate pollution are sent to California's Central Valley skies every year when rice farmers burn the rice chaff off their lands after harvest. The Environmental Protection Agency considers this burning a hazard and is placing restrictions on the practice. Farmers are looking for alternatives, including flooding fields to provide habitat for migrating ducks. The California Rice Industries Association teamed with the North Coast Federation of Fisheries (who had concerns about reduced river flows from flooding early in the fall) to help introduce a bill to the California legislature. This bill, carried by Representative Byron Scher, was signed into law early in 1995 and established guidelines for straw bale construction in California. Ross Burkhardt and John "Balehead" Swearingen and their crew built the nearly eight hundred rice-straw bales donated to Real Goods by the rice growers. One day over lunch, Ross and I calculated that two hundred thousand homes per year could be built with the straw currently being burned in Northern California!

DAVID ARKIN

A cornucopia of reused and recycled materials can be found in a visit to the restrooms at the Solar Living Center. A band of Meadowood trim encircles the room. This finishboard is manufactured from rye grass by Leonard Opel and his son in Albany, Oregon. Using an old plywood press, they add an isocyanate resin and press 4- by 8-foot panels 5/16 of an inch thick. The resin currently costs fourteen times what the typical exterior plywood glue does, but does not off-gas formaldehyde, which is one of the leading toxins implicated in "sick building syndrome." Meadowood carries Germany's strict "Blue Angel" rating for low toxicity. We see use of agricultural fibers in building materials as a sign of the future of products currently being manufactured of wood and wood byproducts.

During a visit to Recycletown, a used-materials yard in Santa Rosa, Jeff and Tim noticed the hundreds, if not thousands, of old toilet tank covers there and wondered if they could be used to tile the restroom floors. We then deemed them too slippery for the floor, but I suggested a wainscot of them, and that's what we did, including a few marbles for filler at the occasional missing corner. The sinks came from a used building material store in the Bay Area, and the countertops are made of recycled bottle glass with a small amount of Portland cement as a binder. Made to order by Counter/Productions of Berkeley, the glass is

Seeking to minimize the environmental impact of construction often led Real Goods to the same solutions that were found in the creation of a climate-responsive building. Although rice farmers are looking for alternatives to burning the chaff in the fields after harvest, currently over one million tons of carbon dioxide and particulate pollution blacken Northern California skies annually. Instead, two hundred thousand homes could be built with the rice straw burned each year.

poured into a mold and then ground to a smooth finish in a process similar to finishing stone. The bits of bottle glass, especially at the front edge, are little windows into the material. Urinals made by the Waterless Company are just that, saving 40,000 gallons per year.

The ultimate restroom material one can't help but notice is the toilet partitions of 100 percent postconsumer HDPE plastic. Shredded milk jugs and such, paper labels and all, are melted into panels 1/2 inch thick, with bits of color spiraling from their center. This, in combination with some warping, creates an exciting vertigo experience not found in your average loo! A sign on Highway 101 touts the Solar Living Center's "weird restrooms," and indeed each day brings visitors enticed by the building's unique facilities.

We also designed several elements of the project in such a way that construction waste could be used in subsequent phases of the project. An example of this is the formwork, which we were able to reuse for light shelves, framing of overhangs, and the few wood stud walls in the project.

While the Douglas fir in the project was certified sustainably harvested, all of the redwood is reclaimed from dismantled lumber mills and beer and wine tanks. Ours was procured by Joe Garnero of Recycled Lumberworks in Ukiah, 15 miles north of Hopland. This clear, straight-grained wood is old-growth timber cut over half a century ago. We laminated some of this redwood into the curved fascias on the stepping roofs and planed some for the exterior trim, but most of the trellis structure has at least three faces of the material in its "as-found" condition.

Among the systems that minimize impact is the graywater recycling equipment on display in front of the restrooms. Wastewater from the restroom sinks is piped separately from the toilets to this filtration system, donated by AGWA Graywater Systems, which irrigates gardens and lawn in the oasis. Toilet waste, known as blackwater, is piped to the municipal sewage treatment facility adjacent to the SLC. During design, we suggested that the Hopland Public Utilities District (PUD) consider a model biological sewage treatment facility on their site and become part of the demonstrations.

The list of low-impact products and methods we used goes on and on. We also took what might be best described as an "attitude" that reduced some construction impacts. This was

Closing the circle of recycling means using and reusing old materials in new ways. The Solar Living Center's restrooms take recycling to new heights of social responsibility. The Meadowood trim is manufactured from rye grass (an agricultural byproduct), the countertops are made of broken bits of bottle glass, the toilet partitions are formed from shredded and melted 100 percent postconsumer HDPE plastic bottles, and the wainscotting is constructed of—what else?—hundreds of old toilet tank covers.

JEFF OLDHAM

to "live with our mistakes." Things don't always turn out just as you expect. The sanded concrete finish and some of the stepped foundations are examples of things that didn't quite turn out. After exploring some cover-up solutions, we elected to just let them be, rather than tearing them out and repouring, which often happens in construction. The walks are what they are. The footings are stained with an iron-sulfate fertilizer wash, giving them a rich red-brown tone to complement the PISE™. Loosening up on some of the specifications without sacrificing the overall quality enabled us to focus resources in other areas.

Adam: For me, one of the more compelling aspects of this project was that the phrase "design for low-impact construction" truly encompassed all aspects of this project—from building design to site design. It is quite amazing to consider the level of detail with which Real Goods laid out their vision for the SLC, and perhaps more amazing that they had the fortitude to stick to their principles through some undoubtedly tough decision making (in chapter 5 you will find a substantive explanation of some of the building's climate-responsive strategies and mechanisms).

Bruce: It was easy to identify two material uses in the structure where we could ease the environmental impacts: concrete and wood.

Concrete depends upon its principal bonding component—Portland cement—to become what it effectively is: cast-in-place rock. But the manufacture of Portland cement requires huge amounts of energy and extensively generates both greenhouse gases and particulate pollution. We found that we could substitute fly ash (the waste product from coal-fired power plants) for a quarter of the cement in our concrete mix, thereby lessening the cement usage and making productive use of a "trash" material. With tongues firmly in cheek, we also displaced some of the concrete volume in the thick footings with "consumer flotsam and jetsam," including old stereos, 8-track players, answering machines, and worn-out plastic toys, though the effect was far more symbolic than material.

The use of lumber was hugely reduced by using straw bales (from the nearby rice-growing region of the Central Valley) for the 400 feet of north and west walls.

DAVID ARKIN

The goal of designing for low-impact construction and the goal of involving everyone and having fun dovetailed when the footings were poured. "Consumer flotsam and jetsam" (such as this 8-track) donated by Real Goods customers displaced some of the concrete volume. A more practical innovation was the substitution of fly ash for one quarter of the Portland cement, which is the principal bonding component of concrete. The manufacture of Portland cement is energy-intensive and polluting, while fly ash is a waste product from coal-fired power plants.

(The thick straw bale walls were also, by wide consensus, more beautiful and far more insulative than comparable stud walls.)

Everyone at Real Goods was also emphatic about using "sustainably harvested lumber" (SHL)—meaning grown, cut (but not clear-cut), and milled locally and with respect for ecosystem health. This made for a few procedural problems with acquiring the material, as SHL is not yet in high demand and therefore not regularly present in the construction marketplace. The situation is perhaps analogous to the status of organically grown produce twenty or thirty years ago: It was available, but only at higher cost, irregular quality, and in only a few outlets. Real Goods paid a modest premium for using SHL, but as a result has taken a step to make it more of a mainstream commodity.

Jeff: In the mission to produce a model of sustainability, the process itself had to be environmentally sensitive. Tim Kennedy, my assistant, was indispensable in many ways, such as researching products, getting quotes and supplies to the site, finding used materials, and so on. One of his key responsibilities was to do the environmental tracking and recycling. My job—and maintaining the quality of the project—would have been impossible without Tim's contributions. The entire team was asked to be aware of the finiteness and toxicity of fossil fuels. We minimized the amount of fuel spent to get materials and personnel to the job. We maintained our equipment to avoid leaking fluids on-site. We developed a new sensibility about recycling construction materials. The general contractor, Tom Myers of TDM Construction, was exemplary in this process. It was a real joy for me to work with Tom and his crew. I appreciate the professional ethics that they practiced. Their subcontractor, North Coast Construction, also devoted themselves to the mission of building a demonstration center that exemplified the principles of sustainability. These contractors had no previous experience in this arena, but they were anxious to tackle sustainability issues and learn green building principles. They told me that they knew this was the "future" and they wanted to get in on the ground floor. When people start building this way, they want to be the ones who have been doing it for a while. It was a thrill to watch them break out of the good-old-boy mold and fully adopt the principles of sustainable, saner, alternative construction systems. I watched them experiment with form-releasing materials that were vegetable- rather than petroleum-based. We learned that Crisco quickly drains down form stakes in the summer sun and that the time of use is sometimes more important than the material used. Everybody kept a very positive spirit during these experiments. This was an opportunity to show "What if?" as well as an educational experience for us. I think everyone walked away with a new understanding about how to build and a respect and pride for a job well done.

The Lumber Story

Jeff Oldham

WE WANTED TO USE SUSTAINABLE BUILDING MATERIALS for this project, and lumber was one of the primary areas of concern. Living in the Pacific Northwest, we are surrounded by bald mountains that provide a stark display of the desecration of our forests. We are very sensitive to what is going on and wanted to make sure that we did not contribute to bad forestry practices. We tried to use recycled, reclaimed lumber whenever possible, and when this was not usable or available for an application, we would use certified sustainably harvested wood. We were very fortunate that the Institute for Sustainable Forestry set up one of the first certified timber harvest plans in California in our area in time for this project, and they coordinated the certification, logging, and purchase of the wood for the Solar Living Center.

Because the sustainable forestry industry in still in its infancy in this region, it was necessary to buy logs directly off the log deck from the logging operation, rather than through a supplier. After purchasing the logs, we were responsible for getting them delivered to the mill, milled to our specifications, delivered to the Standard Structures factory to be made into glu-lams for the arched roof, and then delivered to the Solar Living Center site. Very early in the bid stage of the project, we hit a snag concerning the availability of this lumber. The loggers were ready to move on to other areas, and we either needed to claim some wood or not.

Ed Winkelmann of North Coast Structures offered to take responsibility for the lumber, if we assured him that we would pay for it if the contract was not consummated. We agreed, and Ed extended himself to purchase the lumber. He talked with the Institute of Sustainable Forestry, trying to understand "how many logs does a guy buy to get so many board-feet of lumber?" These framing contractors had never purchased lumber in this way before. They took the information given them to the best of everybody's knowledge and purchased accordingly.

When the lumber was milled and graded, the culls were quite a bit more than expected. As a matter of fact, they approached 50 percent. We remilled to achieve a better grade and saved a lot of wood, but still came up short. The logging operation had already shut down, so we had to buy more lumber elsewhere. We went to Berry's Saw Mill in Cazadero. Berry is not certified as a sustainable forester, but practices most of the principles of sustainable forestry. We were able to buy the makeup batch that we needed, which amounted to a couple of units of lumber.

Ed was left holding the bag for a few thousand dollars for the additional lumber. Since he was doing Real Goods an enormous favor, taking the responsibility for purchasing the lumber before receiving a contract, Tom Myers and I felt that we should share the responsibility with Ed. So we each chipped in $1,000.

The moral of the story is, use sustainable lumber, but try to buy a finish-milled product. Buying logs in the forest carries its risks. The industry is not mature enough yet in our area to afford that luxury, but if the market maintains demand for such an end product, then supply should soon develop. We also found that the premium on SHL was about 30 percent, but this premium translated to less than 2 percent of the project at large. I feel that 2 percent is an extremely small price to pay, a bargain in fact, to be supporting sustainable forestry practices, and to help the market mature.

One of the forgotten tenets of sustainability seems to be that, in order to maintain a system, the participants must willingly engage in its processes. Probably the best way to do that is to make it fun. The collaborative design/construction team of the Solar Living Center almost always remembered this goal. Below, Adam and Norm Bourassa work with a model during "a particularly fun period of Heliodon testing."

Goal 4. Involve Everyone and Have Fun

David: My greatest joy through the entire design and construction of the building was having a role not unlike that of a team captain. I was there primarily to synthesize and coordinate all of the professionals, building systems, and subcontractors; to facilitate communication and resolve differences. Perhaps being the oldest of twelve children prepared me well for such a position, but in any event I had great fun in it. Credit enough cannot be given to John Schaeffer and Real Goods for pushing us as much as we pushed them in setting and achieving the goals of this project. In ancient as well as recent history, many have suggested that the process is just as important as the product. This project is testimony that these goals are not mutually exclusive; that in fact, they are mutually beneficial.

Adam: My involvement was largely during schematic design, and for most of the process I was directly involved only with David and Sim. This was a tremendously fun period of creative explorations, model construction, and empirical testing. But due to our physical distance from the client, my exposure to the rest of the participants in the project was somewhat limited.

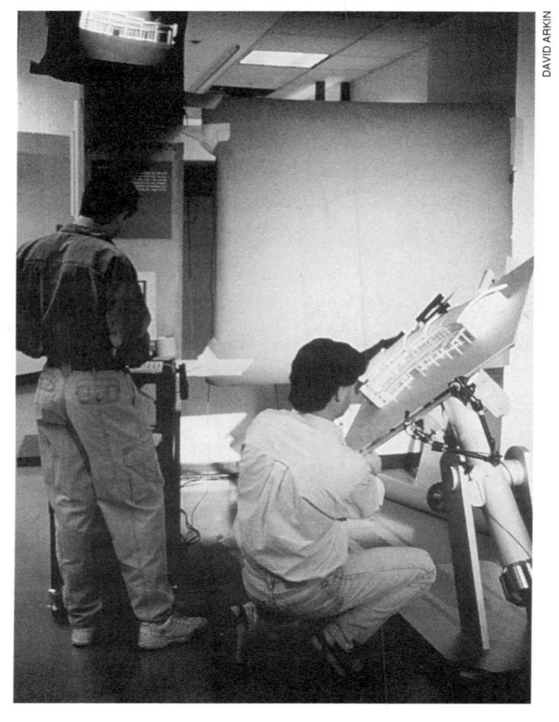

DAVID ARKIN

At one point during schematic design—coincidentally during a particularly fun period of Heliodon testing—we got wind that our proposed curved building was deemed overly expensive, and that it was thought that perhaps we should develop a simpler approach. I remember Sim and I looking at the latest round of glorious slides and video recordings depicting the inside of our curved building under various sky conditions, and he turned to me and said, "That's it. We're bringing all of this stuff up there right away and showing them why this building is worth having!" Sure enough, a meeting was scheduled for the next week, and we went loaded with a multimedia presentation. As I entered the meeting room full of board members, there was a distinct air of tension as we seemed to be at a potential impasse with the future of the design. This atmosphere was quite contrary to what I had heard about our relationship with the client. Nevertheless, this was my first impression of Real Goods. We quickly proceeded with our presentation. As I started the video, I became completely absorbed in my description of the building. I went through countless slides and solar studies, and was so fired up about the project that I lost all track of how long I had been speaking. At the conclusion, the lights came on and there was nothing but silence. I immediately had a horrifying thought that I had just killed the project with my overzealousness, when John Schaeffer turned his chair around to the rest of us and said, "Well, it looks like we're going to have to find a way to pay for this thing!"

From this point, the atmosphere completely changed and I had my first sense of how involved everybody really was with this project. It was immediately fun again. I think this can only happen when everyone is involved and pulling for a common vision. And although I'm sure everyone has their share of headache stories from this project, it really has been a fun process.

Bruce: We stopped keeping track, fairly early, of who had which bright idea, and the spirit of innovation and fun was always with us.

One day I was walking across the site in the blistering September sun, having just addressed a myriad of framing problems. We were in the thick of actually building a structure that curves and wanders in every conceivable line, using mostly unconventional materials, and it was not easy. As we walked back to the construction office, Tom Myers spontaneously put his arm around my shoulder and said, "Wow! I'd forgotten that building is *fun*!"

When no one tries too hard to claim credit for the good stuff, and no one is too willing to start laying blame for the bad stuff, extraordinary things can happen. Like, well, having fun.

Jeff: From the beginning, when we chose to involve all of Real Goods' employees in this project, we realized the wealth of ideas and experience contained in their input. We wanted to give them a sense of involvement and ownership so that they would be proud, excited, and supportive during the development. Their input was solicited for site and design team selection. We identified a few sites along the Highway 101 corridor that would be acceptable for us to build on. We asked the employees to give us their opinions about the sites and vote for the one they believed would suit us best. At the same time, John circulated his six-page vision statement for employee input, then revised and recirculated it for additional comments. The employees had a couple of

DAVID ARKIN

Constructing a building with both a curved plan and roof took as much head-scratching as nail-pounding. Here, contractor Tom Myers (right) confers with Stacey and Ira of the North Coast Structures crew.

weeks to review, comment, and vote on the presentations from the five different architectural firms who submitted designs to the competition.

We chose Sim Van der Ryn and Associates, had them finalize the master plan, and quickly moved on to developing a scale model of the entire site. We wanted this model to be a detailed image of how the completed Solar Living Center would look. The model was showcased in our temporary Hopland store. We invited the community to come and offer their input. The model helped everyone visualize the project and created excitement and community ownership. We released some publications into the Hopland area. We made presentations at Public Utility District and Chamber of Commerce meetings. We wanted to involve the community and enlist their support. We were very happy to gain the support of Hopland, and Hopland was excited to have Real Goods become a part of the community and welcomed us with open arms and warm hearts.

Throughout the whole process, we involved our customers and shareholders. We constantly talked up the project and printed running progress reports in all of our catalogs and publications. We solicited input through all stages of the project. We talked about our vision for the project at shareholder's meetings, soliciting their ideas, and also their junk merchandise to displace concrete in the footings. We gave shareholders two tours of the site, one in the beginning "dust bowl" phase and again at the 1996 shareholders' meeting, showing them their site at completion. Truly a grand opening!

I would say my biggest regret and largest mistake was not involving the store staff as much as we should have. I remember when Nancy Hensley, the store manager, joined David and me for lunch while we were going over some details, frankly pretty far into the project. Nancy looked at the plans and said, "Wow, this is cool. I've never seen these before." David and I looked at each other, our jaws dropped, and we both simultaneously realized that we'd made the biggest error we could have made. Fortunately, with dumb, blind luck (and perhaps a bit of good planning), we had pretty much hit the mark of what Nancy wanted. There were some things she wanted changed; unfortunately, it was too late to change one or two of those. The primary problem was that we really did not consider foul weather conditions in planning access between the storage building and the store.

My number one goal on future projects will be to keep the principals more involved, and to extend the definition of principals beyond the owner to include those who are most intimately affected by the project. The best ideas will come from those who will be living with the final project; they know what works. They are the ones we need to make happy. If we can give them an atmosphere that is comfortable and stimulates their imagination and creativity, then we have created a successful marriage of form and function.

Goal 5. Measure (and Celebrate) Our Successes and Failures

David: All natural systems employ feedback mechanisms that continuously tune and refine their responses to changing conditions. This metaphor is appropriate in understanding both the design process and the ongoing operation of a building.

In design, we paid great attention to everything at and near our site, including the climate, culture, production and availability of materials, and so on. This information became the launching point of a design process that revisited each of these elements in turn, as well as Real Goods' needs and desires.

This continued through construction, when we were able to make changes as opportunities presented themselves. Using Fetzer's PISE™ instead of stucco on the straw bale walls was one of these opportunities. Adding a skylight to house Peter Erskine's *Secrets of the Sun* solar calendar was another.

During construction, Tim Kennedy kept careful logs of the miles traveled by all the vehicles arriving at the site, including the pickup trucks of the contractors and subs. North Coast Structures, aware of these concerns, encouraged their crew to carpool to the site (one carpenter who lived in Oakland, over one hundred miles away, camped inside the Kids' Cave tunnel). With this information, we can total the embodied energy in our building in comparison to typical highway commercial buildings. We can also compare life-cycle energy use and determine at what point the energy used in operating the building exceeds the energy used to build it. In typical buildings, this point is reached after three to five years. At the rate we are using energy, this point won't be reached at the SLC for over dozens of years (due, of course, to the low energy usage, and not to any increase in embodied construction energy). As the publication *Environmental Building News* has noted, small additional expenditures for greater energy efficiency quickly pay for themselves and keep paying back. The SLC is testimony to the logic of this sort of thinking.

As the building moves through its first year, the store staff has taken note of the performance of the building relative to their interaction. They lower the hemp awnings on hot fall days when the low sun angle could overheat the showroom. They open the high clerestory windows on summer nights to flush the heat out of the building, but at some point late in the fall, leave them closed to hold in the heat. The showroom requires the awareness of its users in order to remain comfortable, and in doing so does not deny them this opportunity. Rather, they are finding that this vigilance heightens their awareness of the nature around all of us at all times. This is, perhaps, the true benefit of climate-responsive architecture, in how it can transform our lives.

NAME: Burkhardt COMPANY: Skillful Means Builders

Weekly Resource Monitoring Form

Due to the nature of this project we must monitor and be aware of all the "hidden" resource costs of this building. This form is to assist you in monitoring your consumption and to identify sources of waste. I will try to look over your shoulder to help out but if you have any questions please ask.
Tim Kennedy, asst. project mngr.

Personal commute or equipment use:

DATE	# People	MPG	Miles Traveled or Total gallons	Fuel Type	Comments:
8/28	2	18	50	UNLD	Ross, cy
8/28	1	25	10		Becky
8/29	2	18	50		Ross, cy
8/29	1	25	10		Becky
8/29	1	24	55		Ben
8/30	1	18	50		Ross
8/30	2	20	50		Peter, cy
8/30	1	25	10		Becky
8/30	1	22	55		Ben
8/31	1	18	50		Ross
8/31	1	20	50		Peter

DAVID ARKIN

Real Goods maintained a log of the miles traveled by all the vehicles arriving at the construction site in order to calculate the total embodied energy in the building and determine when the energy used in operating the building exceeds that used to build it. A typical commercial building reaches this point in three to five years. Due to its exceptionally low energy usage, the Solar Living Center won't exceed its (also low) embodied construction energy cost for dozens of years. Monitoring of the building's performance provides useful feedback, allowing improvement and offering lessons for others engaging in ecological design.

Adam: In the spring of 1995, when the building was largely designed but not yet under construction, I departed the country to teach for a year at a university in England. In some ways this was rather frustrating in that I did not get to witness any of the construction process (and I am still begging my colleagues for photographs of the process). But one of the benefits of my absence was that upon my return—timed perfectly to attend the grand opening—I experienced the full power of the building with no buildup. And although I remember one of my first thoughts as I walked toward the building was, "Wow, it sure looks small!" I was truly thrilled when I was finally able to step inside.

I knew this space so well . . . a space I had modeled perhaps five separate times in various detail. And each of those times, I had peered into the building model through a tiny hole and wished I could stand inside for just one minute to really evaluate whatever strategy I was currently trying to resolve. I must say, finally realizing this wish was a powerful experience.

Is the building a success? According to the client and the visitors, undoubtedly yes, and this certainly brings me great joy. The occupants seem to be comfortable and happy to be in the building; it meets their needs appropriately and appears to be using a minimum of fossil fuels. I continue to remain curious about the detailed performance of our daylighting and passive conditioning strategies.

In October of 1996, a class in "Passive Cooling" led by Gail Brager from UC-Berkeley embarked on a one-month study of the Solar Living Center. In order to gauge the building's daylighting and thermal performance, three students (Graham Carter, Jeff Hou, and Prerna Jain) monitored various aspects of the SLC for ten days. Although the duration of the monitoring period was limited, it did occur during an unusually warm period and revealed a few noteworthy findings.

Their primary findings concerned the effectiveness of the ventilation and thermal mass strategies. Data indicates that the clerestories are successful at inducing cross-ventilation, and thermal stratification sensors show interior stack effect to account for a 5.4 to 14.4 degree Fahrenheit temperature gradient between occupant level and ceiling level. Temperature probes in the straw bale walls indicate they are performing not only as good insulators but additionally as thermal mass, aiding in diurnal thermal coasting.

The group also conducted a series of modeling exercises to examine whole building energy performance and relative humidities. Using the program CALPAS3, the team compared the SLC to a standard construction building of the same configuration. They found the SLC to consume roughly one-fifth the energy of the standard, characterizing the SLC as a low-low energy building. Perhaps their most interesting findings concerned the effectiveness of the evaporative coolers. Perplexed that the staff was not using the coolers even during periods when they felt uncomfortably warm, the group learned that running the coolers made the interior feel muggy. Subsequent analysis showed that even though the external climate is generally relatively dry (30 percent humidity), when occupant transpiration is taken into account interior humidity can climb to over 50 percent. Analysis showed that if all five evaporative coolers are run simultaneously, relative humidities can approach 80 percent! Clearly, there is a lesson here about such cooling even in dry climates.

Overall, the building seems to be performing well, and thankfully, much as we had anticipated. But I feel it is vitally important that we be open about any shortcomings in the building's performance. Without full disclosure of issues and features that didn't succeed, people are destined to repeat our mistakes and nothing will have been learned.

Bruce: The whole dern project was and is a huge, unqualified success. So there.

The biggest "failing," it seems to me, is in the system within which we were working. The letter and enforcement of building codes grow increasingly burdensome as time goes by, but I'm not sure the public is getting appreciably better or safer buildings as a result—though they are definitely more expensive buildings. And we have also become accustomed to using entirely manufactured materials for everything in the building, from foundation to roof to wall surfaces to doorknobs. The idea of using local, handmade, unprocessed, or waste materials (such as fly ash, straw bales, earth, hand carvings) is generally viewed askance by the construction industry. To some extent the conservatism is warranted, for we do have to be certain about life safety in every sense of the word.

But it is worth pointing out that structures all over the world of stone, earth, and straw (and other plant fibers) have been around for decades or even centuries, but have never met any code requirements (and still wouldn't!). It is my personal hope that the presence of those solid old buildings—and the SLC—will help loosen the entrenched conservatism of the building, lending, and insurance industries so that environmentally benign architecture can become the norm, not the aberration.

Jeff: Visitor feedback to the project has been extraordinary. The tours are filled with people who are just shaking their heads in awe. People find it easy to absorb, and addictive. Everybody goes home having learned something that they can begin to apply in their own lives and homes. In that respect, I think it is an enormous success. Real Goods has always said that "knowledge is our most important product." If someone can simply visit this site and come away with a bit of knowledge that they didn't have when they arrived, then all of our jobs were done well. Indeed, I think that is what the outcome indicates, that we really did produce a site that is conducive to learning, makes understanding simple, and demonstrates solar living in a visible and accessible way.

The staff is truly excited about working at the site. They look forward to arriving at work in this building. Certainly, it would be hard to say that most people look forward to getting to work, but I would have to say that our staff look forward to spending their day at the Solar Living Center. If you have got to work somewhere, I have never visited a place that would be more desirable than this place. The employees are very proud of their building, and they feel deeply involved with it. The design requires the interaction of the staff to maximize its potential. They have to open and close doors, windows, and shutters at the proper times to ventilate the building as needed. They turn the lights off and on when it is required (except for the main lighting, which is daylight dimmed). The staff is happy to do all these things; in fact, they prefer to do it themselves. All too often in automated, so-called "smart buildings," we see the controls and sensors overridden by the staff, because they don't quite meet their demands. Obviously, a computer can't guess their comfort level and lighting requirements. At the SLC, we feel that people need to interact with the building so that it can suit their needs, and they can take part in the process and be part of the organism of the building itself.

The Collaborative Flow

David: You have just heard four different voices discussing the same project from four different perspectives. The many areas of achievement of the Solar Living Center would not have been possible by any one individual's effort. Collaboration and teamwork are key to integrated ecological design. As is often the case with construction or any other sort of project, close friendships develop in the pursuit of a common goal. This certainly happened during the building of the Solar Living Center, and the joint authorship of this chapter has been a wonderful reunion for the four of us.

A final thought is the acknowledgment of the truth of Sim's axiom, "Form follows flow," which is his ecological twist on late-nineteenth-century American architect Louis Sullivan's well-known slogan, "Form follows function." In the case of the SLC, the flow was more than merely energy and matter; it was also the design process and interactions within the team. By constantly responding to each other, to the site, and to the design, each of us became part of a building process that in retrospect felt very natural. This same character—which is evident in the form of the finished building—is very much, we believe, the result of this collaborative flow.

JACK HOWELL

A relative newcomer to Real Goods, **Mark Winkler** is the director of the Solar Living Center. His task is to provide the education and hospitality to ensure the fulfillment of visitors to the site.

CHAPTER 7

Making the Most of Your Visit

Mark Winkler

In the end, we will conserve only what we love, we will love only what we understand, we will understand only what we are taught.—*Lao-Tzu*

WHEN IT COMES TO IMPROVING THE QUALITY OF LIFE, there is no future in being shy. That's why Real Goods chose to build the Solar Living Center next to a busy highway. We also chose landscape design and architecture with striking visual appeal and placed our solar arrays and wind generator in plain view. That way, anyone who is looking for us will find us, but more importantly, people who are not looking for us will find us. We want people to feel curious enough to turn in at our front gate, especially if they have never heard of Real Goods. After all, we do feel a sense of urgency in our effort to encourage an ever-widening circle of people to consider renewable energy and other healthy choices. Thousands of people are visiting and many share their appreciation of the Solar Living Center with us. It may be the sight of a row of solar panels tracking the sun, the unusual shape of our building with its wall of south-facing windows, or a glimpse of our ponds and gardens. I suppose much of the credit for making people curious could go to our collection of five car bodies, each of which sports its own tree. Love 'em or hate 'em, they do give people pause. Be they cliché, eyesore, or inspiration, they are at least an aggressive enough image that people give thought and respond. My favorite observation came from the man who noted that while California's redwood region is known for having the "drive-through tree" it was nice to finally see the "grow-through car."

LAND & PLACE

Please stop if you are ever in the neighborhood. When you do, we hope you will have some time to spend. Since there aren't a lot of people who actually live in Hopland, many of our visitors have been zooming along at high speed for at least an hour or two. We hope to provide some refreshment from the hurrying mind-set. The first thing you'll notice is that rather than choosing fossil-fuel–based asphalt for our driveway and parking lot, we have gravel. Please feel free to go slow and to think of our roundabout driveway as a country road. Observe the amazing Willow Dome on your left; scan for the exotic leaping jackrabbits! Since the driveway makes a very short country road, by the time you've changed your pace, you'll have reached the parking lot. Note that there are two charging stations available for electric vehicles. So far, they aren't getting much use, but we look forward to the day when two is not enough. If it's hot out, you might like to try standing under the Agave Cooling Tower near the entrance, which emits a fine mist and offers a drinking fountain. It also serves as a good place to socialize and meet your fellow travelers. The restrooms are just up the hill, if that's the first order of business, and the bonus is that they answer the riddle, What has five toilets, but two hundred and twenty-four toilet tank lids?. . . Ah, the joys of recycling!

A grove of "grow-through cars," a gravel (not asphalt) driveway and parking lot, and two electric-vehicle charging stations announce to arriving visitors that the Solar Living Center is definitively not about fossil fuel consumption.

The welcome sign outlines a few points of interest, including directions to the areas for dog walking and for smoking. Thus far, no other special interest groups have lobbied for their own spaces, benches, or hydrants, but we stand ready to

LAND & PLACE

Reconnoiter under the Agave Cooling Tower while you decide what to do first. The landscape soothes, protects, inspires, and teaches visitors as well as those who work here.

respond when the need is clear. You may want to make your way up to the store immediately, which is both understandable and to be applauded. However, there may be other factors to consider. Do the kids need to exercise first? Do the adults? Perhaps a tour, to get a better feel for the place? If you decide to have a look around the grounds first, there are a few ways to approach the prospect. We offer guided tours daily; the times are posted near the welcome sign. If you missed the tour, you may strike out on your own by using the self-guided tour brochure available at the entrance and in the store. Roaming, pausing, reading, and relaxing are all encouraged, and if you're here when fruit is ripe, tasting is just fine too. Another option is to rent one or more of the audio tours that are available in the store and use them to gain insight into the creation and design of the Solar Living Center.

In addition to highlighting the landscape design, architecture, and power system, a tour of the grounds may also bring you into contact with a bit of nature. The combination of a seasonal stream to our north, open fields to the east, a vineyard to the south, and the water features and ponds on our property, has proven to be quite attrac-

Guided tours are offered daily to help visitors gain insight into the design and function of the Solar Living Center. Grown-ups may find that they learn as much in the children's play area as their kids do about the cycles of the solar year, the benefits of renewable energy, and how to keep cool in the summer sun.

tive to wildlife from the surrounding area and to both resident and migrating birds. Even much of the existing aquatic life in our waterways came to us spontaneously, as bullfrogs and bluegill arrived in the floodwaters we experienced during the first winter that the ponds were in place. It is pleasant indeed to arrive in the morning and see a great blue heron and a great egret striking tai chi poses as they hunt in the reeds where the tadpoles are thick. A green heron spent the whole month of August with us, patrolling the shores of the ponds and up the streambed to the Oasis Fountain in front of the store. I've also noticed that the tadpoles attract the elusive ten-year-old-bicycling-Hoplanders, who, when approached in a nonthreatening manner, turn out to be open to communication about interspecies activities. And since the bullfrogs are invaders here, actively eating everything that fits in their very large mouths, I'm always happy to see the herons feeding. The ponds have also drawn a belted kingfisher and many swallows, which gather mud for nests in the spring and, thankfully, eat lots of insects.

In my first year here, I've already seen a variety of raptors as well. These welcome visitors have included one bald eagle, a kestrel, a Swainson's hawk, a red-shouldered hawk, and the occasional red-tailed hawk. There is also a wonderful pair of white-tailed kites, who

Welcome to Real Goods' Solar Living Center! We hope you enjoy your visit and are inspired to include the use of solar power and other sustainable practices in your daily life. This brochure will lead you on a stroll around our buildings and gardens. For more in-depth information, please inquire in the store.

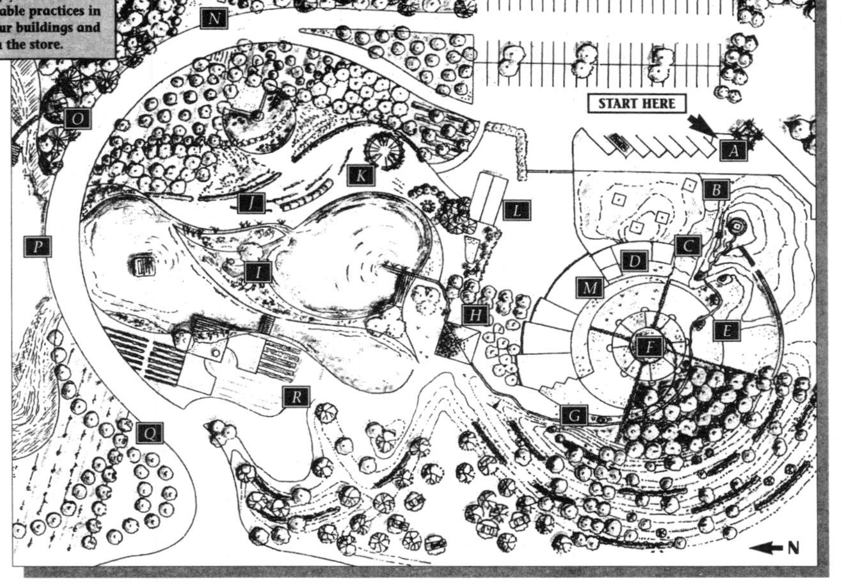

AGAVE COOLING TOWER
You are standing in the flood plain of Feliz Creek and the Russian River on land that was, until 1994, a Cal Trans dump site. If you are hot, step under the mist of the Agave Cooling Tower and have a drink of water!

PV KNOLL AND WATER FEATURES
From our high water table, we use solar power to pump 35 gpm into the redwood tank on the hill. The water then flows through a series of features on the property, providing cooling and masking the highway noise as it goes. All power here is provided by sun and wind. Our system consists of a 10kW solar photovoltaic array provided by Siemens Solar and a 3kW wind generator.

RENEWABLE ENERGY CONTROL CENTER
The engine room features our Ananda power center and controllers and Trace Engineering inverters. Our power system allows us to sell our excess power to Pacific Gas and Electric Co. when the sun is shining and buy it back when its not. This provides a net gain for us and allows us to use them as our storage system. The exterior of our building is finished with PISE™, which is pneumatically impacted stabilized earth. This mixture of soil and cement has been sprayed over the straw bale wall beneath (see item M).

THE RESTROOMS
Our restrooms are designed to feature several recycled materials. The countertop contains recycled glass, the Hardie panel cabinets are a mixture of cement and newspaper, and yes, the wainscotting is made of used toilet tank lids!

PLAY AND LEARN AREA
In the play and learn area you are invited to try experiments designed to help you feel how much muscle power it takes to generate electricity, experience the threat of rising oceans due to global warming and play engineer in the sand and water floodway.

OUR AXIS POINT AND SOLAR CALENDAR
The entire Solar Living Center is laid out from this central point. If you turn toward the building, there are great natural acoustics and singing is encouraged! Note the stone pillars on the western berm marking solstice and equinox sunsets.

OLIVE BOSQUE
This grove of Manzanillo and Russian olive provides fruit, scent and shade as a continuation of the oasis atmosphere. The earth berm and plantings are designed to mitigate noise from the highway and serve as part of the circular framework for the central fountain.

J MEDITERRANEAN ORCHARD
This is the Mediterranean climate orchard & chaparral area. It features drought-tolerant plantings such as Jerusalem Sage, Lavender, Santolina, a Feijoa hedge, dwarf olive hedge and numerous bulbs, such as Alstruemeria and Iris, which go dormant after flowering.

I PONDS
The ponds were dug not only as landscape features which serve as storage for irrigation water, but the soil they provided was used to help raise the building site above the flood plain. The ponds have now been naturalized with the arrival, by flood, of perch, bluegill and bullfrogs, and they attract many species of birds.

H BAMBOO PYRAMID
The Bamboo Pyramid is one of several shade structures designed of living plants, in this case Timber Bamboo, which will be pruned annually in the shape and proportion of the Cheops pyramid of Egypt.

K HOPS TIPI
As a circular shade structure with living walls and bench, this over-sized Tipi, shaded by hops and other vines, provides a "room outside". To the south, on the slope below the storage building, is a small grove of Dawn Redwood, the only deciduous cousin of our native Coast Redwood.

L THE PARKING AREA
We chose a gravel parking lot to avoid the embodied energy in a fossil fuel based asphalt lot. The reeds and grasses in the central marsh area act as "bioremediation" to remove heavy metals and pollutants which drain in from the parking lot.

"We shape our buildings and thereafter they shape us."
—Winston Churchill

Please feel free to stroll the grounds. Explore our buildings and enjoy yourselves! For more complete information, please consider taking one of our tours. Thanks for visiting the Solar Living Center.

R KITCHEN GARDEN
Espaliered Apples, Asian Pears and Cherries are some of the perennial features of this intensive production garden. Cut flowers and vegetables will serve our future bed-and-breakfast, planned to overlook the ponds nearby.

Q NUT COPSE
The nut copse, with various species of delicious nuts and blueberries, is just one manifestation of our landscape design as a demonstration of the permaculture approach to a development where the great majority of plantings provide useful food, herb, or fiber.

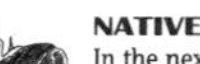

P NATIVE WETLANDS
In the next phase of our landscaping, we will restore a wetland area along the northern edge of our property. This will create an excellent new habitat for wildlife, particularly birds, and provide us with further opportunity for nature study as part of our ongoing education program.

O WILLOW DOME
Another example of our living structures is the Willow Dome, which at the age of three years will be woven into an arching shade structure. becoming a virtual upside-down willow basket measuring thirty feet across!

N NORTHERN FOREST
The northeastern corner of the property represents the northern latitudes with its evergreen trees, coastal and Sierra redwoods, and cedars. Looking back to the southwest, Duncan Peak dominates the horizon as our most prominent landmark.

At this point, you may stop if you wish and visit the store, or continue on the walk around the perimeter.

M BUILDING DESIGN
Our building is designed to take full advantage of light and heat from the sun. The walls are made of rice straw bales covered with a mixture of soil and cement which creates a wall with an R-67 insulation factor. The building features a high-performance Hypolon rubber roof, 600 tons of thermal mass for temperature control, and beautiful use of natural daylight throughout. Feel free to ask our staff to explain the workings of the building and our Rainbow Sundial, where you can bathe in solar rainbow!

Printed on recycled paper with soy-based ink

nest nearby and are reliably seen hovering and diving for prey along the railroad tracks to the east. Many underappreciated turkey vultures hang around, cleaning up roadkills along the highway. My favorite memory of the Solar Living Center must be the morning this winter when I arrived as the early sun was just growing strong enough to bring our tracking arrays of solar panels into place facing east. A turkey vulture was sitting on a nearby fencepost with its black wings spread wide to absorb the sun's warmth, angled identically with the panels. It was a moment of visual poetry that spoke volumes about balance and reminded me of what I like about this place. It also made me laugh, because it looked so staged, like we'd brought him in from the bird actor's guild. Even for a guy who gets nervous when anything cosmic comes up in conversation, it was a nice little moment. Just the kind I hope you might have here, and it gives me cause to think about the wisdom of building business places that are also living places that welcome nature inside.

Now let's assume you've had a nice time out by the ponds and you're ready to head for the building. If you have children with you, be prepared for a pleasant (and potentially educational) delay at the sand-and-water play area near the Oasis Fountain. It is hard even for grown-up kids to pass it by, especially if the weather is warm. Once you are in the building, if the sun is out you can check solar time by locating the colorful image cast by our Rainbow Sundial. If the rainbow glows in the western half of the building, it is still true morning; if it is in the eastern half, it is afternoon. At solar noon, when the Sun reaches its zenith, the image falls exactly on the true north-south line that runs in the front door,

With water restored to this once-fruitful, then barren landscape, nature began to take over in repopulating its niches. The ponds have attracted native wildlife, including the bluegill swept in with the floods. Great blue herons, belted kingfishers, and even a bald eagle come to feed on the fish and amphibians. Other raptors hunt the smaller birds and animals who make the reclaimed landscape their home.

BAILE OAKES

through the store, and out the back. If you brought your camera, the wash of rainbow light makes for some great photographs. You'll also want to inspect the "truth window" in the southeast corner of the store, with its view into the inner workings of our straw bale walls, although for the kids it may require a revamping of the story of the Big Bad Wolf. A favorite interior view of mine is to stand at the western wall and gaze back along the gracefully stepped and curving ceiling.

If you've come for information, we have a very resourceful staff and a library filled with excellent books which will help with both the "how-to" and may-be even the "why-to" of solar living. There is also always at least one technician on duty to assist you in understanding the products and options of renewable energy systems. In fact, our company maintains an entire Renewable Energy department that is just a phone call away if you need advice about saving or creating energy. Another neat trick, if you're social by nature, is to engage other visitors in conversation. I'm continually delighted by the knowledgeable and friendly people I meet on our tours. I'mcertain I've learned more than I've shared, at it is always uplifting to hear about a permaculture project in Australia, solar architecture in Turkey, or a bird sanctuary in Missouri. There's a distinct lack of sermonizing going on, as most people are having a good time pursuing what they clearly see as the sane approach to living, and they are happy to share what they know with anyone who's interested.

LAND & PLACE

Doom and drudgery it is not, and we may even be in danger of forming an affirmation program and taking to the road with a touring company of "Up With Green People." Anyway, it beats getting depressed over the state of the world and it's nice to know that lots of people are doing what they can. Are we going to be able to pull off this evolution/revolution in human behavior fast enough to truly deserve the best seats on Earth? Here's hoping!

When it is time to go, you may want a few insider tips about the surrounding environs, and our

Inside the store, find a library well-stocked with information on the "hows" and "whys" of solar living; products designed to help you conserve energy, create energy using renewable sources (including human power), and enjoy the energy you've gained; and a staff brimming with enthusiasm and advice.

staff would be happy to help. The area in and around Hopland has lots to offer, in a small-town kind of way. There are several good places to eat, with not a single fast-food franchise in sight. There is a historic hotel and numerous excellent wineries where you would be more than welcome. Hopland also has its own premium brewery and pub, and as of this writing, weekend excursion rail service has been reestablished to our little town. Just be careful crossing the street and don't try to make a left turn from the side street next to the hotel. It is a busy highway that runs through town and people tend to go way too fast. So if you're heading out, we hope you'll feel like taking a deep breath, easing through town, and giving the slow lane a try.

We also hope you'll want to come back again, as we fully expect that who we are and what we can do here will continue to evolve as we develop and balance our Solar Living Center. The possibilities may not be endless, but they sure appear to be wide open.

As you leave the Solar Living Center, notice that even the exit sign is illuminated by solar-powered compact fluorescent lights.

The Country Store of the Future

Nancy Hensley

Susan drives in under the Country Store of the Future sign to begin her day. When I asked her what it's like for her to work at the Solar Living Center, she immediately said, "it's like being at a party without the alcohol and hors d'oeuvres."

> Watch, look at the faces of these people coming up the walkway. They're smiling. People are always telling us how beautiful it is here. I feel fortunate to have been here for the 'birthing' of the store, to watch it grow. Being here helps us to feel a part of the changing seasons because we have nature all around us.

Thom coasts into work on his bicycle. His thoughts about working at the Solar Living Center opened my eyes even though I have been here with him for a year.

> It reminds me of when I was a kid in Florida and houses were very manual; they were built with common sense. You live with the building, opening windows and closing doors, paying attention to your environment instead of flipping a switch and consuming tons of electricity to stay comfortable. We interact with the building to tame the elements. We are on friendly terms with the elements here, actually. Without the heat outside, the building would get too humid. We watch the temperature of the walls, the floor, and the people around us. If they are hot, we are going to be hot, so we react. We open up the windows and doors to flush out the warm, stale air, then close them to let the walls and floor cool us down again. We might need to turn on a fan at night to draw more cool air from outside. We are becoming sensitive again to the things around us. The plantings and water in the landscape reduce the stress in our lives. Something about them helps us feel safe and serene. I'm not sure why, maybe it's negative ions. But anything clean and pretty makes your spirit rise. Even the texture of the building adds to the beauty around us. People pull off the highway ready for an adventure, and the place just seems to encourage that. They are encouraged to reach up and attain their goals.

As he said that, we both looked up and noticed Duncan Peak towering over us.

The place actually makes the business run more smoothly, because the customers are in the same elements of beauty and balance that we are. Once they get to the cash registers, they feel good. Something has happened to them. By the time they get to the sales desk, they are at ease, grateful.

Stephen is enthusiasm embodied.

It is a wonderful privilege to work with the living presence of the Solar Living Center around us. We have brought an entire, lush, verdant oasis microclimate to surround the building we work in. And it is still in its infancy! This surrounding has an impact on my experience inside the building. As I work inside the amazingly cool store, I am always aware of the life around me. My wonder at the passive solar aspects of the building only grows with the day-to-day tasks of opening and closing the various apertures in the room. I cannot think of anything that I could want out of the building that the designers didn't already think of.

Aaron worked at a Chevron station before he came to Real Goods. I asked him what it was like working with the customers who come to visit us.

I'm not really comfortable calling them customers. To me, they are people coming from all over the world to their Mecca. They are the learned and the students. They are highly motivated and very conscious. I like to think that something happens to everyone who passes through the front gates. They gain a sense of inspiration and beauty from being here. Being here certainly has had a tremendous effect on me! I have met so many incredible people

Nancy Hensley was working at the local food co-op when John Schaeffer told her he needed help. John was running Real Goods out of his garage with five other people, two computers, and two telephone lines. Since September of 1989, Nancy has worked at Real Goods as a Telephone Sales Representative, Customer Service Agent, Warehouse Packer, Receptionist, Special Events Coordinator, first Dean of the Institute of Solar Living, and Retail Division Manager. She has moved the store three times, and is presently the Solar Living Center Store Manager.

and I love the two-way exchanges that happen. It's grass roots and it's powerful. There is a very strong feeling of thinking globally and acting locally. People are looking for ways to create new traditions. They are thinking about how excessive power consumption may affect future generations. It is so nice to see people coming back again, still walking to the beat of their own drum, but feeling a bit more in harmony with the world. No, they aren't customers—they are extended family.

Bill has been working for Real Goods almost since the beginning in Willits. Someone he met at the Solar Living Center told him that there were no good jobs around. Bill responded in his warm Arkansas drawl, "Well, I've gotta good job." The other guy's reaction was, "But being in your position, teaching people about all of this is like being a rock star." Bill couldn't agree more.

It's like being chained to a tree but it pays better. It's the same message we had when we were protesting but we are making a living at the same time. I get to talk about it all day. I love it.

People appreciate this place maybe even more than we expected. Visitors come here expecting us to be able to answer just about any question; they are looking for instruction. When we give tours, we are listened to. It's great to be part of an organization where that happens. It pushes us to keep on top of the learning curve. It keeps us sharp and fresh and that suits me just fine. If I were a millionaire, I'd still want to be here teaching. People are starting to see that the only viable solution to the world's energy production problem is to re-individualize power production. I can't imagine anything I'd rather be doing.

Everyone depends on **Doug**. He always has the answers we need.

I like being surrounded by natural daylighting in a cool place. When it's 100 degrees outside, I enjoy assuring people that we don't have air conditioning. We only marginally need to turn on two small fans at night to vent the building, or to make a fire in the wood heater in the winter to take the chill off. This is a wonderful place to work. I love to watch the kids playing, or to grab a couple of artichokes from the garden on the way home from a hard day at work.

As you can see, this place in the sun attracts incredible people. I could never have imagained how much information would be traversing through here when I first saw the raw property. But I think that is its purpose: to gather vital information and give it back to the world. The people who work here feel that purpose so strongly, it's hard to keep them from working too many hours per day. I am honored to be a part of this extraordinary group of pioneers.

After three long years of dreaming, fantasizing, planning, and building the Solar Living Center, the grand opening in June 1996 provided a great sense of accomplishment. What was striking, however, was that it generated much more of a sense of beginning than one of completion. It is clear from the comments from our first summer's visitors that we have generated a sense of hope, optimism, and inspiration as well as a desire to see the Solar Living Center replicated in strategically placed sites around the world.

Chapter 8

John Schaeffer

If you have built castles in the air, your work need not be lost, that is what they should be. Now put foundations under them. —*Henry David Thoreau,* Walden, *1854*

The Solar Living Center is a place of far greater significance than just somewhere to buy a few environmental products. It represents an oasis of possibilities. Our goal was to provide the raw material from which experimentation into cutting-edge products and new ideas of sustainability could take place. When Siemens Solar donated 10 kilowatts of photovoltaics to us, it was with the understanding that they could use the site to test out new modules. As new technologies come off the drawing boards and into the early adoption stage—from electric vehicles, to new storage batteries, to hydrogen power generation, to new ways of gardening—we will be there ready to test and evaluate their efficacy. We want to encourage students of all kinds as well as theorists, visionaries, and inventors to use the Solar Living Center to test their new ideas.

There is much still to be built and developed, even at our first Solar Living Center. In 1998, we hope to begin work on our Education and Learning Center, which will house a renewable energy museum showing the history of solar energy use. It will be home to exploratorium-like interactive displays that will help children and adults learn about new technologies. It will become the classroom for our Institute for Solar Living and a confer-

Praises from Visitors

to the *First* Real Goods Solar Living Center

Dear John Schaeffer: Ever since I attended the grand opening of the Solar Living Center, I've deeply involved myself in the area of ecological design. I consider the event a turning point in my life, and I want to thank you for it. The people, the actions . . . it all felt right, guilt-free, life enhancing, healing. Again, thank you.

Robert Hickling

"We must be the change we wish to see in the world." —Gandhi. He'd be proud!

Molly Tirpak, San Francisco, CA

Where we're all going in our near future!

Desire Beauchemin, Desire, CA

Came all the way to visit the Solar Living Center by train and bus from Louisiana. It took me two days to soak it all in. It was well worth it. Want to come back with friends and family.

Tracy Gallagher, Baton Rouge, LA

Wonderful!! I worship at your shrine—great tour and staff. How *did* you teach the frogs to croak "Real Goods, Real Goods"?

Mary (a lifetime member)

Have heard about what you do and wanted to be further inspired. IT WORKED! This is truly a magical and inspirational place!

Rebecca and Daniel Ullis, Oakland, CA

They said I could go anywhere I wanted for my birthday—I made them bring me here! I love you guys!

Jill Farmer, Eureka, CA

ence center for organizations with complementary missions. It will house our food service outlet and feature organically grown produce from our own agricultural endeavors. In 1998 or 1999, we plan to get started with our 2,500-square-foot Solar Bed and-Breakfast, which will be completely powered by its own solar and wind energy system. The house will feature many of the products from the Real Goods store and catalogs and will allow visitors to experience solar living firsthand, with energy-efficient lighting, superefficient appliances, a composting toilet, natural bedding, a sustainable-living library, and an impressive array of products made from industrial hemp fiber and other ecologically produced materials.

Also in 1999, we plan to restore the wetlands between the road and Feliz Creek. To highlight the fact that 80 percent of the wetlands in America have been destroyed by encroaching development, we want to provide a sanctuary for local wildlife and bog plants with a unique observation platform for children and adults to learn about wetland ecosystems. Around the same time, we plan to build on the southern end of the property to provide additional space for like-minded businesses to demonstrate and sell their wares. It is only through the creative synergies between many businesses working together toward a common goal that we can hope to achieve critical mass to convert the planet to a sustainable future where renewable energy replaces our last remaining sources of fossil fuels.

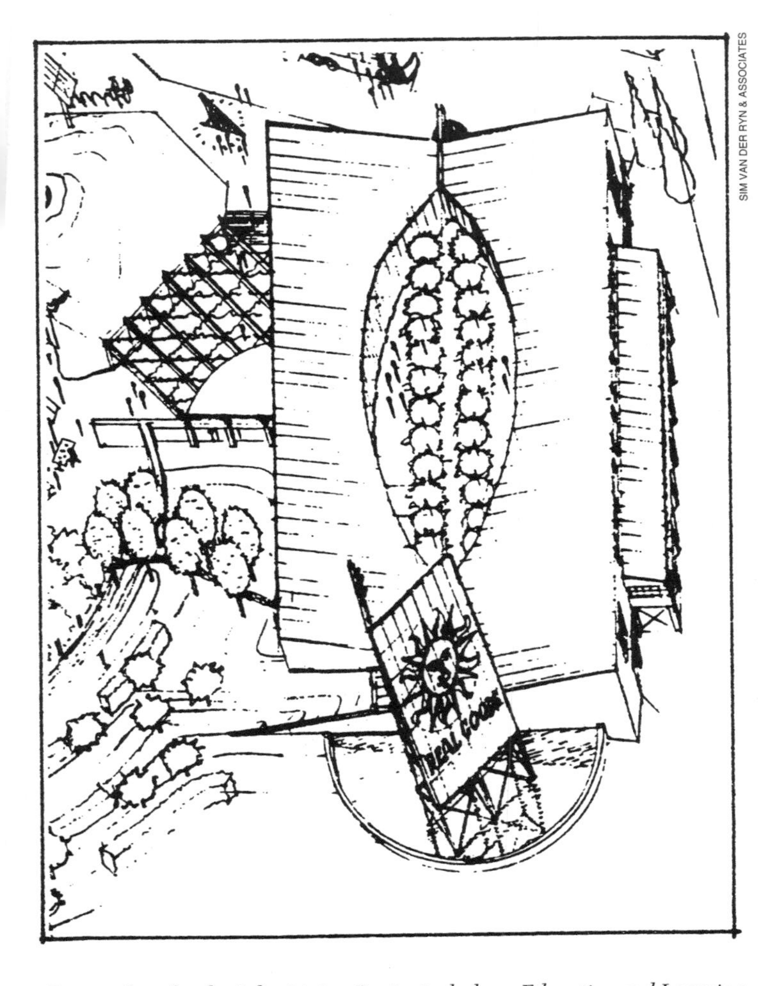

SIM VAN DER RYN & ASSOCIATES

Future plans for the Solar Living Center include an Education and Learning Center, slated to begin development in 1998. It will house a museum and hands-on science center devoted to the history and future of renewable energy. Classrooms for the Institute for Solar Living, a conference room, and a food service outlet featuring produce home-grown in the on-site sustainable agriculture endeavors will share this space. Built and furnished with ecologically sound methods, materials, and appliances, powered by its own renewable energy systems, and processing the wastes its occupants produce, a Solar Bed and Breakfast is planned that will allow visitors to experience solar living firsthand.

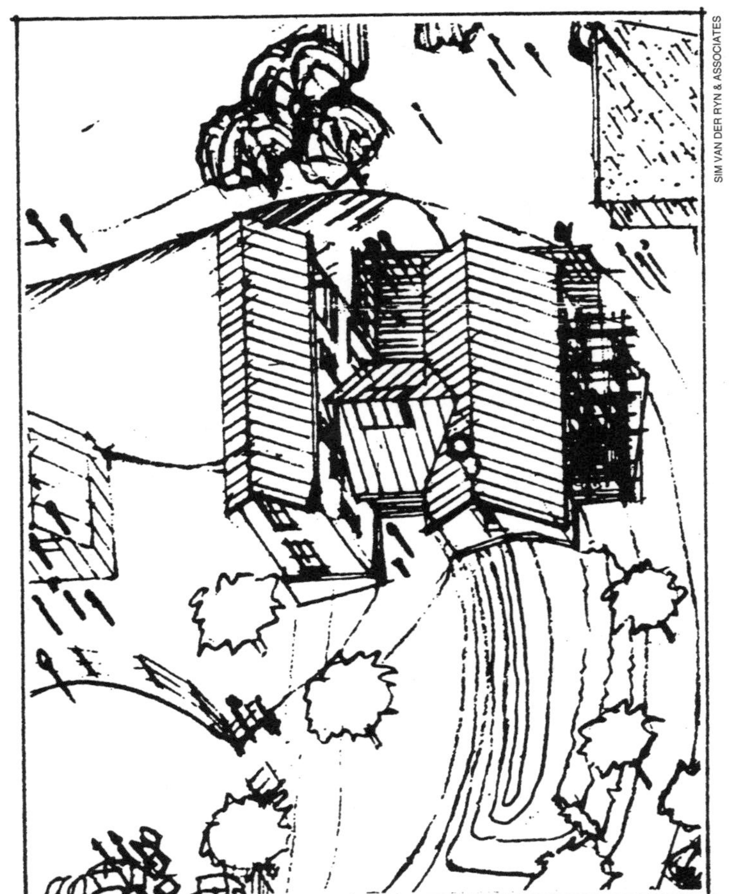

SIM VAN DER RYN & ASSOCIATES

But we mustn't stop here. We need to let a thousand Solar Living Centers bloom around the world. It has become abundantly clear to us with our first SLC that we have awakened a sense of hope, passion, and inspiration in all the visitors who enter our vision. And surprisingly, there are not many places like this in the world. This kind of enthusiasm, promise, and hope needs to be replicated and instilled into people in all walks of life and in all locations around the planet. Our immediate targets for development of additional Solar Living Centers are the Pacific Northwest, the Eastern Seaboard, the Rocky Mountains, the Midwest, the Southeast, and the Southwest. This would bring seven locations to the United States and make visiting an SLC a fairly easy trek for most Americans, vastly increasing exposure to a new, sustainable, regenerative, and healthy way of thinking. We aim to do this not by ourselves, but by piggybacking on like-minded organizations, businesses, nonprofits, and associations whose missions are closely aligned with our own. By creating synergistic partnerships, we will all be able to get started for a much smaller investment and increase the exposure of solar living enormously.

It all started from a combination of hope for an energy-efficient future and feelings of guilt and hypocrisy that we were not "walking our talk." What has evolved is a whole far greater than the sum of the parts of all the incredible energies that came together to make the Solar Living Center possible. Our slogan that "knowledge is our most important product" has proven out. We hope that we have started a trend that cannot be stopped until renewable energy is more commonplace than fossil fuels and until a sustainable future can be assured for coming generations.

Contributors and Sponsors

Real Goods is more than the sum of its parts. It is a publicly traded company listed on the Pacific Stock Exchange (RGT) and on NASDAQ (RGTC). Stock can also be purchased through any stockbroker or from another shareowner on the Real Goods web site.

For more information on Real Goods:

Head Office

Real Goods Trading Company
555 Leslie Street
Ukiah, CA 95482
telephone: 707-468-9292
fax: 707-468-4807
email: realgood@realgoods.com
website: www.realgoods.com

Solar Living Center

Real Goods Solar Living Center
13771 South Highway 101
Hopland, CA 95449
telephone: 707-744-2107
fax: 707-744-1342

Real Goods Store in Eugene, Oregon

Real Goods
77 W. Broadway
Downtown Mall
Eugene, OR 97402
telephone: 541-334-6960
fax: 541-334-6982

Contributors

Arkin Tilt Architects
David Arkin, AIA
1062 Stannage Ave.
Albany, CA 94706
telephone: 510-528-9830
fax: 510-528-0206
email: arkintilt@aol.com
website: www.arkintilt.com

Ross Burkhardt
PO Box 1436
Ukiah, CA 95482
telephone: 707-462-3734
email: ross@pacific.net

Counter/Production
1075 Dwight Way
Berkeley, CA 94710
telephone: 510-843-6916

Peter Erskine
1100 Palms Boulevard
Venice, CA 90291
telephone: 310-396-4615
fax: 310-396-9083

Adam Jackaway
Climate Responsive Design
2954 San Pablo Ave.
Berkeley, CA 94710
telephone: 510-704-0706

Bruce King
Structural Engineering
209 Caledonia
Sausalito, CA 94965
telephone: 415-331-7630
fax: 415-332-4072
email: ecobruce@aol.com

Land & Place
Stephanie Kotin
Christopher Tebbutt
11800 Anderson Valley Way
Boonville, CA 95415
telephone: 707-895-2111
fax: 707-895-3442

Mendocino Engineering
Terry McGillivray
4501 Deerwood Drive
Ukiah, CA 95482
telephone: 707-462-9372

North Coast Structures, Inc.
PO Box 1650
Windsor, CA 95492
telephone: 707-838-4345

Baile Oakes
Sculptor
Box 203, Westport, CA 95488
telephone: 707-964-7721
fax: 707-964-8258
e-mail: oakes@mcn.org

Otto Design Group
1850 N. Hope Street
Philadelphia, PA 19122
telephone: 215-291-0767
fax: 215-291-0726

Rammed Earth Works Associates
1058 Second Avenue
Napa, CA 94558
telephone: 707-224-2532
fax: 707-258-1878

TDM Construction
Tom Myers, Principal
144A Cherry Street
Ukiah, CA 95482
telephone: 707-468-0928

Touch of Grace
Mary Buckley
PO Box 642, Ukiah, CA 95482
telephone: 707-462-5971
email:
mary_buckley@redwoodfn.org

Van der Ryn Architects/
Ecological Design Institute
Sim Van der Ryn
10 Libertyship Way, Suite 185
Sausalito, CA 94965
telephone: 415-332-5806
fax: 415-332-5808
email: ecodes@aol.com

Sponsors

Ananda Power Technologies, Inc.
14618 Tyler Foote Road
Nevada City, CA 95959
telephone: 916-292-3834

California Rice Industry Assocation
701 University Avenue, Suite 205
Sacramento, CA 95825-6708
telephone: 916-458-5206

In-Line Plastics, Inc.
12247 FM 529
Houston, TX 77041
telephone: 1-800-364-7688

Insteel Construction System, Inc.
2610 Sidney Lanier Drive
Brunswick, GA 31525
telephone: 1-800-545-3181
fax: 912-264-3774

James Hardie Building Products
26300 La Alameda #400
Mission Viejo, CA 92691
telephone: 714-582-0731

Leviton Manufacturing Co., Inc.
59-25 Little Neck Parkway
Little Neck, NY 11362-2591
telephone: 707-763-9141
fax: 707-763-9141

New World Manufacturing, Inc.
PO Box 248
27627 Dutcher Creek Road
Cloverdale, CA 95425
telephone: 1-800-523-8853

PG&E Energy Center
851 Howard Street
San Francisco, CA 95105
telephone: 415-973-7268
website: www.pge.com/pec

Pittsburgh Corning Corp.
800 Presque Isle Drive
Pittsburgh, PA 15239
telephone: 412-327-6100

S.E.S. (Solar Electric Specialties)
PO Box 537, Willits, CA 95490
telephone: 707-459-9496

Siemens Solar Industries
PO Box 6032 , Camarillo, CA 93011
telephone: 805-482-6800

Skylark, Inc.
Virbela Flowforms
W 2463 County Road, ES
East Tray, WI 53120
telephone: 414-642-9665
fax: 414-642-2661

Small Power Systems
74550 Dobie Lane
Covelo, CA 95428
telephone: 1-800-972-7179

Trace Engineering
5916 195th Street NE
Arlington, WA 98223
telephone: 360-435-8826

Waterless Company
1223 Camino Del Mar
Del Mar, CA 92014
telephone: 1-800-244-6364